Bastard or Playmate?

*Theater Topics* is a yearly publication dedicated to research in and into theatre. Thematically organised, each issue centres on a different subject. *Theater Topics* presents a platform for current research, while aiming to stimulate new developments. *Theater Topics* is oriented first and foremost towards the Dutch and Flemish context.

*Theater Topics* is an initiative of the Department of Theatre Studies of the University of Amsterdam; the Department of Arts, Culture and Media of the University of Groningen; the Institute of Theater, Film and TV Studies of the University of Utrecht; and the Theater Instituut Nederland (TIN). *Theater Topics* is published by Amsterdam University Press.

Series editors:
Maaike Bleeker
Lucia van Heteren
Chiel Kattenbelt
Christel Stalpaert
Rob van der Zalm

Final editing:
David Depestel


*Theater Topics* is een jaarlijkse publicatie over onderzoek in en naar theater. Elk nummer brengt onderzoek bijeen rond een specifiek thema. Het doel is om enerzijds lopend onderzoek grotere zichtbaarheid te geven en anderzijds, door middel van de thematische opzet, het onderzoek nieuwe impulsen te geven. *Theater Topics* richt zich daarbij in de eerste plaats op onderzoek dat plaatsvindt binnen de Nederlands/Vlaamse context.

*Theater Topics* is een initiatief van de leerstoelgroep Theaterwetenschap van de Universiteit van Amsterdam, de afdeling Kunsten, Cultuur en Media van de Rijksuniversiteit Groningen, de opleiding Theater, Film en TV-wetenschap van de Universiteit Utrecht en het Theater Instituut Nederland en wordt uitgegeven door Amsterdam University Press.

# Bastard or Playmate?

## Adapting Theatre, Mutating Media and the Contemporary Performing Arts

Edited by Robrecht Vanderbeeken, Christel Stalpaert,
David Depestel and Boris Debackere

Amsterdam University Press

The publication of this book is made possible
by a grant from the University of Ghent.

Cover design: Studio Jan de Boer, Amsterdam
Lay-out: Het Steen Typografie, Maarssen

ISBN        978 90 8964 258 5
e-ISBN    978 90 4851 317 8 (pdf)
e-ISBN    978 90 4851 674 2 (ePub)
NUR        670

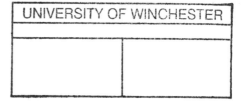

Every effort has been made to obtain permission to use all copyrighted illustrations reproduced in
this book. Nonetheless, whosoever believes to have rights to this material is advised to contact the
publisher.

# Contents

# Introduction

## Perhaps the Medium-Specificity of the Contemporary Performing Arts is Mutation?

*Art is often a bastard, the parents of which we do not know.*
Nam June Paik

Artistic media seem to be – more than ever – in a permanent condition of mutation. Mutation is a term borrowed from molecular biology and genetic science referring to the permanent change in the DNA sequence of a gene. Mutations in a gene's DNA structure not only alter the connectivity within the DNA sequence but might also change a protein produced by a gene. In much the same way, we inhabit an ever-mutating media landscape where once separate media levels are interconnecting in novel configurations and where different media devices and forms shape-shift in a most surprising way. Take the example of the applause, one of the devices that 'belong' to the live performing arts. The act of clapping is an expression of approval or admiration towards live performers. However, we found ourselves applauding before a machine in Kris Verdonck's *Actor #1* (2010). It is obvious that Verdonck's creations are situated in the transit zone between visual arts and theatre, between installations and performance, dance and architecture. This not only affects the mutual relation between these media but also our attitude towards their mutating devices and forms. Have you ever found yourself applauding in a museum, before a 'dead' painting? Did you ever wonder why (not)?

The rise of mutating media is an evident consequence of the fact that artists have been searching for innovation and controversy throughout the twentieth century. The avant-garde idea that started as a revolt against the long-established traditions and prevailing institutional codes also entailed a radical deconstruction of the supposedly separate media levels. Artists challenged one another to combine daily life with tradition or to mix artistic and popular media. The boom of multimedia (combining and crossing over into various media) not only liberated art from its canonical disciplines, it also turned it into a vast diversity of experiments. Concurrently, technological revolutions brought about a re-enactment of old media like film and theatre, as well as a sweeping influx of new media.

Thanks to these transformations, artists now have an extensive set of instruments at their disposal. But what is more important, they also became highly aware of the nature of media and their differences. They investigate the limits and possibilities of the media they use and experiment with the crossing over, upgrading and mutilating of media. Or they explicitly explore the unknown intermedial space between existing media, searching for the hybrid beings that occupy these in-betweens. Needless to say, this condition of transgression and mutation fits perfectly well with the spirit of the age: globalization, migration, transculturalism, the end of grand narratives, the fading of traditional values and the steep rise of individualism. The dynamic postmodern plurality of contemporary society goes hand in hand with a fast-evolving diversity in contemporary art.

This diversity, however, implies a major challenge for art theory. The lack of general traditions and overall tendencies make it impossible for scholars to analyse contemporary art in explicit terms or paradigm examples without the risk of severe reduction or even sheer speculation. This, by the way, explains why a non-category like 'media art' has become successful or why concepts with suggestive prefixes are so common today – e.g. 'the post-medium condition' (Rosalind Krauss), 'postdramatic theatre' (Hans-Thies Lehmann) and 'altermodernism' (Nicolas Bourriaud). The only general thesis that remains largely undisputed, therefore, seems to be the diversification of art itself.

This issue of *Theater Topics* takes the theme of mutating and adapting media as a starting point for a twofold inquiry into the so-called contemporary performing arts. First, we take it as an opportunity to discuss what makes its diversity specific. Some underlying mapping questions are: What are the different domains that take part in the evolution of the contemporary performing arts? How did basic aspects of theatre evolve? How did historical traditions in drama adapt to new cultural contexts? What are these mutants, and what is their added value? How does the stage contextualize media that are normally used elsewhere? How do old media – i.e. their aesthetics, canon, technology and methods – get remediated in contemporary performances? In sum, what are the challenges, restrictions and implications of a deep play with old and new media on a stage? Obviously, the different contributions included in this volume cannot provide an extensive answer to all these questions. But the case studies and the lines of thought they develop do give an exploratory overview of the scope of the topic.

Another question that was, in fact, the main incentive to create this book is: Does mutation eventually lead to a contamination or even a disintegration of what we call theatre, or rather to a revaluation and thus to a confirmation thereof in the long run? In other words, does mutation turn theatre into a bastard or a new playmate? By way of a preliminary answer to this question, the claim we want to put forward with this book is that basically mutation is what the contemporary performing arts stands for: a playground for innovation in which what is already done is constantly put at stake. Rather than deconstructing this thing called 'the contemporary performing arts' into an unknown 'other', mutation in fact generates them, as its very offspring – the otherness – is exactly what we take to be the contemporary performing arts. Put differently, in academic-scholastic terms: mutation is what makes theatre medium-specific today.

Of course, mutation is a principal driving force of innovation for contemporary art in general. In our view, however, it is especially important for the contemporary performing arts in particular, not only because it takes central stage here but also because its outcome coincides to a much larger extent with what we essentially take to be the 'contemporary' performing arts. In fine art, for instance, the crossover with other media like film, music, theatre or architecture generated new forms: video art, sound art, performance art, installation art. But these developments should be understood as extensions, hybrids actually, which enabled fine art to reinvent and redefine itself into a new and broader heterogeneous artistic field that gathers a new generation of experiments with classical media (sculpture, drawing, painting, etc.) next to these new forms. In the case of the contemporary performing arts, on the contrary, there is hardly anything else but these newly created forms (in which classical elements are often integrated – or replaced by newcomers).

One of the reasons for this is that, to this day, the distinction between 'classic' and 'contemporary' is upheld in performing arts: theatre companies still perform classical plays or interpretations thereof, while in the case of fine art, the 'classics' belong to the museum of art history. Consequently, newly created work in classical media is considered to take part in 'contemporary' fine art (or else it might qualify as 'amateur art', even if it is 'professionally' made...). Another reason might be that, in evolutionary terms, theatre as a medium seems to be very robust. It can, therefore, easily allow radical experiments without (completely) losing its identity. For instance, many contemporary experiments revolve around breaking away from the standard structure of theatre, which goes back at least to the Greek amphitheatre: a stage, an audience, performers, a live event, a play, a play time. Performances in situ or in public space, interactive theatre, marathon plays, etc. mainly – if not only – make sense as a variation. What makes them special is defined in relation to the standard structure that functions as a signifying gravitational force in the background. The same goes for so-called intermedial experiments: the very description 'intermedial' already lays bare a relational concept with respect to classical theatre, which also implies that the success of these experiments depends on the originality of the adaptation they provoke. Therefore, what is 'intermedial' in relation to classical theatre is what makes the contemporary performing arts medium-specific in its quest for authenticity and individuality. In evolutionary terms: it is all part of a process of selection and fitness in order to keep the experienced audience persuaded, surprised and ignited in relation to what they are already acquainted with. At the end of the day, these are the central criteria for acceptance and lasting impressions as a contemporary performing arts piece.

The first chapter in this volume – *Theatre Between Performance and Installation: Three Contemporary Belgian Examples* – elaborates on this central aspect of mutation as medium-specificity. Christophe Van Gerrewey thus opens up the discussion of the standard structure of theatre as the DNA of new creations to come. He focuses on the importance of the architectural domain of the theatre compared with the institutional context of the museum by means of a discussion of installation, performance and archive mutated to a theatrical situation. Van Gerrewey develops his comparison based on an analysis of three contemporary productions from Belgium: *Viewmaster* by Heike Langsdorf, Ula Sickel and Laurent Liefooghe (2007-2010), *End* by Kris Verdonck (2008) and *You are here* by Deepblue (2008).

Next, we included three chapters that study the topic of mutation and adaptation from a broader perspective. Instead of a clear-cut focus on the complex crossovers between artistic media, the dynamic and intertwining relation between theatre and political reality is taken into account. The first of these chapters is a nosedive into history. *The Fourth Wall, or the Rift Between Citizen and Government. Another Attempt at a Conceptual Synthesis of Theatre and Politics* by Klaas Tindemans brings a historical study of the evolution of the relation between actors and audience and how this represents the organization of society – i.e. the relation between governments and citizens. His analysis of the parallels between theatrical and political representation opens up a refreshing perspective on not only the state of the contemporary performing arts but also of present-day politics.

The second chapter on the mutating relation between theatre and politics focuses on the use of recorded images (i.e. film or TV footage) on a stage, and how such hybrids evoke critical perspectives on political reality (and bourgeois theatre). In *Using Recorded Images for Political Purposes*, Nancy Delhalle brings an overview of the different uses and intended effects of staging recorded images throughout the twentieth century: to confront the imaginary realm of the theatre with the hard facts of daily life, to open up the spectator's imaginary world, to tell a story that puts the actors' play in a bigger perspective, to reveal a shocking (hidden) truth, etc. Delhalle illustrates her analysis with two case studies: *Rwanda 94* (2000) by the Belgian enterprise Groupov, and *Photo-Romance* (2009) from the Lebanese artists Lina Saneh and Rabih Mroué. In both plays, new strategies emerge that do not use recorded images to testify but rather to stress the reticular perception of our being in the world under the influence of mass media (and how this transforms the aesthetics of theatre from the viewpoint of a contemporary viewer).

The third chapter on theatre and politics discusses how mutated theatre can enhance its own conditions and, hence, can become a political reality itself rather than just subversively representing one. In *A Campsite for the Avant-Garde and a Church in Cyberspace: Christoph Schlingensief's Dialogue with Avant-Gardism*, Anna Scheer elaborates on the work of a remarkable artist, Christoph Schlingensief (1960-2010), who was capable of turning the metaphysics of political exclusion into performances bigger than life. After a discussion of the production *ATTA-ATTA: Art has Broken Out!* (2003), in order to identify Schlingensief's battle with the avant-garde's legacy, she examines his subsequent hybrid and long-term project *The Church of Fear*. In this work, the boundaries of the theatre space are left behind to engage with the dominant discourses of the social imaginary both in virtual space and with 'activist' events in public spaces. Through radical flirts with exposure and provocation, Schlingensief and his company managed to surpass the distinction between art and activism. But the bastard they created is no doubt an enlightening extension of both.

Following these three chapters on the mutating interplay between reality and politics, we present another trio of papers, this time dwelling on the revisiting of historical elements – aesthetics, classics and styles – in the contemporary performing arts. In the first of these, *Echoes from the Animist Past: Abattoir Fermé's Dark Backward and Abysm of Time*, Evelien Jonckheere traces heritable influences in the work of the Belgian company Abattoir Fermé. In doing so, she demonstrates that by analysing contemporary experiments against a background of (supposed) cultural ancestors – taxidermy, the carnivalesque, curiosity cabinets, shamanism, etc. – a vivid interpretation can be developed that sheds a new clarifying light on a dark oeuvre that became famous for its art of mutating. Paradoxically, it is the use of these pre-modern elements that gives the performances of Abattoir Fermé their contemporary air.

The second chapter of this trio also explores the issue of interpretation. In *Folding Mutants or Crumbling Hybrids? Of Looking Baroque in Contemporary Theatre and Performance*, Jeroen Coppens considers the baroque as a tool to interpret contemporary art. By way of comment on the current neo-baroque discourse with respect to mutating media, Coppens argues that an actualization of the baroque ought to be based on the perspective that baroque art produces (and thus is famous for) rather than on formal analogies. To make his case, he offers an analysis of the baroque vision that is present in the hybrid theatre work of Romeo Castellucci: are the mix of meanings and the blurring of the borders between reality and illusion in *Tragedia Endogonidia* a resuscitation of baroque experiments with the *bel composto* – the beautiful union of multiple media?

In the third chapter on the breeding of historical elements, the floor is given to two artists: Sarah Kenderdine and Jeffrey Shaw. In *Making UNMAKEABLELOVE: The Relocation of Theatre*, they explain how they took a classic drama – Samuel Beckett's prose work The Lost Ones – as well as the inventions of early cinema (e.g. the *Kaiserpanorama*, a stereoscopic cylindrical peepshow) as a starting point to create a machine theatre called UNMAKEABLELOVE (2008). This high-tech installation offers an interactive and physically immersive three-dimensional space of representation that constitutes an augmentation of real and virtual realities. The initial confrontation that takes place in Beckett's short story between ourselves and another society of lost ones is resurrected in a cyber realm of physical and psychological entropy.

In what follows, we present a set of chapters that discuss – each in a different respect – the diversity of what could be called post-medium species. However, in order to avoid vague debates on the degree of mutation of different contemporary experiments – is it an adaptation or does it present a new line of life in the pedigree of media? – we opted for a mapping borrowed from an old typology from evolution theory. In this so-called mutation theory, advanced at the beginning of the twentieth century by the Dutch botanist Hugo de Vries, a basic distinction is made between three types of mutation: progressive mutations (the appearance of wholly new properties), retrogressive mutations (the loss of a trait) and regressive mutations (an activation of a trait long latent in the species). By the 1920s, however, the development of genetics refuted all the main principles of the mutation theory and thus reminded scientists of the easily forgotten truth that our intelligence can hardly compete with the complexity of reality. Nevertheless, the fact that this typology died out in biology is at the same time a good pretext to revive it as a simplistic but useful pedagogical instrument.

Closed-circuit television (CCTV) art is but one example of progressive mutation. In *Witness Protection? Surveillance Technologies in Theatrical Performance*, Elise Morrison discusses the genre of 'surveillance theatre'. These performances are characterized by the significant integration of technologies of surveillance into the form and content of live theatre works. Surveillance technologies are welcomed as a new characteristic that challenges artists to probe progressive mutations by remediating the phenomenology of surveillance in a theatrical setting. In addition to being evocative of a host of contemporary social and political hot-button issues – issues of control, discipline, CCTV evidence, freedom, etc. – these technologies can serve as particularly effective tools with which artists can stage formal provocations to habitual conceptions of both theatre and surveillance.

The so-called 'documentary theatre' can also be considered part of the family tree of progressive mutants. In her chapter *The Work of Art in the Age of its Intermedial Reproduction. Rimini Protokoll's Mnemopark*, Katia Arfara provides not only an intriguing illustration of what documentary theatre can be but also how it can be brought into being by the medial crossing of painting, video art and theatre. Based upon an actual railway model – at a scale of 1:87 – Rimini Protokoll's *Mnemopark* stages a hybrid theatricality while calling into question the very place of the spectator and, therefore, questioning the very notion of perception from an intermedial perspective. The reproduction of Swiss landscapes by new media technologies such as micro-cameras allows the director Stefan Kaegi to examine documentary theatre through the pictorial landscape tradition.

In addition to this case study, we also include, as a deviation, if you will, or as a twin variation on the line-up we presented so far, an interview with Stefan Kaegi by Frederik Le Roy. In *Rimini Protokoll's Theatricalization of Reality*, Le Roy further elaborates on how mutation is also induced by the employed strategies of appropriation of different types of documents such as films, news media, radio plays, video footage, diaries, photos, etc., as well as of different cultural traditions and popular stereotypes.

Next, we turn to two studies of retrogressive mutation: how can the loss of certain traits create new kinds of theatrical descendants? Typical of retrogressive mutation is that certain features are left behind (or put to the background) so that a free play of other elements can induce an emersion of new constellations. In *Digital Landscapes: The Meta-Picturesque Qualities of Kurt d'Haeseleer's Audiovisual Sceneries*, Nele Wynants analyses the artistic spirit that motivates the versatile oeuvre of Belgian artist Kurt d'Haeseleer. According to Wynants, whether it concerns an experimental short film, the VJ or live cinema of a music performance, an interactive installation or the videography of a performance, all of his works appear as (digital) landscapes as a result of their outspoken pictorial cinematography. In his self-proclaimed 'visual machinery' *S\*CKMYP* (2004), for instance, the observer is dropped into a kaleidoscopic labyrinth, driven through a fragmented landscape of screens by the mesmerizing voice of the author as a narrative guide. In terms of retrogressive mutation, this means that the actors' play is largely put aside in favour of the creation of theatrical landscapes that await the spectator's gaze.

Another example of retrogressive mutation is found in the exceptional work of French media artist Julien Maire. In *The Productivity of the Prototype: On Julien Maire's Cinema of Contraptions*, Edwin Carels presents one of the first extensive discussions of the groundbreaking work of a promising artist who became famous for developing what can be called medial prototypes. Like d'Haeseleer, Maire also moves away from drama and the actor's play, not to create pictorial landscapes but to experiment with performances and installations in which the technological medium is the protagonist. By means of experiments with the ontology of audiovisual media, Maire produces a new, specifically post-medium image quality.

Finally, to conclude our application of mutation theory on the contemporary performing arts, two examples of *regressive* mutation are tackled: how can the activation of a (long latent) property go hand in hand with the genesis of new artistic strategies? In cases of regression, full attention is given to certain components of the medium of theatre by implementing constraints or by using reductive approaches. This, however, might seem at odds with the idea of creating something new and diverse by means of the art of mutation which normally implies, and thus is associated with, the maximization of instruments, stratification, abundance of media, etc. Yet, the fact that mutation in terms of maximization is so common already explains why a method of minimization offers an original alternative. In *The Theatre of Recorded Sound and Film: Vacating Performance in Michael Curran's 'Look What They Done To My Song'*, Marco Pustianaz draws our attention to a modality of theatre where the realm of recording (a song) instead of the event itself can 'come to pass' before a spectator. In his performance-installation, the Scottish artist Michael Curran performs the myth surrounding a song by framing its absence. The mise-en-scène of the loss of the original performance (the live music session) is produced through a re-installation of a space that displays memory traces of the initial event: films of a recording session, a recorded soundscape and the remains of the recording studio with the abandoned set.

In a second example, a regressive mutation is created not by an evocation of something that is vacated but by a focus on repetition. In *Doubled Bodies and Live Loops. On Ragnar Kjartansson's Mediatized Performances*, Eva Heisler examines how the performance-based works of the Icelandic artist Ragnar Kjartansson re-invent the practices of 'liveness' and 'endurance' associated with 1970s performance art. It is argued that Kjartansson's use of exuberant repetition within the context of theatrical conventions mediatizes the liveness that historically has been fetishized in performance art. The article closes with a consideration of Kjartansson's *The End*, a six-month painting performance at the 2009 Venice Biennale that, in its staging of a romantic image of the painter in his studio, extends the artist's preoccupation with mediatized live performance and, as with all of Kjartansson's work, presents a conflation of theatre and performance art.

With this last case study of the piece *The End*, our reconnaissance of the specificity of the diversity of the contemporary performing arts is also coming to an end. With the fourteen chapters we have introduced so far, we hope to have shown that the enigma of mutation encloses many surprising dimensions and directions. Moreover, we hope that the reader will consider our central thesis: that mutation is not only the drive behind the contemporary performing arts into something 'new' or 'other', but it is actually also a good candidate to comprehend its very medium-specificity. Finally, by way of disclaimer, we challenge the reader to question the rudimentary typology developed above. One of its implications is that mutation need not necessarily be conceptualized as crossbreeding between media, since it can also be conceived as a process of self-fertilization (in terms of the rise and loss of traits, or the explicit activation of existing ones). Indeed, it might very well be the case that we have been far too enthusiastic in interpreting new evolutions in performing arts as something intermedial rather than something genuinely specific for theatre in a contemporary modus. Maybe our vision was often too limited, too preoccupied with other media, too fascinated also with the baby bliss of new media to understand that also theatre would adapt in its own right – at the same pace we all try to – to the drastic evolutions our society has been going through?

In any case, as an antidote to the temptation to overstress mutation – we confess our susceptibility to this in the preparation of this book – we conclude the book with an interview by dramaturge Tom Engels with the German director Antonia Baehr. In *Between Solitaire and a Basketball Game: Dramaturgical Strategies in the Work of Antonia Baehr*, a discussion unfolds that demonstrates that there are also artists who work with different media without necessarily wanting to combine them.

Robrecht Vanderbeeken
Christel Stalpaert
Boris Debackere
David Depestel

# Theatre Between Performance and Installation

## Three Contemporary Belgian Examples

Christophe Van Gerrewey

> *Wenn heute viele sensible Menschen ihre Aversion gegen das Theater damit begründen, dass ihnen dort zuviel vorgelogen wird, so liegt das Recht dazu nicht in seinem Zuwenig, sondern in seinem Zuviel an Wirklichkeit.*
>
> *Denn der Schauspieler überzeugt uns nur, indem er innerhalb der künstlerischen Logik verbleibt, nicht aber durch Hineinnehmen von Wirklichkeitsmomenten, die einer ganz anderen Logik folgen.*
>
> Georg Simmel, 'Der Schauspieler und die Wirklichkeit' (1912: 5)

In the age of mechanical and especially digital reproduction, the factual and material presence of the artwork is very relative. It is no longer truly necessary to be close to the real work in order to study it, interpret it or aesthetically appreciate it. Every act of theatre seems to form an exception to this instance. Of course, the theatrical performance can be reproduced in film (or in words or images), but everyone will agree that watching these documents will never be a true match to the experience of sitting in the theatre. Exactly this architectural domain of the theatre is of importance here, even more so than the formal characteristics of the medium of the theatre.

The importance of the place where the artwork is revealed and for which it is made can be shown by comparing the theatre with its two derivatives: the installation and the performance. Both installation and performance art have nothing to do with the theatre. They are made for, and in reaction to, the museum. The inevitably spatial installation 'installs' a space in a space: it establishes and settles itself as a new space in the already existing space of the museum. Even when the installation is made for the public space, and not for the museum as an enclosed building in *stricto sensu*, the installation reproduces a much smaller version of the already existing – and nowadays nearly global – sphere of art. The same goes for the performance: an artist decides to make a work of art with his own body. He or she moves and behaves temporarily as a 'normal' person could move. But the artist is not a normal person, since he or she works inside the museum – or rather, the Museum, understood as the art world. A performance is more than an everyday set of peculiar movements, however, precisely because of the Museum context. Understood in this sense, the museum is the eye that watches the artist as he or she produces or moves – the museum is the basic tool that starts every form of mechanical or digital reproduction. The performance and the installation are made with only this initial public in mind: the museum itself, the invisible camera that is the institutional art world. The old esoteric riddle concerning the twig that is breaking somewhere deep in the woods without anyone hearing it does not exist in the sphere of the visual arts. When a twig breaks without anyone hearing it, it might as well have never happened and the twig might as well have never existed. But when an installation is made or a performance is enacted without anyone witnessing it, the installation or the performance is still seen by the eye of Art. The institutional and spatial context in which the installation and the performance come into being ensures their birth, existence and survival. The museum, after all, is – historically seen – a place of conservation and documentation. The museum exists so that things do not get lost, independent of their audience or their actual importance. Indeed, in the archives of many museums, works of art (or other artefacts) do exist that no living person has ever seen or will ever see. That is why the installation and the performance are somewhat violent obligations to the museum to do its conservatory work. In these cases, the museum does not select (by way of the conservator or the curator) something from the outside world in order to preserve it, but someone comes from this outside world and steps into the museum, sometimes even without being invited, in order to be preserved.

The theatre does not have such an auto-conservatory impulse. The theatre does not have a 'real' and 'spatial' warehouse and, as such, it works completely without an archive. Even more so: what truly defines the theatre and distinguishes it from all other art forms is that it can never create its own documentation or archive. Of all the art forms, it has succeeded the worst in adapting to the laws of mechanical or historical reproduction. The theatre has no material history, since the theatre building and the theatrical tradition are, historically speaking, not historiographic inventions. The theatre is indeed like the twig that breaks deep inside the forest: if there is no audience to hear and watch it, it might as well have never existed.

Many art forms and many artists have shown themselves to be jealous of this unique feature of the theatrical medium. In this sense, the installation and the performance are both somewhat desperate attempts to distort the actions of the imperturbable museum by injecting it with life that does not immediately become an image. But in reverse, in various contemporary theatrical productions, this particular characteristic of actions taking place on stage in front of a seated audience is mingled with practices that originate clearly from inside the museum. This has, of course, been the case ever since the birth of the museum and of modern art, but when the individual arts change, so do their mutual influence. It is, however, too easy to simply invert the argument here by stating that the theatre wants to receive from the museum, as if both are playing the card game of happy families, a sense of history and storage. The theatre cannot and does not want to prevent that everything that happens inside of its boundaries immediately disappears forever. There is more at stake when installation and performance techniques are set in a traditional theatrical constellation. Three contemporary Belgian productions – *Viewmaster* by Heike Langsdorf, Ula Sickel and Laurent Liefooghe (2007-2010), *End* by

Kris Verdonck (2008) and *You are here* by Deepblue (2008) – can enlighten this specific and intriguing case of mutating media and artistic codes and conventions.

*You are here* by Deepblue is, just like *Viewmaster* and *End* (to some degree), a theatrical performance – that is to say, it maintains the emphasis on a short time duration that the classic theatre play installs, and it takes place inside a certain theatre architecture. There is a stage, and then in front of the stage there is a seated audience that cannot or should not move during the play – say between 8:00 and 9:15 pm. *You are here*, however, starts in a back-to-front way. The theatre space is decorated with curtains in such a way that the audience first has to walk behind the scene. There the spectators, standing, have to wait and see what happens. Their perspective resembles a three-dimensional version of the old PacMan computer game: on the floor lies a grid of 31 x 25 batches of white A4 papers. On about ten fields in the grid, small towers of varying height are erected, built with something that resembles, from a distance, bricks. At first, the scene is empty: the two performers, a man and a woman, are busy between the rows of seats. They are stretching red thread over the chairs at both ends of each row – probably because these chairs do not offer the correct and desired perspective on the narrow stage. Meanwhile, an electronic sighing sound fills the room. Now and then, under the ceiling of the stage, a small red lamp brightens.

Then the two performers finally set foot on the stage. Heine Røsdal Avdal and Mette Edvardsen are both dressed in a white polo shirt, blue jeans and white sneakers. They start clearing a path, again not unlike PacMan, through the white grid of papers. They pick up, seemingly independent of each other, batches of paper so that holes appear in the grid. The teleology of PacMan – eat everything as soon as possible, in a race against the clock, until the screen is empty – does not apply here: sometimes the grid is repaired, when some papers are laid down elsewhere. The clearout has a different purpose: when a path appears, the performers step aside so that the audience can finally walk to its secure seats, carefully in between the rows of papers and the small towers on stage.

Avdal and Edvardsen continue removing or rearranging the papers, and temporarily they uncoil red thread on the stage. The audience can now clearly see that the strange bricks are actually old-fashioned archive boxes. Another thing that now catches the eye is a screen of red LEDs high above the centre of the stage. The 'system' that seems to control *You are here* and its performers 'communicates' with the audience by means of this screen, but the messages that are transmitted never reveal the true nature of the system. 'System activated', the audience reads, or 'New situation created', 'Process information' and so on. Orders are given, situations are described and difficulties are diagnosed: there is an interface in front of the audience, but it never becomes clear what lies behind it.

During the last part of the performance, the small boxes are handed over, one by one, to the audience by the performers, not without some detours in between the still not entirely removed papers. 'Pass sideways', says the screen hanging above the stage. The first archive boxes, when opened by a 'spectactor', show tiny but beautiful and tactile scale models of rather classic scenographic situations: an audience, a stage, some actors or performers. It is as if an image is made of the spatial and conceptual conditions of *You are here* – indeed to show where we are, as the title has it. But later on, quite slowly, the boxes start to show not where we are but where we could be. The audience discovers more and more improbable scenic imaginations: mountain sceneries full of soldiers, a man mowing the lawn, a miniature version of the LED screen, or a man who has already partly left the box: only his legs are still dangling at the side. The 'real' performers, meanwhile, look now and then surprised but concentrated at the audience – and their activities continue. The last boxes hint at a closure of the performance: they show an arrow pointing in the direction of an emergency exit, or a forest of traffic signs. When all the boxes have passed through the hands of the audience, one final box is revealed from behind the scenes. This box is much larger and heavier than all the previous ones. The performers do not hand it over, but keep it in their hands, showing it to every member of the audience. What is now revealed inside the box is the original setting of *You are here*, reduced about twenty times. The papers on the floor of this model prove to be small coupons, good for a free drink in the bar just outside the actual theatre for each visitor. And here yet another representation of the performance is shown on a television screen: with some delay, every spectator can see him- or herself some moments before, right at the moment when the last box was opened before his or her eyes.

With *You are here*, Deepblue has enacted the archival impulse during a theatrical performance. In contemporary art, the cataloguing of art or artefacts has become a valid and regular practice in itself. Mostly in the form of an installation, artists simply show in a pseudo-scientific way a possible approach to a small part of the remnants of the past, be they real or invented. In his essay on the collecting of books, *Unpacking my Library*, Walter Benjamin has rightly stated the memorial aspect of every (personal) collection: 'Every passion borders on the chaotic, but the collector's passion borders on the chaos of memories. More than that: the chance, the fate, that suffuse the past before my eyes are conspicuously present in the accustomed confusion of these books' (Benjamin 1999: 41). Putting together a pile of objects that one has gathered personally over the years (or, rather, unpacking as Benjamin did and as happens in *You are here*) is indeed a chaotic kind of activity that makes frequent use of several individual memories. In the museum, however, and in an installation inside the museum, the archive or the collection installs a sense of historical time – not the time of an individual, but the time of mankind itself. The archive, the collection and the index are the tools that history uses to establish itself as an identity in the museum by creating the illusion of transparency, chronology and/or completeness.

The theatrical regime is of a different kind. There is no such thing as historical time inside the theatre. The expectations of the audience are totally different, just like the features of the art form – and both are continually preserved by time and space, by the duration of the show and by the architecture of the theatre. During *You are here*, hundreds of possible stage scenes are shown to the audience, together with the unpacking (during the first parts of the performance) that is necessary to reveal these possibilities. The audience – and this is the important difference with an artistic installation in the museum – has no clue about either the origin of the objects or the working method of the archival system. Are we being shown forgotten ideas of Deepblue, sketches of other possible performances? Is this an homage to previous artists, a case of contemporary but not outspoken referentialism? Or is this an enactment of the total end of history and of art history, and evidence that art can still continue after it is proclaimed dead? We do not know. As said before: the theatre does not work for the sake of collecting history but for the sake of entertaining an audience. That is why, in You are here, the introduction of archival impulses or the technique of the installation acquires a comparable status to other narrative elements in a play. When we watch Uncle Vanya by Chekhov, we do not know exactly why Vanya has made such a mess of his life, or why he has allowed himself to get locked up inside this existential deadlock. There is only the chaos of memories, and his memories are not the memories of the audience. The audience can watch and listen, but it will always be confronted with a loss, as it has no contact to the time before the play, before Vanya became unhappy, or – likewise – before the performers of Deepblue or the anonymous master of their performance machine started collecting all these theatrical remnants and scale models. Moreover, there is no time after the play either. When the audience has left You are here, it can still watch the television screen, but it will know very well that what it sees is truly over, exactly because the audience has experienced that same thing only moments before. That is why theatre does not leave the audience with empty hands. The audience starts to watch theatre (or every other art form) with empty hands, but the workings of theatrical space and time slowly and magically make the hands of the audience even emptier than they already were. To give meaning to this emptiness is the value of the theatrical experience.

In You are here, the magnitude of this valuable loss is reinforced by the initial nearness of the audience to the archive: the spectators are allowed to see the archive at close quarters, from another viewing angle than later on during the performance. The same goes for Viewmaster, another example of a theatrical constellation that lingers between the visual regimes of installation and performance. This stage play takes place inside an architectural construction that makes use of the so-called 'Pepper's ghost illusion', a nineteenth-century 'machine' that was used on stage to call forth ghosts and phantoms. In order to make this illusion real, the viewer needs to have clear sight of a first room through a large glass partition, without being able to look into a second, adjacent room. These two rooms are separated by another glass partition, slanted in relation to the first. When these two rooms are strategically lit (that is: simultaneously or not simultaneously), the audience sees how a body appears at another spot than where it is actually standing – indeed like a ghost or a phantom. In a certain sense, the Pepper's ghost illusion is a precursor to cinema: in a movie theatre, we see a body where it is not physically present, but we also see this apparition at another moment in time. The Pepper's ghost illusion can only show a body that is actually there at the moment, but only a couple of metres removed from the place where it appears in the eyes of the audience.

*Viewmaster*, performed by Heike Langsdorf and Ula Sickel and designed by architect and artist Laurent Liefooghe, takes place inside such a machine. This whole of adjoining rooms, wooden walls and glass partitions is placed inside a space without a real theatrical infrastructure: there is no stand, and there is no proscenium. That is to say: the Pepper's ghost illusion is the proscenium, and as soon as the performance starts, the audience sits down on the floor or on chairs in front of it. Just like in *You are here*, the viewers are at first allowed to visit the machine while all the lights are still on. By doing so, the artists do not pretend to keep anything back: the trick is exposed, nothing is hidden, and everyone can see for himself what is there. When everyone is seated, the lights go out and the performance starts. First, the theatrical machine presents itself: the separate parts are illuminated separately from inside. Nothing happens that is impossible, and this is thoroughly shown. Then the bodies of the two performers appear. One of them stands in the left room (which is invisible for the audience), left of the slanted glass partition; and the other performer is standing in the space that lies directly in the audience's line of view, behind the slanted glass partition. Depending on the internal lighting of the Pepper's ghost illusion, one body, another body, or two bodies at the same time appear in the perspective of the audience. What we see is now really impossible: it is out of the question that two women are standing on the same spot, or that a woman is standing on a spot where, only one moment later, as the light changes, another woman is standing. The classic postmodern motif of the bi-location, which shows one person simultaneously in two places (one is reminded of many of the movies of David Lynch) is reversed: in this instance, in one place, two people are standing. *Viewmaster* calls into being a specific kind of melancholic wonder: once upon a time, the audience that witnessed this illusion must have really been frightened by what it saw. A contemporary audience, however, is used to these kinds of things. Because we have been able to study the machine beforehand, because we have become somewhat blasé after a century of full-blown visual culture, we almost feel ashamed when we realize we do not feel more – more wonder, more disbelief, more enchantment.

The architecture that is being used in *Viewmaster* reminds one of the installations by visual artist Dan Graham, such as the classic *Square Room Diagonally Divided/Two Audiences* from 1981: a square room divided by a glass wall as a diagonal in two triangular rooms. One triangle has white walls; the other one is covered in mirrors. Two audiences can enter: they look at each other, mirrored and distorted by both glass and mirrors, seeing themselves reflected in the faces and bodies of others. But the real difference between *Viewmaster*'s and Graham's approach is more remarkable and lies on a less formal level. That difference is the absence of a chronology: Graham does not install a sequence and does not use a performative track. Inside his installations, there are no lights that flicker. In Graham's pavilions, the visitors have their own freedom of action, and indeed, only their movements guarantee some action. The work of Graham, and the work of the visual arts in general, does not concern itself directly with motivated action or co-ordinating time. In *Viewmaster*, however, we witness the presence of an 'author' – indeed, a 'view-master' – who enforces a regime that creates conditions in space *and* in time. It has been the dream of many artists to make art that seems to have no author. When, for example, visual artist Ilya Kabakov speaks of the 'total installation' (1995: 251-255), he is thinking exactly of this: an artwork that is so 'total' that every trace of the author seems to have disappeared. And indeed, artistic installations often do have a ready-made or everyday quality about them, like for example the *Wirtschaftswerte* made by Joseph Beuys in 1980: a collection of shelves, objects and paintings on the wall. It is important to notice that only space and material can obtain an anonymous or authorless status this easily. Nothing can distract the mind as profoundly as architecture does, since the movements of the body are not restricted in any way, and the course of things never becomes fixed. As soon as a specific development of time is introduced, as is the case with theatre, the existence of an author becomes imminent.

In the case of *Viewmaster*, the artistic regime and the auctorial intention execute a montage live and on the spot. *Viewmaster* is a theatrical performance, with a beginning and with an end – and in between, according to convention, the daily aspects of human life are neglected. That is not the case in Graham's pavilions which stand in the public space: one can, for example, have a fight inside one of these constructions or eat a sandwich or make a phone call.[1]

In *Viewmaster*, after the machine and the performing bodies are properly introduced, a narrative is developed, with fitting, subtle and sometimes even ironic allusions. A lounge cover version of *Come as You Are* by Dani Siciliano is played, originally performed by the rock band Nirvana. Again, this phrase reminds us that no invisible tricks are being played. Slowly, the movements of Langsdorf and Sickel become increasingly frenetic and faster, and the effects of the machine become more intense and explicit. The suspicion arises that something is happening inside of this Pepper's ghost illusion, something that starts and that ends properly, as real and classic stage plays tend to do. This desire for a story is not entirely fulfilled by *Viewmaster*, but it is put inside an ironic perspective when the performers re-enact scenes from famous movies, from the likes of *Inland Empire* (2006) by David Lynch or *L'année derrière à Marienbad* (1961) by Alain Resnais. The audience can hear the sounds and the dialogues from these movies, but it still sees the bodies of the performers. This explicit reference to (experimental) movie classics tries to historicize the mechanism of *Viewmaster*: the Pepper's ghost illusion is positioned inside the history of film, mechanical reproduction and representation – a history that coincides almost entirely with the history of the modern world. Through a specific combination of elements from different media and art forms (performance, installation, cinema, theatre), *Viewmaster* strengthens the artistic illusion, precisely by confronting the audience with everything it has chosen to believe in as soon as it agrees to subject itself to the codes and the rules of each art form. The illusion is strengthened paradoxically because it makes no effort at all to hide its own illusory character.

At the end of an important conversation that Boris Groys has conducted with visual artist Ilya Kabakov on the occasion of an exhibition of Kabakov's theatrical installations, the philosopher and the artist address these issues of art and theatricality. Installation, says Groys, is in its very structure the space of memory. 'It is very important,' Kabakov says,

> for any viewer to experience a feeling of trust in what he is being shown. This is simple with a painting – if it is not a fake – that is always hanging on the wall; it possesses an eternal presence. As far as the theatrical production is concerned, and in particular the theatrical installation, then, of course, we can believe that they were the productions of that very same Meyerhold [the name Meyerhold is used here by Kabakov as a simple and well-known example], but for us it is a completely empty sound and we must exert more effort to resurrect our memory that is very weak.

'In summary,' Groys reacts, 'it can be said that like the theatre, the installation reveals either the memory about an event, or the anticipation of it.' And Kabakov concludes: 'But it never shows the present: it awakens either memory or hope, but it never satisfies us in the present' (Kabakov & Groys 2006: 13-22).

The difference between installation and theatre needs to be refined here, albeit slightly. Every art form does show, to a greater or lesser degree, an illusion that shortly afterwards completely disappears. But whereas an installation or other forms of material visual art do remain present afterwards as an artefact, the theatrical performance is gone forever. In theatre, not only the actors and their movements or enunciations are temporary apparitions, the décor and the entire 'materiality' of theatre are as well. Anyone who leaves the theatre takes everything with him and destroys all that is shown by his leaving. An installation, on the other hand, remains as a museological artefact – a real presence that can be remembered but that at the same time is still there. By showing the audience this longer endurance and material presence of the installation on the one hand and the both spatial and temporal illusion of film on the other hand, *Viewmaster* succeeds in enlarging the tragic contrast that lies at the core of every act of theatre: something that was only a moment ago eminently 'there' in reality is gone the next second. Its staging of the present reality is, because of the specifics of human experience in the theatre, indeed never satisfactory. It creates, therefore, a very specific mixture of loss for the past and hope for the present, in a way that only theatre can.

A third stage play that illuminates the balance between loss and hope is *End* by Kris Verdonck, exactly because it stretches the rules and the workings of the stage play to an even greater degree than *You are here* and *Viewmaster* do. *End* takes place inside a classical spatial theatre structure: stage, audience, curtains in between. It could be called an installation consisting of ten performances. These performances are set on stage directly behind each other: each 'performer' (which in this case will prove to be an incorrect term) has one vertical plane to work and move in, and the planes run parallel from right to left. The ten different pieces depict ten ways – so Kris Verdonck has stated explicitly in interviews and accompanying booklets – to imagine the end of the world. End shows, at random, the ten commandments of the Apocalypse:

1. A black-and-white movie of clouds floating by is stretched against the backdrop of the stage, across the entire width of the podium.
2. A man falls down, at regular intervals, from a great height, and plumps down heavily on a small elongated and slightly increased stage.
3. A cabin, the upper half in glass, the lower in metal, slowly moves forth; inside the cabin, a man is recounting and describing the most horrendous tableaux into a microphone.
4. A woman moves slowly and unnaturally, in contorted positions, from right to left, and is being held up by metal cables.
5. A small flame ignites at the right side of the stage and then crosses the stage in a straight line.
6. A stake, crowned with four white megaphones, each oriented in another direction, files past; the megaphones bring forth sharp, high and loud sirens.
7. A woman in a made-to-measure suit drags a packet wrapped up in white cloth; the packet has the dimensions of an adult and now and then folds into two equal parts.
8. A gigantic petrol engine gets itself going with a deafening noise, and then travels – panting, vibrating, uncontrollably rotating, floating through the air – across the stage.
9. A man in a made-to-measure suit pulls forth a heavy load by means of an armour around his upper body; this load is not visible but it does shift and grate audibly.
10. A man hangs in the air, about three metres under the ceiling, and swims breast stroke; he dances, turns around, thrashes about.

These ten little performances are never shown all at once, but on the other hand, they are seldom seen entirely independent of each other. Nevertheless, they do not compound. Now and then some things do happen that might seem to belong together, but these connections are arbitrary or coincidental. The ten performers (or the 'ten performing objects') do not interact. Sometimes, for example, the woman in the made-to-measure suit does walk with the same pace as the little flame next to her, but this might as well have not taken place, as her movements do not entail any motivated action that have an impact on the flame next to her. She makes nothing happen.

What it comes down to is giving meaning to the individual performances: End cannot be a 'combined play' in the literal sense of the word; it is only the multitude, the enumeration and the parataxis that counts. So what do we see, after we have realised, some fifteen minutes into the play, that these ten little performances will keep on going and will not interact with each other? What is happening, coloured by our knowledge – given at first instance by the title of the play – that we are watching a (tenfold) enactment of an end or of *the* end?

1. A threatening, angry, polluted sky, in which the clouds become more and more unnatural?
2. A man falling or jumping out of a building or an airplane?
3. A neurotic, traumatized man, in a kind of post-nuclear 'pope mobile' that protects him from radiation, while he has to tell without stopping his endless anecdotes and stories – also to the two little birds that fly around like the canaries in the coal mine – in his little cabin?
4. A woman who is handed over to the torments of bone cancer, excruciating temperatures, mental torture – or a cyborg that is not correctly adjusted?
5. A fuse that is burning up slowly, heading for a batch of explosives or for the last remnants of a gigantic holocaust, on the way to its final extinguishment?
6. The derailed announcement of alarm, danger, disaster – pointlessly continuing to go off, even after the human beings by and for whom the messages have been composed are exterminated?
7. A grieving widow, on the road with the corpse of her husband, searching for a place where she might bury the dead in a dignified way?
8. An incarnated, runaway engine, furious, escaped from the straitjacket of a gigantic car, no longer controllable by human force?
9. A man on the run with his possessions, fleeing the police, a plague of insects, chemical warfare or a terrorist threat?
10. A human body floating around in a jelly-like material, in which it can only swim, thrash about or seemingly fly?

The way(s) in which we try to give meaning to the tableaux of End show that they are intriguing pieces that, however, lose much of their appeal when they pass by for the second time. This can be explained by the fact that End is a museological continuum, which we would like to be able to enter and leave at any moment. But the laws of theatre stop us. If we left the play before it ends, our leaving would be interpreted as a breaking of theatrical conventions. This imprisonment within the laws of theatricality constitutes the value of End: it shows how the end of the world is endless in itself. What we call history is a continuous and paradoxical enactment of a possible end. By doing so, End shows how this other ending, not the end of the world but the end of End, the end of the performance, is artificial but liberating at the same time. The quality of End lies in the fact that the audience, after some time has passed, longs for only one thing: the end of End. This makes End indeed 'bad' theatre, but not in the traditional, somewhat bourgeois and dismissive sense of the word. We do not hope for this terrible play to be finally over simply because the acting is bad, the story is boring or the setting is ugly. Nor are we disgusted with all the atrocities that are being shown. Rather, the opposite is true:

we are disgusted by the disgust that does not come and that does not lead to a catharsis. The historical time of the installation (a time without an end that is constantly and invariably evolving in the present moment) is placed in direct confrontation with the theatrical time of the stage play (a time that does not exist in the present time, but that is always longing for either a past or a future, in which the events of the present are either explained or developed).

One of the most famous texts on the theatricality of modern art was written by the American critic Michael Fried in 1967. In 'Art and Objecthood', Fried criticizes minimalist art, which he likes to call 'literalist' art. The minimalist art of artists such as Donald Judd or Robert Morris tries to involve the beholder and make him or her as conscious as possible of the fact that he or she is watching a work of art. 'The literalist espousal of objecthood,' writes Fried,

> amounts to nothing other than a plea for a new genre of theatre, and theatre is now the negation of art. Literalist sensibility is theatrical because, to begin with, it is concerned with the actual circumstances in which the beholder encounters literalist work. [...] [T]he experience of literalist art is of an object in a *situation* – one that, virtually by definition, *includes the beholder*. (1967: 20-21)

According to Fried, this 'new' theatricality of art does nothing less than kill art – or at least theatre and art are at war with each other in a very vehement way, making many victims. Fried concludes his essay by 'breaking down' his claim into three propositions or theses:

1. The success, even the survival, of the arts has come increasingly to depend on their ability to defeat theatre.
2. Art degenerates as it approaches the condition of theatre.
3. The concepts of quality and value – and to the extent that these are central to art, the concept of art itself – are meaningful, or wholly meaningful, only within *the individual arts*. (ibid.)

The validity and value of these propositions on the evaluation and theory of the visual arts have been discussed and refuted properly since the 1960s. As a matter of fact, in a strange irony of recent art history, Fried has written the programme of minimalist art exactly by critically attacking it. The weaknesses and dangers that Fried happened upon when examining the new minimalism became the qualities that these artists (and their more favourable critics) ascribed to their work. As Thierry De Duve has stated, the work that Fried criticized was already – and intentionally – critical of the 'greenbergian' modernist theories that prompted Fried's criticism (1987: 179). In short, the fact that each artwork creates a 'situation' together with every single viewer that views it is nowadays no longer seen as a problem or as a diminution of the autonomy of art.

Nevertheless, performance or theatre theory could benefit from imitating the historical fate of the 'Fried case'. At the beginning of the twenty-first century, 'classical' theatre finds itself – maybe not in general but certainly in the case of *You are here, Viewmaster* and *End* – in a situation comparable to that of 'modernist' art of the 1960s. Whereas then, as Fried argued, theatre approached and even penetrated into the visual arts, nowadays the visual arts (the installation, the performance, the archive) do the same thing with the theatrical arts.

One first exercise in this art-historical mimicry would be to pose the same propositions about theatre as Fried did about the visual arts. This could develop along the following lines, and actually with very minor adjustments:

1. The success, even the survival, of the theatre has increasingly come to depend on its ability to defeat the arts.
2. Theatre degenerates as it approaches the condition of the arts.
3. The concepts of quality and value – and to the extent that these are central to art, the concept of art itself – are meaningful, or wholly meaningful, only within *the individual arts*.

Secondly, it is also possible to write a criticism of these rigidly modernist statements. As the avant-gardist or modernist attacks on theatre have been entirely recuperated, the same goes for the artistic or visual influences on contemporary theatre. Either the historical avant-garde has tried to 'threaten' theatre by trying to get rid of identification or reality effects, or cultural evolution and history itself have come to stand in the way of what everybody understands as 'theatre'. But in both cases, theatre has proven that it can stand the test, like a kettle of boiling water that cannot be cooled down, no matter how large the amounts of ice that are added.

In a way, there is no such thing as interdisciplinary art – there are, indeed, only 'individual arts'. This means that any form of fear for the contamination of a single art form is not realistic and even futile.

The fate and the critical reception of Michael Fried's writings have shown[2] – and art history and criticism have explained – that the visual arts were not defeated by theatre; quite the contrary, as the 'new' theatricality of the visual arts was actually not so new at all and proved to be an improvement or reinforcement of typical artistic mechanisms. In the same manner, the examples of *You are here, Viewmaster* and *End* show that theatre will not be killed by the visual arts but that the visual arts might make theatre stronger. What could be feared as a devaluation of the theatrical presence on stage and a diminishment of the importance of 'the eye of the beholder' and the audience actually amounts to an expansion of these effects.

A paradox installs itself: the stranger the 'new' artistic element seems to be to classic theatre, the stronger the theatrical experience becomes in the end. The (so-called) mutation of the theatre is only one of the many conceivable subjects or narrative elements to become a cog in the big machinery that we call theatre. The fixed and recurrent work of theatre remains in place.

Historically, the theatre has always been the place where everything that concerns us appears in a very intense, concentrated and three-dimensional manner, and subsequently disappears. In a visual and mediated era like our own, artistic strategies like the performance, the installation and the archive – not only the artworks themselves but also the mechanisms that are used by them – have become an important part of daily life. These artworks and everything they represent or deal with are part of our contemporary reality. That is why they return on stage, in theatrical performances of the likes of *You are here*, *Viewmaster* or *End* – not as elements of this reality, but as elements of a new work of art. It is only here that the presence of these elements can be brilliantly but artificially summoned, and immediately afterwards be gone forever. Time and again, we are a little bit closer to an understanding and an appreciation of what we have seen.

**Christophe Van Gerrewey** is a member of the scientific staff (FWO) of the Department of Architecture & Urban Planning at Ghent University. He is preparing a PhD on postwar architectural theory and criticism. He has published widely on architecture, literature and the arts in books, monographs and magazines such as *Etcetera*, *OASE*, *De Witte Raaf* and *Metropolis M*.

## NOTES

1 For the sake of completeness: there also exists a version of *Viewmaster* as a 'real' installation, as an installation that is not governed by theatrical time. This Pepper's ghost illusion has also been shown in more museological conditions, where it can be visited during the opening hours of the museum or the art house, when the performers are absent and the audience is free to walk around. The same goes, actually, for the installation that lies at the core of *You are here*. But in these cases, we cannot speak of theatre proper, and thus not of theatre between performance and installation, which is, for the moment, the title and the subject of our investigation.

2 See, for example, Foster (1996: 53).

## REFERENCES

Benjamin, W., 'Unpacking my Library. A Talk about Book Collecting'. In: W. Benjamin, H. Arendt (ed.), *Illuminations*. London, 1999 [1955].

De Duve, T., 'Performance Ici et Maintenant. L'art Minimal, un plaidoyer pour un Nouveau Théâtre'. In: T. De Duve, *Essais Datés I. 1974-1986*. Paris, 1987.

Foster, H., *The Return of the Real. The Avant-Garde at the End of the Century*. Cambridge, 1996.

Fried, M., 'Art and Objecthood'. In: *Artforum*, 5 (June 1967), p. 12-23. Republished in: M. Fried, *Art and Objecthood. Essays and reviews*. Chicago, 1998.

Kabakov, I., *On the 'Total' Installation*. Ostfildern, 1995.

Kabakov, I. and B. Groys, 'The Theatricality of the Installation and the Installation of the Theatrical'. In: I. Siben (ed.), *Ilya & Emilia Kabakov. Installation & Theater*. Munich, 2006.

Simmel, G., 'Der Schauspieler und die Wirklichkeit'. In: *Berliner Tageblatt und Handelszeitung*, 7 Jan. 1912. Accessible online at *Georg Simmel Online* <http://socio.ch/sim/verschiedenes/1912/schauspieler.htm>

# The Fourth Wall, or the Rift Between Citizen and Government

## Another Attempt at a Conceptual Synthesis of Theatre and Politics

Klaas Tindemans

Denis Diderot, the eighteenth-century French philosopher who also took a special interest in theatre, gave the following instruction to stage actors: 'Don't think about the spectator anymore, act as if he doesn't even exist. Imagine there is a big wall at the edge of the stage separating you from the parterre. Act as if the curtain was never raised' (1970: 453). In all the theatre theory that was to follow, this imaginary wall was known as the 'fourth wall'. Diderot writes this at a time when both the theory and practice of theatre and drama in France – and elsewhere – are subject to profound changes. He develops a different idea about theatrical credibility and 'naturalness' – an idea which, as I will try to demonstrate in this paper, reaches much further than the stage and the theatre venue. An idea about politics not as a spectacle but as a democratic event which, in *ancien régime* France, for the time being exists only in theory. This new type of theatre, by contrast, is already coming into being in practice.

### The Debate on Citizenship for Actors

In December 1789, a remarkable debate takes place in the *Assemblée*, the provisional parliament governing revolutionary France (Friedland 2002: 3ff.). The representatives in this assembly are discussing the question of whether the right to vote should be given to 'actors, hangmen and Jews'. The people's delegates rapidly reach consensus on voting rights for hangmen, perhaps because Robespierre already foresees he will need them in a few years' time, but the discussion regarding the actors is very lively.[1] During the debate in the *Assemblée*, pamphlets circulate expressing abhorrence at the notion of allowing actors citizen's rights. The English observer Edmund Burke, a notorious conservative, probably gives the most accurate account of the motives for this fear when he suggests that the French Revolution is an illegal political theatre performance: '[The representatives of the *Assemblée*] act like the comedians of a fair before a riotous audience; they act amidst the tumultuous cries of a mixed mob of ferocious men, and of women lost to shame...' (quoted in Buckley 2006: 72). Illegal because it is an aesthetic

horror, in which both the action and the images violate any distinction between dramatic genres. And according to Burke, dramatic genres are a perfect representation of the harmony of the natural order. In other words, since the revolution produces such horrible theatre and even owes its success to this monstrous theatricality, actors, who are of course directly responsible for this wicked form of performance, must not be given citizen's rights. This is the point conservatives obviously want to make.

But, under Robespierre's terror, this antirevolutionary reluctance regarding actors and theatre gains a perfect mirror image. His *Comité du Salut Public* and the Parisian *sections* which provide the infantry for his short-lived ascendance to power were ordered explicitly to combat theatrical excesses, in the first place to 'unmask' – the word is chosen deliberately – plots (Maslan 2005: 125ff.). For my argument, it is sufficient merely to see that in this debate the confusion over the theatrical nature of revolutionary politics takes very concrete shape. Put more generally, the emancipation of the actor as a fully-fledged citizen, as a subject with political rights, signifies no more, nor any less, than a peak in the radical changes that are taking place on both the theatrical and political stages in continental Europe in the eighteenth century.[2]

## The Fourth Wall and the Question of Representation

But what has this idea of a 'fourth wall' to do with this problematic relationship between politics and theatricality, which is raised in anecdotal form in the debate about citizen's rights for actors? The keyword is 'representation'. This notion is usually associated with two societal phenomena. The first is the representation of the people, of the nation, of the assembled citizens in a parliament: the elected members of parliament represent us, as citizens. In the second place, already less general, representation has something to do with artistic objects, with a work of art – a sculpture, a picture, a theatrical performance – referring to a field of signification different from the matter of the object itself. In drama, this object – insofar as it is connected with the actor – is traditionally called a 'character': a constructed human figure that is given physical form and is thus represented by a living actor. The existence of a relationship between political and theatrical representation has been made clear by this remarkable parliamentary debate itself. But there is more. The important question can be raised of whether this relationship, this tension, still exists today. Or rather: the question of whether this assumed relationship tells us anything about the state of the art of theatre and, more especially, of present-day politics.

## The Metamorphosis of the Actor

Although at the time of the 'second birth' of European theatre in the Middle Ages, the Church is inclined to be positive about the educational potential of 'live performances' of instructional stories from the Gospels, it very quickly changes its position. The low social status of actors – who continuously change their roles and function and do not fit neatly into the static mediaeval concept of man – is only one of the reasons for this. The condemnation of theatrical representation is much more fundamental. The physical portrayal of biblical figures, especially of Christ, the son of God, appeared to lead to the possibility of transforming a uniform message into specific narrations, into concrete characters, which, purely by their physically specific nature endanger the unique image of God in his Trinity (see for example Duvignaud 1999: 147ff.). It is no coincidence that Orthodox iconography provides a more correct example of Christian representation: the icons of Christ all show the same face, with only slight variations. Just as the Host during the Holy Mass transforms into the real body of Christ at the moment of Consecration – the so-called 'transubstantiation' – it is commonly believed, until late in the seventeenth century, that a stage actor undergoes a true metamorphosis, that he has to feel his passions as if real in order to show them, without the 'as if' that Stanislavski considered to be the central point of his theory of theatrical transformation.[3] And this is of course unthinkable. The very Catholic eighteenth-century rhetorician Bossuet asserts that only the suffering Christ, in the garden of Gethsemane or nailed to the cross, can choose consciously between switching off his feelings and enduring his sufferings. Christ chooses to endure his pain, but if a mortal human being pretends, especially in front of a naive audience, to choose between the experiences of different feelings, he is pretending to be as divine as the son of God himself. The fact that the actor, like Christ, knows very well how the drama will end only adds to the blasphemous nature of acting. The Church does not condemn the actor for playing false but rather for playing real (Friedland 2002: 5, 17-20).

But this notion of acting-as-metamorphosis changes profoundly during the second half of the eighteenth century. The actor François Riccoboni and the writer Denis Diderot reject almost simultaneously the idea of 'transubstantiation' on the stage. 'When someone has the bad luck to truly feel what he is trying to express as a feeling, he isn't capable of acting anymore,' says Riccoboni, to the dismay of the majority of his colleagues. Both Riccoboni and Diderot think that actors should imitate feelings; they should not look for the truth – le vrai – but for the 'appearance of truth', le vrai-semblable (Friedland 2002: 21-23). By observation and training, actors should analyse and imitate all external signs of a passion, without suffering from the inner chaos that accompanies real feelings. It all comes down to technical skills. This was later to be called Diderot's paradox: the less real feeling in the actor, the more actual feeling in the spectator.[4]

This radical change in the attitude of the actor does not appear suddenly but is the result of changes in drama, in the subject matter of the theatre itself. The eighteenth-century philosophers and their artistic allies write drama that deals with the reality of a developing bourgeois society: they no longer deal with mythical passions and tragic fate but with real social relationships. Their drama stages recognizable tableaux as something artificial, with as much craftsmanship and as convincingly as painters' pictures. But this change in aesthetic need – the best French examples are the bitter comedies of Beaumarchais – encounters another problem. The interior architecture of the early modern theatres is in no way suited to these tableaux. From the end of the sixteenth century, the demarcation between audience and actors is very vague in the French theatre. Even in the *théâtres à l'italienne*, with their horseshoe-shaped auditoriums and their frontal stages, members of the audience sit on *banquettes* on stage, in the midst of the performance itself. The most prestigious seats are those where the rest of the audience can see them best: on stage. Moreover, the members of the audience (especially aristocratic youngsters) who buy these expensive seats react to everything that happens during the performance with hand-clapping and whistling, and witty and stupid comments. So it is understandable that an actor prefers to let loose his ecstatic passions, as if in a trance, mentally liberated from all this noise. During the eighteenth century all this changes, in parallel with the changes in acting attitudes and dramaturgy: the *banquettes* are removed from the stage, then seats are put in the parterre, then these chairs are fixed to the floor. A smart pricing policy prevents social conflicts in the stalls: the seats in the stalls are sold at high prices while the noisy common people are to watch from the highest balconies. The step from these practical changes to theory – the notion of a 'fourth wall' – is consequently very small. An imaginary wall, transparent to the spectators, black to the actors, means the players no longer have to shout down this noisy audience. From now on they can concentrate on each other, on creating the *tableaux*, aesthetically and technically as believable as possible (Friedland 2002: 23-28; Ravel 1999: 156ff.).

A certain irony of (art) history means that the most beautiful examples of Diderot's idealized *tableaux* have been immortalized in the art of painting, like *Le Serment du Jeu de Paume* from the most famous revolutionary artist, Jacques-Louis David. This *tableau* shows the room where the representatives of the 'third estate' swear that the gathering will not disperse until they are recognized as the only *assemblée* to be qualified as the embodiment and the representatives of the French nation. The architecture in this painting is adapted to the political dynamics, the theatrical power of the spokesmen ordered along dramatic rather than hierarchical lines, while every beholder of this painting clearly knows that these artificial interventions are deliberate effects. It is the idea of *vraisemblance* that counts, of a theatrical representation of the nation, not the real passion of the historical moment. This is about a sacred moment, but only in a metaphorical sense. The conscious theatricality of this experience is further demonstrated by the fact that David, who happened to be a zealous accomplice to Robespierre's despotism, never finished the painting. He never accomplished this *tableau*, not only because some of the characters shown fell into disgrace – like Mirabeau – but also, and more importantly, since this kind of theatricality goes absolutely against the anti-theatrical ideology of unconditional virtue the radical Jacobins stood for (Buckley 2006: 38-42).

## The Metamorphosis of the Political Body

It was implicitly clear from the motives behind the transformations in eighteenth-century theatre under Diderot's influence that a change of artistic paradigm only takes place alongside other profound shifts in society. The crisis in theatrical representation is at the same time the crisis in political representation. Since the Middle Ages, the relationship between political power – monarchy – and the community on which this power is practised is expressed in terms of 'embodiment'. In this context, the British historian Ernst Kantorowicz developed the concept of the *King's Two Bodies* (1997). A monarch has a mortal 'body physic' and an immortal 'body politic', which is the incarnation of this political sovereignty. In England, this distinction is very strictly respected. When, around 1640, King Charles I confuses the two aspects and begins to consider his person as the unique embodiment of sovereignty, he effectively signs his own death sentence (Koschorke et al. 2007: 119ff.). In France, this distinction has a weaker foundation, but the history of the States General, in which the three estates – clergy, nobility and bourgeoisie – assemble at regular intervals at the invitation of the king, shows that here too there is a difference between body physic and body politic, at least until 1614 when the States General assembles for the last time before the fatal meeting of 1789. The *Roi Soleil*, Louis XIV, intended to eliminate this subtle distinction, however.

The early modern history of the States General and the preparations for the States General of 1789 show a concept of political representation that, just like the theatrical metamorphosis dealt with above, links up seamlessly with a theological idea of 'transubstantiation' (Friedland 2002: 29-51). The nation is staged – at least that was the intention (also of Louis XVI in 1789) – as an organic totality, in which every member and every organ knows and fulfils its function perfectly. The architecture of the room in Versailles where this assembly was to gather shows a perfect image of this anatomy. The attendants at the court of Louis XVI studied the models of the sixteenth and seventeenth century meticulously. The representation of the nation in the States General should in the first place express its unity and embody it as perfectly as possible – in the literal sense. This aspect is probably more essential than the theatrical processions and the liturgical imagery – the spectacle. During the preparations for this unique political event, which lasted almost a year, the local communities, neatly divided by estate, appoint their representatives. These local *assemblées* also publish a list of their grievances to be handed to the king in the form of *cahiers de doléances*, a kind of complaints book that also included all the compromises concluded within the estates and finally between the three estates. The King must not be confronted with division, since he has to react clearly to the organic nation of which he is the head. The representatives at the final session in Versailles are bound strictly by these *cahiers de doléances* and are subject to a so-called *mandat impératif*. They cannot modify their points of view during an informal or a public discussion without feedback from their rank and file. And this, from a practical point of view, is simply impossible. So true debate is effectively excluded (Friedland 2002: 97-102).

The very lively discussions between and within the three 'members' of the body of the States General, between April and June 1789, deal almost exclusively with the nature of this mandate, because the third estate is heading for a radical transformation of the 'body politic'. Of course, the *cahiers de doléances* do not mention this question at all. Emmanuel-Joseph Sieyès, the most influential ideologue of the French Revolution, writes in his famous pamphlet *Qu'est-ce que le tiers état?* that the representation of the third estate is the only one able to express politically the 'general will' of the French people. The first and the second estates – clergy and nobility – are by definition not able to do this, since their privileged status makes it impossible for them to be 'representative'. A proportionate relationship has to be established, both quantitatively – representation as a function of demographic number – and qualitatively. Sieyès considers landed property as the foundation of political rights – between the community, the nation and her representatives. Sieyès postulates that the mandate of these representatives cannot be 'imperative', since it constitutes a delegation of power. More precisely, it is not power itself that is delegated, since power is, as Jean-Jacques Rousseau stated, 'unalienable', but rather the expression and the execution of power.

Under the *ancien régime*, the King is the visible body, the incarnation of the people, whereas, after 1789, this people itself becomes the sovereign body and the *Assemblée* 'only' a provisional representation since, from a practical point of view, it is not possible to have everyone around the discussion table. So the irony is that at the moment the relationship between nation and representation is conceptually reversed, a fourth wall is built on the political stage – Sieyès was to dominate this debate decisively for some time – between the elected representatives and the population they are representing. Just as in the bourgeois theatre of Diderot, the population can watch from the public gallery, but it cannot and may not react directly during the meeting of the *Assemblée* (Friedland 2002: 124-164).

During the most critical years of the revolution, from 1789 until the fall of Robespierre in July 1794, the debate on the content of representation – on the penetrability of the fourth wall, one might say – continues to spread. Even though one might conceive of the debate on the expression of the general will by an autonomous, representative institution as the recognition of political diversity, Sieyès' aim is to achieve unity, unity as the result of unrestrained discussion. This presupposition may even be fatal when one takes into account the 'sovietization' of the French Revolution – i.e. the growing influence of the *sections*, the spontaneous committees of Parisian *sansculottes*, which would finally end in the totalitarian form of Robespierre, l'*incorruptible*, the incarnation of virtue. 'Virtue' as the actual meaning of the general will, to be defined only by Robespierre's 'party', the *Comité du Salut Public*, which was a kind of politburo. Or, in other words: the revolutionary dynamics ultimately leading to institutional politics – contrary to 'incarnated' or 'organic' politics – would finally end, during the Reign of Terror, in a barely modified version of the monarchic incarnation of power in the person of Robespierre.[5] This was a truly tragic irony, as Georg Büchner was to dramatize fifty years later in his virtuoso play *Danton's Tod* (Buckley 2006: 120-142).

## The Paradigm Shift in Theatre

One could say, without much exaggeration, that both Diderot's theatrical reforms (the death of the passionate actor) and the French Revolution (the death of the sovereign monarch) have reached the status of 'myths of origin'. Both developments lead to a paradigm shift regarding the nature of both theatrical and political representation, which was only truly revealed in the twentieth century. This postulate naturally requires closer scrutiny. In the case of theatre, every renewal in the twentieth century, from Konstantin Stanislavski and Bertolt Brecht to Jerzy Grotowski relates, in one way or another, to Diderot's rift between the player and the audience on the two sides of the fourth wall, no matter how zealously all these practices and theories are committed to launching a movement of emancipation.

Stanislavski develops a method that should lead to what he calls the actor's 'solitude in public' (1987: 82; Wiles 1980: 16-17). He puts forward an unconditional fiction, an 'as if' as a mental guideline for every concrete choice in acting, in every detail of the acting in the ensemble. This actor reacts only to the impulses that the theatrical space, including his co-actors, offers him. In this way, Stanislavski refines the relationship with the audience, since he starts with the idea that any non-motivated theatrical action, any action that is not the consequence of a preceding impulse, is implausible. And modern theatre exists thanks to a seamless *suspension of disbelief*: this is why the fourth wall, which precisely circumscribes the limits of a scenic space, is so essential. Fiction and the acceptance of fiction – these are the dynamics of theatrical representation.

For completely different reasons, Bertolt Brecht, who, even more than Stanislavski, was driven by the idea of the emancipation of both the player and the audience, has conserved the fourth wall, even when his actors address the audience directly. It is out of the question that the audience should participate in the action on stage, not even in terms of approval or disapproval. The change in political attitude in the spectator, his readiness to believe in a 'doable' world and to fight for this revolution himself, has to happen outside the theatre, in the streets, at home or in his workplace, in real society. From a purely technical point of view, Brecht breaks through the fourth wall and his actors are no longer 'lonely in public', but his spectators listen, by preference attentively and silently. Even when most theatre historians give him credit for breaking through the fourth wall, by replacing an internalizing psychology with an epic attitude in the player, distancing himself from his character, Brecht sticks to a structural difference of consciousness between players and spectators (Wiles 1980: 82-85). He struggles with this statement, but as long as he follows his own logic he cannot avoid it. The Brazilian stage director and teacher Augusto Boal describes this evolution. According to the Aristotelian tradition – which to Boal means always, even in Brecht's theatre – the spectator cedes his power to the character who subsequently acts and thinks in his place. In Brecht, the spectator still cedes his power, but now it is to a character who no longer masks the artificiality of his construction – he remains visible as an actor. Most importantly, this actor doesn't think in the spectator's place.

In his theatre practice, Boal goes one (radical) step further with the aim of direct intervention in situations of social inequality. His spectator does not cede power at all, neither to think nor to act. The fourth wall has disappeared because the audience has disappeared, and the spectators play themselves, they themselves take all the dramatic decisions, but they nevertheless remain aware of the fictional theatrical framework they are acting within. In other words, the invitation to a suspension of disbelief – this time not directed to a nonexistent passive audience but to itself – doesn't disappear with the fourth wall. To paraphrase Boal's own rather pathetic words: theatre is the rehearsal for the revolution, but theatre can by no means be identified with the 'real' revolution. So the modern idea of representation as coined by Diderot, which in specific aesthetic cases such as naturalism led to a strict fourth wall, remains standing in spite of the disappearance of the passive, silent audience. Theatre is a different language than the language of political discourse, but this language could possibly – this is at least Boal's objective – challenge this political discourse if the revolutionary conditions are there (Boal 2000: 119-156).

But apart from this now somewhat naive-sounding demolition of the wall between audience and actors, some non-Marxist theatrical experiments have also 'dismissed' the audience, including experiments such as those by the Polish director Jerzy Grotowski in the Sixties. Grotowski combines an extreme form of physical training, focused on the expressiveness of breathing, with a very precise dramaturgy in which the Bible is often confronted with moments of crisis in European history. Facing the body and the texts as objects of signification, the spectator, by Grotowski's logic, has to tie the two extremes together. Moreover, he puts his audience in a 'dramatic' position, for example as living beings confronting the dead characters of the actors. But there the problem arises that a spectator is never able to know the physical or dramaturgical history he needs when he is made finally and entirely responsible for the interpretation. Grotowski's spectator can never play his role. In 1969 he made his last production for an audience and spent the rest of his life teaching. He did not really dismiss the audience, he just demanded too much from it and the spectators evaporated as a result of intellectual and sensory overheating (Wiles 1980: 137-157). Again, there is a certain irony in the fact that the Marxist Boal also returns to education, though unlike Grotowski he had never actually left it.

To put it simply, this struggle with the fourth wall – the constant refrain in the development of European theatre in the twentieth century – was lost. Nobody managed to break through this 'literal' fourth wall. Spectators expect a representation, more precisely a readable representation that does not give them the impossible task of acting or interpreting. They expect a minimal framework, a community, a unity to which they belong, together with the actors. Or, more accurately, the spectator accepts the structural divorce between himself and the stage – he even demands this divorce – as a condition for signification in the context of the artistic representation he witnesses.

## The Paradigm Shift in Politics

The question of whether this 'fortification' of the fourth wall implies that the bourgeois revolution in the arts – Diderot being its successful theoretician and the 'fourth wall' being a somewhat cumbersome symbol – or this bourgeois mentality, now definitively belongs to the culture of European civilization appears to be a rather ideological issue. In order to address it, one should focus on that other bourgeois revolution, the development of representative democracy. When Sieyès claims as early as 1789 that only a representative institution such as the *Assemblée* is able, even by definition, to formulate the 'general will', he not only affirms an inevitable dualism in the idea of sovereignty – the so-called rift between politics and the citizen – but does so much more fundamentally than any journalist could imagine. In his statement, Sieyès clears the way for an 'aesthetic' concept of political representation, as historian Frank Ankersmit calls it (1990: 267-291). Ankersmit claims that the democratic political order can only exist by way of a representation that is specifically *not* a literal image of the unity of the community – a community that is totally imaginary anyhow. Just as a work of art is created by observation and training – as Diderot demands of the actor – the political order in representative institutions is also only created in an artificial way. A political system is a construction, one might say, that delves into a cultural repertoire of 'great metaphors' – e.g. the body, nature – but which at the same time, because it is conscious of the figurative nature of this repertoire, has to demonstrate its own constructed nature.

Representative democracy has a number of instruments at its disposal to do this, instruments which should, according to philosopher of law Hans Kelsen, accentuate the difference between the sociological nature of society and the rationality of the political order (1981a: 4-113). A concept such as the majority principle – the majority decides, the minority accepts – is only conceivable if a construction exists whose purpose is the protection of minority rights, which can demand qualified majorities, and which can order the postponement of a decision or a second reading. In contrast to the position of most revolutionary ideologues, representation should not aim at the visibility and creation of the unity of the political community, but in fact should aim to shape the diversity of the nation – natural and voluntary diversity. For the same reason Kelsen, writing in the 1920s, favours a constitutional anchorage of political parties, as was effectively done in the German Constitution (1981b: 26-37; 53-68). Even when, with some exaggeration, this type of representative democracy now theoretically constitutes the only legitimate form of political order, democratic institutions are under serious pressure, the pressure of legitimization.

## Representation and the Challenge of Populism

Nowadays, this crisis is more subtle than in the 1920s or 1930s, when certain parties openly rejected representative democracy and shamelessly appealed to the Soviet principle or the leadership principle.[6] Contemporary populism, rarely bound to specific political parties, suggests a simple connection between society and politics, mostly linked to a very simplified image of both social community and political order. The existence of different centres of power outside visible, constitutional politics – big business, social consultation, the medical-pharmaceutical complex, etc. – is ignored or denied, so in the eyes of this populism the complexity of a political construction that tries to take this pluralism into account, let alone justify it, is equally illegitimate. To close this rhetorical circle, political power is reduced to an essential unity, no longer around a symbolic character like a king but around such symbolic notions as 'security' and 'identity'.

Even when, as has been mentioned above, Sieyès assumes the unity of the general will and, by doing so, accepts in principle the incarnation of the general will in one person – Robespierre – his early and pointed plea in favour of the independence of the parliamentary mandate makes any fixed metaphor and, more importantly, any substantial content of the representative organs in a democratic system, structurally problematic. It may be said that the creation of a rift between politics and the citizen, between institutions and the community, represents a larger contribution to the theory and practice of democracy than the Copernican revolution that transforms the people into a sovereign. The recognition of this dissension – both factually and normatively – is not a popular theme. Populists prefer to organize plebiscites or look noisily for scapegoats with an even weaker social empathy than the noisemakers themselves. Procedures are not a preferred topic of debate – though it will always come down to procedures, as voluntarism is not productive – when combining insights into a society that originate from those who make the society run (those 'experts of daily life') with political and legal formalism, with the need for abstract legitimization. The populist discourse continues to look for la vérité in the image that politics present, whereas politics itself can only exist if it ceases looking for this truth and, conspiring with its rank and file, opts for vraisemblance. This is not a plea for hypocrisy, at least not without nuance, but for credibility and modesty. Representative democracy is modest, just as the contemporary theatre maker can only be modest. But that is a different issue.

**Klaas Tindemans** is a dramaturge and a philosopher of law. He works as a lecturer and researcher at the theatre schools of Brussels, Antwerp and Tilburg and at the Vrije Universiteit Brussel. He is dramaturge with the Antwerp-based players' collective De Roovers and he writes theatre plays.

NOTES

1   Jews remain provisionally excluded, they will only be recognized as full French citizens two years later. In the case of the women's vote, not on the agenda of this meeting, the French Revolution would even turn back the clock two years later: their local voting rights, in existence since the Middle Ages, are abolished until 1944 (see Pernoud 1980).

2   I limit myself to France, since it is there, around 1789, that the rifts are most explicit and visible. England decapitated its kings in a theatrical way, one century before, but the Houses of Parliament subsequently left the monarchy intact and parked it in a constitutionally safe place (Manow 2008: 16ff). Afterwards they 'restored' the the-

atre, i.e. they reduced it to an entertainment for the new bourgeoisie. The German Enlightenment invented a new genre, the bourgeois *Trauerspiel*, with Lessing as its most important author. But their political environment was hopelessly fragmented. Georg Büchner said, late in the nineteenth century but very much to the point, that the country looked like an onion: only layers and no longer anything in the middle (Büchner 1987: 55). England doesn't like revolutions, in Germany revolutions always look like wet fireworks – loud explosions but quickly extinguished. But democratic France genuinely originated from a revolution; this is at least what the French themselves like to believe, rightly I think.

3 The 'as if' is a crucial element in the acting method, as developed by Konstantin Stanislavski. More than just a recognition of the fictional nature of the dramatic situation, it serves as a dynamic element in the enhancement of the theatrical imagination: 'By using the word *if*, I confessed honestly that I was only giving you a supposition. The only thing I wanted to accomplish is that you should say what you would have done *if* the supposition about a lunatic behind the door had been a proven fact, and that you should feel what everyone in these given circumstances ought to feel' (Stanislavski 1987: 49-50).

4 In fact, the meaning of 'paradox' here is weak: an unusual point of view, going against the *doxa*, about the actor (*sur le comédien*). Later interpretations of this text gave it a stronger meaning, so it became the paradox of the actor too (*du comédien*).

5 Probably the sharpest expression of these dynamics is the 'anti-Leninist' vision of François Furet (Furet 2007: 328-380).

6 I certainly do not subscribe to the 'revisionist' thesis of a (causal) connection between the two ideological postulates – on the contrary. This connection was one of the topics of the *Historikerstreit* in (West) Germany between 1986 and 1988 (see Verbeeck 2001: 23-42).

**REFERENCES**

Ankersmit, F., *De navel van de geschiedenis. Over interpretatie, representatie en historische realiteit.* Groningen, 1990.

Boal, A., *Theater of the Oppressed.* London, 2000.

Büchner, G., *Leonce und Lena. Kritische Studienausgabe, herausgegeben von Burghard Dedner.* Frankfurt am Main, 1987.

Buckley, M. S., *Tragedy Walks the Streets. The French Revolution in the Making of Modern Drama.* Baltimore, 2006. `

Burke, E., *Reflections on the Revolution in France,* Indianapolis, 1987.

Diderot, D., 'Discours sur la poésie dramatique'. In: D. Diderot, *Oeuvres complètes III.* Paris, 1970.

Duvignaud, J., *Sociologie du théâtre. Sociologie des ombres collectives.* Paris, 1999.

Friedland, P., *Political Actors. Representative Bodies and Theatricality in the Age of the French Revolution.* Ithaca/London, 2002.

Furet, F., *La Révolution française*. Paris, 2007.

Kantorowicz, E. H., *The King's Two Bodies. A Study in Mediaeval Political Theology*. Princeton, 1997.

Kelsen, H., *Der soziologische und der juristische Staatsbegriff. Kritische Untersuchung des Verhältnisses von Staat und Recht*. Aalen, 1981a.

–. *Vom Wesen und Wert der Demokratie*. Aalen, 1981b.

Koschorke, A., S. Lüdemann, T. Frank *et al.*, *Der fiktive Staat. Konstruktionen des politischen Körpers in der Geschichte Europas*. Frankfurt am Main, 2007.

Manow, P., *Die politische Anatomie demokratischer Repräsentation*. Frankfurt am Main, 2008.

Maslan, S., *Revolutionary Acts. Theater, Democracy, and the French Revolution*. Baltimore, 2005.

Pernoud, R., *La femme au temps des cathédrales*. Paris, 1980.

Ravel, J. S., *The Contested Parterre. Public Theater and French Political Culture, 1680-1791*. Ithaca/New York, 1999.

Sieyès, E.-J., *Qu'est-ce que le tiers état?*. Paris, 2009.

Stanislavski, K., *An Actor Prepares*. London, 1987.

Verbeeck, G., 'In de schaduw van Auschwitz en de Goelag-archipel. De Historikerstreit'. In: P. Dassen and T. Nijhuis (ed.), *Gegijzeld door het verleden. Controverses in Duitsland van de Historikerstreit tot het Sloterdijk-debat*. Amsterdam, 2001.

Wiles, T. J., *The Theater Event. Modern Theories of Performance*. Chicago/London, 1980.

# Using Recorded Images for Political Purposes

Nancy Delhalle

Today, more than ever before, the availability of recorded images and the interactive opportunities they provide have made it possible for theatre professionals to focus on form and aesthetic approach. Such artistic work with recorded images still essentially relies on the use of digital, video or film images on stage. Theatre stages are full of screens and offer countless visual experiences that may be fascinating or even aggravating. Among members of the artistic team, there are now a number of comparatively new functions such as 'video artists' or 'image directors'.

This might lead us to the hasty conclusion that form takes pride of place, in some new updated version of art for art's sake. It should be recalled, though, that technical devices have always been used on stage. In the twentieth century, however, they acquired a higher degree of autonomy; they were freed from a purely functional dimension (such as lighting the actors) to achieve an artistic function of their own. They became free-standing elements of the language of theatre. In this development, recorded images powerfully contributed to the transgression of boundaries between the arts at the end of the twentieth century. This kind of transgression had actually already been experimented with by the avant-gardes in the 1920s and 1970s. No theoretical consideration on the use of media on stage can ignore the fact that as a living art, theatre is a hybrid that has always incorporated other arts and new techniques.

That said, technologies developed so fast during the twentieth century that their use on the stage resulted in the blurring of commonly recognized landmarks. When faced with performances where no actor is present, many spectators will wonder whether it is actually 'theatre' they are witnessing. With *Stifters Dinge* by Heiner Goebbels (2007) or *Les Aveugles* in Denis Marleau's version (2002) – to mention two examples that led to heated debate – it is difficult to determine which standards of reception should be used. Indeed, in both examples there is no actor on the stage. In Goebbels' play, human presence is limited to that of technicians who at the start set up the device through which pianos will play on their own, shift on the stage and produce all sorts of visual and sound effects. For Maeterlinck's play, Denis Marleau also did away with the actor's physical presence and used instead the filmed images of two comedians' faces (for all twelve characters); these images were then beamed onto moulds of their faces on stage. The absence of any human presence and the use of clues and traces fit the diffuse *angst* to be perceived in the text. While in the case of Goebbels, theatre becomes an installation that erases any narrative plot, with Marleau narrative and action are no longer carried by living actors inhabiting the same space-time continuum as the audience. This completely upsets the conventions of drama. Whether they are called 'postdramatic' theatre (Lehmann 1999), theatre in crisis, or the end of theatre, such experiments – taken to the extreme in the instances mentioned, where no living actor is to be found on stage – show that technologies in fact open new perspectives.

Yet, if media have changed the language of theatre, they have also transformed the way we perceive it. We are invaded with images, caught in an unending movement, and we expect the theatre stage to reflect this frenzied pace; to offer a diversified focus of attention. Instead of our eyes focusing on a fixed point as had become the norm since the sixteenth century, we now shift to multiple focuses. A diversity of actions, or rather of activities, on stage and a multiplication of images are current features found in many performances. In most cases we can think that what is at stake is to capture the attention of an audience all too used to the promptings of new technologies such as 3D movies or interactive television and internet surfing. Yet, this might also be part of a quest for a new kind of theatre if we think, along with Bertolt Brecht, that 'theatre, literature, art must [...] create the "ideological superstructure" of actual and effective changes that affect the way of living in our time' (Brecht 1999: 17).[1]

## Fruitful Outlooks

In agreement with contemporary perception frames, recorded images in the theatre have contributed to a renewal of the practice of scenography. Through screens, video monitors etc., images have long been part of the context in which we live. But several stage devices now present instead of three-dimensional elements a backdrop on which digital images are projected. The possibilities these images offer (very slow, almost imperceptible transformations, changing only parts of the images...) make it possible to interfere in the narrative by taking on a descriptive dimension, for instance, or some detail that no longer has to be shown in the actor's acting.

In *Sous le volcan* (2009), as directed by Guy Cassiers and based on Malcolm Lowry's novel *Under the Volcano*, images projected onto the screen which cut through the bare stage both describe places and, along with sound effects, create atmospheres. These are images (both stills and videos, sometimes computer-enhanced) that Cassiers brought back from the very locations in Mexico where the novel takes place. He produces combinations, cuts and juxtapositions apt to take the audience inside the mind of the Consul (the main character played by Josse De Pauw). A mind soaked in spirits, where the course of events is blurred and leaves only traces for the senses: colours, shapes, sounds. Cassiers' images show a world falling apart, a world in which subjective and objective dimensions are confused. Indeed, while spectators slip into the mental deterioration process that calls up the character's visions and hallucinations, they perceive the climate of anguish that prevailed during the Second World War. 'I combine visual and sound elements,' Cassiers writes in the written presentation of the performance. And images indeed do take on the task of describing and contextualizing – both within and outside the narrative – dimensions that are often left out of theatre perfor-mances, while actors play and talk. As he shows on the screen a glass being filled, for instance, Cassiers frees the actual acting of any mimetic dimension, yet he also estab-lishes a succession of very dense interactions between stage and screen so that the de-vice of recorded images is integrated into a renewed theatre language. It is thus not recorded images as such that change theatre language but the connections and interde-pendence between what can be seen on the screen and what is acted on stage.

In most of his recent productions (*Shakespeare is dead get over it*, 2008; *Bérénice*, 2009; *Pleurez, pleurez mes yeux*, 2010), Philippe Sireuil has a rather different approach: digital images are used in his research on a classical repertoire (namely Shakespeare, adapted by Paul Pourveur, Racine and Corneille). *Bérénice* explores the passion between Titus and Berenice, which is defeated by raison d'état since Titus, on becoming emperor, sends Berenice into exile. In Vincent Lemaire's scenography, the stage was divided by a huge canvas on which the image of the actor-character slowly turned into a classical statue (video by Benoît Gillet). This was an allegory of this rigid law, which in turn ap-peared more and more worn by time. As such, there was a reciprocity between the slow transformation of the image on the screen and what Sireuil exposed through the words spoken by his characters, namely, that an external constraint irremediably spoils what we are and turns it into nothingness. From this reciprocity, which increases both the slowness and the burden of what is being acted out on stage (the split between love and power), some sort of immense nostalgia emerges. The audience's attention is not strictly speaking caught by the screen, which only seems to offer a fixed image that is part of the setting. But the spectator's gaze repeatedly stumbles upon this long canvas that obstructs the exit. Now, having looked elsewhere for a while, they will notice that the image has changed. They will then look alternately at the stage and at the screen (where the actor-character is slowly turning into a crumbling statue). Through his di-rection, Philippe Sireuil makes this sort of circling from outside delicately clear. Digital images are used here in a quasi-autonomous way and renew the dialectics between text and stage as theorized by Bernard Dort at the end of the 1980s:

> Thus the issue of text and stage has shifted. The question no longer concerns which of them will prevail. Their relationship, like the relationships among the various components of the stage, can in fact no longer be conceived in terms of union or subordination. A real competition, an active contradiction unfolds in. front of us, spectators. Theatricality is no longer only this 'thickness of signs' mentioned by Roland Barthes. It is also the shifting of these signs, their impossi-ble conjunction, their confrontation before the eyes of the audience of this *emanci-pated* representation. (1988:183)

Inscribing digital images in the staging of *Bérénice* is a way of meeting the challenge Dort points to at the end of his study, namely, how the audience can be 'activated,' yet probably in a less radical sense than the Brechtian practice that prevailed in the 1980s and 1990s. Now fully integrated into theatre aesthetics, recorded images no longer strike viewers as an alternative or competing language which would, for instance, highlight the loss or paucity of communication in our society, as was largely the case in the 1970s and 1980s when videos started to be widely used on the stage. Instead of a dialectical relation or the 'confrontation' mentioned by Dort, we now have an interaction that relies on a multiplicity of forms and produces more diverse effects.

## Testifying and Narrating

Recorded images can thus become components in a network of narrative techniques while preserving some creativity on the part of the audience. In *The Lobster Shop* by Jan Lauwers (2006), they contribute to moving the narrative forward through means other than words uttered on the set. In his analysis of 'stories' and storytelling, at one point Lauwers chooses to restrain the actors' play to screen the fatal scene that leads to a child's death. The bias is more realistic here: the projected images are less formal than the performance on the set and more openly suggest violence. While actors are lying on the half-lit set and hum softly, on the screen two children on a beach engage in wrestling while their parents are strolling nearby (several actors of Needcompany can be identified). Is this really a game? The innocuous context of a family walk may suggest it. Yet the sound effect considerably amplifies the blows. Doubt sets in and is soon confirmed by the look of concern that appears on the faces of the adults on screen. After a while, one of the children falls and does not get up. The adults cannot bring him back to life. This is where the film stops and the actors resume their acting.

Strictly speaking, the film is not necessary for the audience to understand what is at stake in the story told by Lauwers, but it makes its context explicit; without it, the spectators would not know in what circumstances the child died and how this could trigger a sense of guilt. More importantly, it represents a moment of focalization that operates at a different level from the rest of the performance. The play sets out to discuss the grave topic of the child's death and its destructive effect on parents and their environment. Lauwers uses an aesthetics that combines songs, dancing and moments marked by ironic lightness. The stage creates both distance and empathy. United by the adhesion called for by songs and dances, stage and audience are involved in the story, though from a distance. The performance is perceived as fiction and aesthetic achievement, since Lauwers refuses any direct or mechanical effect of art on the world. This gap, this distance is necessary for aesthetic pleasure. It can be described as the locus of mediation.

But then the video cancels this gap. It brings the audience closer to those 'people' on the screen who come across much less as characters. Here, Lauwers plays on the mimetic or indicial dimension that is commonly associated with photography and film. The figures on the video are only partly those on the stage. Next to the actor playing the part of the dead child's father we can see Lauwers with two children, none of whom are visible on the set. Some empathy is thus prompted by the video, creating some sort of identification within a performance from which it is banned, which triggers reflection. While the singing, dancing and acting on the set lead to the audience's adhesion and create a sense of community brought together by art, the video suddenly breaks this aesthetic movement. It brings the audience back to a form of loneliness in front of a violence that is hard to understand. It calls for individual thinking. The use of video in *The Lobster Shop* belongs to a realistic approach that is only a limited part of the performance as a whole and calls upon an ethical questioning on the part of the audience. As with Sireuil, images 'activate' the audience beyond the boundaries of the performance towards an ontological form of reflection (on humankind, violence, freedom...).

## Critical Function

While it is easy to associate such 'activation of the audience' with a Brechtian heritage, effects in Lauwers' play are geared more to meditation than to social critique. Yet in other cases the use of recorded images can lead to a more perceptible critical dimension.

In *Hamlet* as directed by Thomas Ostermeier (2008), filmed images are shown at two levels: in some scenes they are projected on a screen behind the characters, in other instances they are doubled in the foreground but with a fuzzy effect so that the mimetic effect is not obvious. The point is less for the audience to see, recognize or even identify than to stage a perspective. Usually Hamlet himself holds the camera and films characters and himself in some monologues. Imagined by Ostermeier as some dangling and uncouth teenager galvanized by the injustice his father was a victim of, the character is unfailingly accompanied by a camcorder through which he looks at the world. This world as a show by which Hamlet feels repulsed is somehow authenticated by the director beyond the character's subjective point of view. As he uses a microphone to let his actors speak and inserts variety-like songs, Ostermeier reviews the play in light of our contemporary context dominated by reality shows. Here, again, the recorded images are thus fully inscribed among theatre codes but are also an object used by theatre. Through his approach to the play, Ostermeier gives a theatre dimension to filmed images and reaches a synthesis of living art and recorded images – a synthesis achieved through the art of theatre.

Ivo Van Hove's approach to *Romeinses tragedies* (2007) ('Roman Tragedies', after Shakespeare) goes almost in the opposite direction. Here a huge screen hangs over the proscenium and the audience is caught in the simultaneous projection, in close-ups or semi-close-ups, of characters acting on the set. Through a realistic kind of acting that borders on caricature, the actors, who are often positioned directly in front of the audience, strengthen this transposition into the media world that underpins the staging. Stage acting, including as it does recorded images, tends to be obliterated. Through a mimetic quest parallel to that of the television set and the media world into which the political world dissolves, form is meaning. Writing for the stage is influenced by the codes of the media world. As recorded images contribute to suppressing the distance between the viewers and the viewed scene, having spectators up on the stage increases the identification process and connects with the fascination for reality shows that is so typical of our times. Theatre language and recorded images are thus combined and produce a redundancy effect. The blurring of theatre codes and the highlighting of televisual codes point to the disappearance of both the private and the public realms as they are replaced by the realm of the media.

As it heightens our awareness of the general levelling of perception modes enforced by the media, this way of using recorded images somewhat conceals theatre in its essential dimension of a poor or archaic art. Indeed, for a performance to occur, all that is needed is for an actor and a spectator to be physically present in the same place and united by convention in a common process. If it becomes dependent on media, it tends to disappear, at least in its basic principles, and to adjust to what it exposes.

## Political Uses

One of the oldest uses of recorded images in the theatre is part of political theatre. While agitprop largely used documents such as newspaper articles to illustrate its political message, it was probably Erwin Piscator who already in the 1920s extensively experimented with films in the theatre. As he wanted to break away from the myth of art 'offered' to the people, Piscator tried to achieve a synthesis of form and message in the shape of political theatre, or, as he put it at the time, epic theatre. In his staging of the play *Drapeaux* (1924), written by Alfons Paquet in 1918 and focusing on the trial of anarchists in Chicago in the 1880s, he used projected photos and texts that 'drew the lesson of the action' (Piscator 1962: 58). In doing this, he was trying to go beyond the decorative function of recorded images to 'organically' connect film and 'scenic events' (ibid. 64), a goal he had not yet fully achieved in *Drapeaux* but which governed his following attempts.

Piscator used films that he saw as documents testifying to reality, such as the mobilization of soldiers, a parade of European leaders, views of attacks with flame guns and of corpses. He thus showed archive images which, at a time when war films were neither common nor as he said 'fashionable', would 'shake proletarian masses awake' (ibid. 65). He used films to show the validity of historical materialism. Ways of including recorded images were thus duly considered: cinema was to show the interdependence of individuals, society and history.

As he further experimented with this documentary approach, Piscator fully exploited the more realistic dimension that immediately distinguished cinema from theatre. He clearly preserved the specificities of both arts and set them in a dialectical relation. The 'as if' theatre convention was still useful to expose a process – the voting of military credits, for instance – while filmed images introduced a more general social dimension, as they showed the first casualties. In such alternation, the audience's modes of perception were being transformed. Indeed, the film created a gap (Piscator used the word 'surprise') that changed the role of the spectator. The discursive mode (that of the plot, of the narrative) was suspended and the audience had to establish a link between what is said and what is shown. Now this connection belongs more to emotions and feelings than to reason. The sight of bodies on the documentary images creates a relationship to reality that modifies the spectators' position. They are more easily affected. Piscator clearly played on mimesis and catharsis but channelled them towards a political message. All his later experimentations would similarly try to reach the emotions of spectators.

Whether films are didactic, dramatic or provide comments, according to the functions Piscator described (ibid. 166-168), they must be used to find new 'analysis and information techniques'. So the director saw archive films as evidence of reality and used them on the stage as testimonies. He in fact relied on such testimonies to prompt the audience to think about the gap between what is shown on stage and the projected images. He somehow retrieved for recorded images a status that Benjamin had described as lost in his famous 1935 text. But it was also in the 1930s that propaganda techniques were further developed using cinema. And while Piscator did consider his political theatre as a kind of propaganda – i.e. theatre serving politics – Benjamin, like Brecht, had a somewhat different approach: their political theatre was a praxis, a theatre engaged in a consubstantial process with the reality into which it was inscribed. Indeed, Brecht commented on Piscator's work as follows:

> So Piscator does not use the passage from speech to image, which is still abrupt, he merely adds to the number of spectators in the theatre room the number of actors who, while still on stage, stare at the screen [...]. (1999a: 16)

As it combines sensitive questioning (through shocking images) and critical reflection, Brecht's theatre was less directly didactic, relying as it did on a distancing effect. In this respect, while he acknowledged the contribution of technology, and of cinema in particular, to epic drama, Brecht remained rather suspicious about the use of films on stage. Indeed, cinema is likely to foster the kind of illusion and identification that the Brechtian model is supposed to fight: 'What matters is that as it presents a real environment, cinema should not do away with the pleasure to be found in the dialectical game between two- or three-dimensional elements' (Brecht 1999b: 22). Brecht would thus favour the projections of still images and other similar devices such as posters or drawings. On the other hand, his narrative experiments largely borrow from cinematographic techniques such as cuts, framing and editing. He felt that these devices, more closely related to a scientific age, made it easier to perceive contradictions and ideas that underpin his works.

## Tools to Represent the World

Similar questions related to ways of presenting reality in a political perspective motivated the enterprise Groupov launched back in 1980. Feeling that they did not have any reliable tools left to represent the world, this Belgian collective initially worked on what they considered to be remains. After exploring representations of the world based on one kind of truth in this vein (through Paul Claudel and Brecht, among others), however, in 1994 they turned to current events and started staging a major performance based on the Rwandan genocide. Recorded images could not be bypassed here, since a significant part of the performance consists of showing how the Rwandan genocide was presented in the media. Speeches and audiovisual images are therefore an important component in *Rwanda 94* (2000). But the now commonplace use of televisual images to inform and testify is radically turned inside out by their presentation in the theatre. Indeed, the point was to show how the media participated in manipulation both in Rwanda and in Europe. During the performance, next to repeated calls to murder broadcast by Radio Télévision Libre des Mille Collines, we see how in Europe images that reported real facts (beheadings with machetes, for instance) were lost in the flow of media news. The performance deconstructs the impact of media by exposing how they play on perception frames. On the set, a lecturer, Jacques Delcuvellerie, starts a long speech in response to media subscribing to an essentially ethnic distinction with: '*Hutus, qu'est-ce que cela signifie? Tutsis, qu'est-ce que cela signifie?*' (What does it mean to be a Hutu? What does it mean to be a Tutsi?). But theatre will also show the constraints limiting the media: the journalist called Bee Bee Bee, a central character in the narrative interlaced in *Rwanda 94*, will not be able to broadcast the television programme resulting from what she has gone through to understand genocidal mechanisms.

As a constant element of the performance, media images are subjected to a critical dramatic deconstruction resulting in a crystal clear message as can be seen in the words of one of the characters in the Chorus of the Dead:

DEAD 2. –
Hear them, beware
Look at them, but do not trust
These machines that spread information
They infect our hearts
And pollute our minds
A sly hyena starts mooing
Like some cow
We are in their lair
Please beware. (Groupov 2002: 51)

We can see here how the theatrical relationship (in the sense of communication and, specifically in *Rwanda 94*, of a partial participation of the audience) is not considered to be in a dialectical connection with media communication but clearly set above it. This is still obviously the case with the sequence dealing with 'electronic ghosts'. In the plot, one of the elements that leads the journalist into her search for the truth is the scrambling of her television programme with close-up images of victims of the genocide calling for the truth to be established. In contrast to the way Piscator used filmed documents, these images are artefacts, but in the plot they function as though they were parts of reality, whose origins nevertheless remain something of a mystery (since they include dead people talking).[2] Rwanda 94 uses television as an object and exposes its mechanisms. Eventually, while the journalist will not broadcast her programme, the performance is there for us. It retains the freedom of its duration (six hours) and will be shown to various audiences outside the previous censorship enforced in the world of media.

In the relationship between theatre and media, theatre uses recorded images as material and eventually displays its greater power to create a political effect[3]: instead of the dominant discourse that defined the Rwandan genocide as a tragedy nobody could do anything about, what is set out in Rwanda 94 is a sense of co-responsibility. Without developing an alternative truth, the performance shows a plurality of approaches to the genocide, thus questioning dominant notions about the individual and the social dimensions. Through a political set of symbols constructed on stage and the use of media images, Rwanda 94 denies that society consists of isolated individuals and shows how everyone interacts in the web of relations that make up human society. For instance, members of the Chorus of the Dead move about in the room and address their testimony to small groups of spectators, which involves them more closely. This is but one example, but the interdependence of individuals as the matrix of society is one of the leading ideas of the performance that can transform established principles of perception. Indeed, it puts spectators in the position of being always already involved.

## A Subversive Meshing

Lina Saneh and Rabih Mroué's Photo-Romance (2009) develops a completely different way of using recorded images. Set in the oppressive context of present-day Lebanon, the two artists' work aims at developing critical analyses without actually enforcing them. In fact, it is this very double bind imposed by the historical situation that is staged and leads to a new artistic form.

Theatre performance is not questioned as a way of showing the world that would no longer be appropriate to our perceptual frames. It is not modified by the use of media that would open up spectators' imaginary world, disturb their expectations or multiply viewpoints. Media images are the very material of the performance in a clearly political perspective. Here the 'performance' is anchored in its actual referent, namely, the social and political situation in Lebanon.

In Photo-Romance, the use of recorded images does not attempt to recreate a more real referent for an imaginary character, as for instance in Thomas Ostermeier's Hamlet. It makes it possible to interlace a fiction that through its articulation in the plot presented on stage creates a new perception of the Lebanese situation. Recorded images are not used as documenting evidence either. On the contrary, they construct a story which the artists, already in the title of the performance, relate to the most popular fictional genre to be found today – the photo-romance. The performance is indeed inspired by this narrative mode in which the plot develops through a succession of photos while characters' words are framed in bubbles.

From the beginning of the performance two characters, played by Lina Saneh and Rabih Mroué, are sitting in wide armchairs on one side of the set. On the other side stands a big screen. In between, at the back of the stage, a third character sings or plays an instrument. The dialogue between the first two characters immediately provides all the components of the situation. The young woman meets an agent of the Lebanese censorship board in order to be authorized to complete and broadcast her film. A discussion follows in which the censor demands that the director justify the construction of her film and her artistic options. In order to win him over, the woman shows the already filmed images. As she has to justify the editing or the shooting, there are several freeze frames that turn what is shown on the screen into a photo-romance rather than a film.

Yet what is accounted for by the plot's internal constraints (her defending the film) takes a different dimension for the audience. Freeze frames make it possible for the director to comment on the film in progress, and her discourse can be heard in two ways. Within the plot it is meant for the censor who develops counterarguments, which already points to the situation of creation in Lebanon. Everything is scanned to try and detect the lightest indication of non-conformity. The director's answers apparently rely on a reading of the edited shots that seems to be limited to their narrative value. However, the way she speaks conveys a false good faith, a false naivety.

*Photo-Romance* plays on this gap between the uttered words, the images commented upon and the effect produced by them. Beyond the dead phrases used on stage by the two characters with opposed intentions, the audience perceives that elements in the filmed images can be read differently. Spectators then become more actively involved and deduce a third narrative that is less fictional and is directly related to the Lebanese situation. From a number of clues to be found in the dialogues, projected images and comments on them – but also in the absence of things, in what is not said and not shown – spectators construct a more critical representation of Lebanese society. *Photo-Romance* thus develops at the crossroads of three narrative constructs with different fictional status.

Lina Saneh and Rabih Mroué found part of their inspiration in Ettore Scola's film *Una giornata particolare* (1977). Though coming somewhat later than the Italian neorealist school, Scola's film conveys the feel of the late 1930s in showing the latent repression that weighed on Italian society and particularly on marginalized members such as women and homosexuals. The film recounts the meeting between a woman (the mother of several children, worn down by a meaningless life) and a rejected homosexual, who are left alone for a day as others have gone to a fascist demo.

The film on the screen of *Photo-Romance* transposes the plot of *Una giornata particolare* to a Lebanese context with Islam assuming the role of fascism, as women are still confined to household chores and have no rights to their own opinions or pleasure, and homosexuals are still repressed. However, neither the dialogues nor the projected images expose the social and political situation; it has to be induced from tonalities, hesitations or avoiding questions that touch upon sensitive areas, to which the spectators' attention is thus directed. When, for instance, the character of the director explains the connection between her film and Ettore Scola's, the censor's response clearly indicates that the reference to Scola is a sign of legitimacy – all the more so as she adds technical or aesthetic developments about her using a pre-existing work. She subtly concludes: 'All our work is based on the notion that there is nothing new to be invented.' Though this is not laboured, we can see how such an answer fits into the dominant conservative ideology embodied by the censor.

Only careful decoding can reveal the critical dimension within the filmed images. The first images seem to be lifted from a TV news programme. The screen is split and shots of two different demonstrations are shown next to each other. But the commenting words also deserve our attention as they tell us that these demonstrations are organised by the 'two main rival forces in the country' and aim at 'deciding on the identity of Lebanon'. To this end it is further stated that they will converge on a square in the city centre to show 'that there is not one Lebanon but two.' Irony can only be perceived through careful decoding. Indeed, the European spectators' eyes are immediately drawn to those newsreels that they soon understand as a clue to a problem, a conflict they have heard about.[4] These sequences tell them that there is an unresolved issue in this country that is still more or less at war. Now we cannot miss the irony and critical dimension in the commentary – heard in Arabic but with French subtitles: two opposed demonstrations converging to assert their opposition together and turn it into the foundation of Lebanese identity. The underlying criticism is aimed at the media as much as at the recurrent motif of conflicts in Lebanon: identity. Criticism is prompted by irony, and irony is a figure of speech that relies on a permanent double-entendre. Spectators have to supply the missing information, detect the gap and bridge it. The fact that the whole city is out in one or the other of the two demonstrations expresses a bi-polarity with no room for an alternative. People have to belong to one side or another, or else be marginalized. Irony brings out the issue of identity while nothing is explicitly said, but the validity of this is questioned straight away. Such irony points to the problem without actually mentioning it and sets up a reading protocol for the performance as a whole. It makes spectators active and prompts them to play a part in what is about to happen.

The still images shown on the screen point to concrete physical references, those of today's Lebanon (the fiction is set in 2007): streets, rooms within houses, and even the two characters construct a realistic representation of the context. The film, edited into stills, focuses on the two protagonists – the housewife, who is a ghostly presence in a patriarchal society, and the former activist who brings out the situation of the left in Lebanon. They carry the names of the authors, Lina Saneh and Rabih Mroué, which further blurs the all too neatly fictional dimension of the narrative and introduces some sort of continuum between the extra-diegetic reality of Lebanon: what is acted out on the stage and what is shown in the film. The momentum of the performance relies on the blurring of boundaries between fiction and reality. But the process is oriented.

We should also mention that the images are filmed without a soundtrack: in the diegetic context this indicates that the film is not finished. Sitting at a small desk under the screen, and under Arab music, the director reads the replies, which prevents too immediate and too obvious an effect of reality, that of the realist film relying on identification. Such uncoupling of words and images introduces a distance that prompts spectators to pay greater attention to what happens in the gap. Indeed, this is where criticism can step in. Cut off from images, the former left-wing activist's words take on a different value; they seem not to belong to the sort of normal flow to which we are used. Consequently, the political dimension is foregrounded. Rabih Mroué (the character in the film) refers to the many clans and factions that undermine Lebanon while the country seems affected with recurring amnesia: 'Nothing is remembered,' he says. Echoing the marginal situation of the two rejected characters, the film shows a paralysed society that is stuck between extremes (fundamentalism and capitalism) and infected by some minor or ordinary fascism that is conveyed by the introduction of drawings into the film. These drawings point to the family scene that is defined by prejudices, intolerance and moral rigidity. Again, thanks to those commented-upon computer-manipulated drawings, criticism is hidden under the plot and the apparent naivety of its presentation. As can be seen, Lina Saneh and Rabih Mroué use various visual props to expose a collective responsibility, without attempting to develop any systematic discourse.

The performance comes across as a quest in action that relies on spectators' active involvement. The audience follows what is said and debated on the stage, and in order to understand it has to formulate assumptions, for Photo-Romance is anything but didactic. While Lebanese censorship is clearly present on the stage, the performance deflects attention to a diffuse social censorship for which common people are responsible. Instead of a critique of a system, the performance proposes a questioning of people that make up society, their silences, their tacit agreements, their adhesion. Photo-Romance thus shows a local and regional totalitarianism, and through its very form it wagers on the possibility to use forms to ends they were not intended for.

Indeed, through the entwining of theatre and recorded images, the artists question the common assumptions underlying political theatre, about which it was generally agreed that its function is to expose the oppression of one group by another. Now as the issue of representation is the very material of their performance – not just its outcome – Lina Saneh and Rabih Mroué contribute to a new paradigm of political theatre. In committed or political theatre, recorded images are often used to testify, as evidence of some reality. Not so in Photo-Romance. In earlier performances as well, Rabih Mroué and Lina Saneh had already questioned the very notion of representation (e.g. in Qui a peur de *la représentation?* 2006). But the questions they raise – How can we tell a story? How can we speak up today? What is a film? What is theatre? – are also related to a concrete situation. The real is not a vague and undefined world but Lebanon in a context defined by war, fundamentalism and capitalism. Their theatre never conceals its specific anchoring but directs attention to ways of conveying this reality, of providing readings of it that determine a way of acting upon it.

All these elements (theatre, cinema, photos, music…) are taken apart on the stage. Artists thus expose both the media and the way they work. Art organizes representations, but it can also introduce critique into dominant representations. For Lina Saneh and Rabih Mroué, the point is to show that all forms of spectacles and images are relative by foregrounding their nature as constructions that involve choices made on the basis of objectives and interests. As a consequence, no representation can be held as true. The way the two Lebanese artists have worked presents choices and positions that underpin representations. In doing this, they indicate that choosing a representation is indeed a choice that involves a responsibility. This is their way of providing a subtle criticism of this ordinary fascism they perceive in Lebanese society.

Beyond the frequently repeated question 'how can we *say* the world of today on the stage?', *Photo-Romance* attempts to say what is socially 'unsayable' or cannot be said because of specific circumstances. We understand why *Photo-Romance* is less to be received as a performance than as a process, namely, the dismantling of images and discourse. In this, it is also part of the new artistic forms that no longer rely on a finite object. But this form is also political. First, as we have seen, because it works on the juxtaposition of images and drawings as well as of images and words rather than on their logical articulation, it makes a number of critical statements against Lebanese society without ever organizing them into a traceable and therefore easily censored discourse. Next, as they explode the fixed status of any kind of representation, Lina Saneh and Rabih Mroué provide an answer to a Lebanese society that is stuck between conflicting truths where no alternative voice can emerge. In this respect *Photo-Romance* does belong to a new paradigm of political theatre which, as I have shown elsewhere, no longer proposes the representation of a pre-established political construct (Delhalle 2006). This political theatre for today is no longer defined by a unifying answer. Founded on a sociology that aims at renewing the vision of the collective and individual subject, it now posits itself as the new locus of political experience, a praxis that subverts dominant frames of perception. In short, it is a form of theatre that takes some distance from the myth of absolute progress where the collective dimension – the 'we' – is always in an overbearing position, as a somewhat abstract ideal. If it still has an effect on the political principles of our vision of the world, it is no longer as the relay of some party or movement but through repeated breaks – to resist assimilation – and an ongoing debate in which all data are ceaselessly questioned. This new paradigm of political theatre is no longer focused on the issue of power and power relationships but stresses a reticular perception of our being in the world.

As it points to the responsibility of every member of a society in the social process,

Lina Saneh and Rabih Mroué's approach becomes subversive to various degrees depending on the audience. It can easily be imagined that the impact of the performance will be greater with a Lebanese audience. If we want to conclude on the transformation of the aesthetics of theatre under the influence of media, a work such as *Photo-Romance*, which combines an ancient art (theatre) and recorded images, shows the conditions in which theatre can be political today. If this political theatre (also to be found in *Rwanda 94*) uses representations, which is common in contemporary theatre, its effects can act on cognitive structures. In a nutshell, it develops from the assumption that cognitive subversion can contribute to a change in social reality.

**Nancy Delhalle** teaches theatre history and performance analysis at the University of Liège (Belgium). Her specialization is sociology of theatre and political theatre. She is a member of the editorial board of *Alternatives Théâtrales* and of *Prospero European Review*.

## NOTES

1  All quotations from French sources have been translated by the translator of the article, Christine Pagnoulle (University of Liège).
2  For an analysis of these sequences, see Delhalle (2007).
3  In this respect, see Delhalle (2006).
4  I will only consider this European perspective although the artists' ambition is obviously that their production can also be received in Lebanon.

## REFERENCES

Benjamin, W., 'L'œuvre d'art à l'époque de sa reproduction mécanisée'. In: *Ecrits français*. Paris, 1991.

Brecht, B., 'L'essai de Piscator'. In *Théâtre épique, théâtre dialectique*. Paris, 1999a.

–. 'Extrait d'un ABC du théâtre épique'. In: *Théâtre épique, théâtre dialectique*. Paris, 1999b.

Delhalle, N., *Vers un théâtre politique. Belgique francophone 1960-2000*. Brussels, 2006.

–. 'Un miroir inversé. La mise en scène de la télévision dans *Rwanda 94* du Groupov'. In: *Visibles*, 3 ('Intermédialité visuelle'), p. 99-106. Limoges, 2007.

Dort, B., *La Représentation émancipée*. Arles, 1988.

Groupov (M.-F. Collard, J. Delcuvellerie, J.-M. Piemme, and M. Simons), *Rwanda 94*. Paris, 2002.

Lehmann, H.-T., *Le Théâtre postdramatique*. Paris, 2002.

Piscator, E., *Le Théâtre politique*. Paris, 1962.

# A Campsite for the Avant-Garde and a Church in Cyberspace

## Christoph Schlingensief's Dialogue with Avant-Gardism

Anna Teresa Scheer

### *Atta-Atta*: a Melancholic Evocation of the Avant-Garde

> In [19]68 I was eight years old, but I demand that here and now, in 2001, I am allowed to try things out.
> Christoph Schlingensief (quoted in Heineke & Umathum 2002: 33)

Berlin, January 2003: Christoph Schlingensief's theatre performance *Atta-Atta: Art has Broken Out!* premieres in the Volksbühne. A motley group of 'artists', including Schlingensief, record themselves on video as they make an impassioned appeal for the Oberhausen short film festival committee to accept their submission. The scene, which references Schlingensief's beginnings in experimental film, appears to parody the beliefs its protagonists hold with regard to the radical potential of their own filmmaking visions. The next section of the performance sees Schlingensief as a wild 'action' painter, charging at canvases in his studio as his parents look on dubiously from the sofa in the TV room next door. The mise-en-scène – with the parents still visible in their small living room stage left – then opens out onto a camping site with tents, a setting which could be variously interpreted as a cheap vacation site, a place of temporary habitation, a vulnerable site exposed to the elements or possibly to an attack, a terrorist training site, or a mobile military encampment. In this semiotically ambiguous location, Schlingensief situates a group of artists and eccentrics.

In the course of the performance, the camp's assorted commune of oddballs enact strange ritualistic processions, witness the irrational litanies declaimed by members of their group and mimic the performances of well-known artists. Joseph Beuys with his hare, Hermann Nitsch's orgiastic experiments and Marina Abramovic's physically challenging works, familiar to the contemporary audience in terms of their photographic documentation, are clearly referenced in the piece. A giant inflatable tube of black paint invades the campsite and is wrestled to the ground by Schlingensief and the inhabitants who succeed in deflating its presumably malevolent intentions. The site manager announces over the intercom: 'Everyone should leave the campsite toilet as they would wish to find it'. Throughout the performance, a pre-recorded black-and-white film shot in amateur style is visible on two screens above the stage. It shows a film director (Oskar Roehler) as he awaits a group of actors who slowly gather at the Brandenburg Gate. They set off on a night stroll through Berlin, the purpose of which is not identified until they seem to enter the doors of the theatre, where they change into Ku Klux Klan costumes, apparently intending to invade the auditorium. One actor, Herbert Fritsch, does in fact appear onstage (in a suit), his movements followed in real time by a camerawoman. He grapples with Schlingensief, who finally leaves the stage, before he comments disparagingly on the prior performance and releases a number of chickens from their cages onstage, yelling 'Freedom!'.

The adumbration of live performance, pre-recorded film and live-video recording serves to disorient the audience's perceptions, not only in terms of what is actually happening in present time and what has occurred elsewhere, but also with regard to their expectations of the various mediums. The lack of perceptible purpose in the film heightens the suspense created for the audience as they see its protagonists enter the theatre foyer and attempt to prefigure what sort of denouement this may precede. As Marvin Carlson has suggested, live-video recording, 'makes possible a kind of visual experimentation that is impossible either in video or film by bringing the means of live transmission into the very space that is being transmitted' (Carlson 2008: 24). The notion of theatre operating as a 'hypermedium' has been discussed by Freda Chapple and Chiel Kattenbelt, who argue that it can offer 'multiple perspectives and foreground[ing] the making of meaning' for an audience as a space 'in-between realities' that constitute diverse media (2006: 20, 24). Put another way, theatre provides a potential space for reflexivity, both synchronic and diachronic, in its multimedial and multilayered stagings that extend beyond corporeality to generate a series of complex resonances for its audiences.

The resonances generated by *Atta-Atta* begin with the staccato phonetics of its title, which echoes those of the nihilistic art movement Dada and simultaneously references the name of the Saudi terrorist Mohammed Atta. The brief account of certain features of *Atta-Atta* unmistakeably points to Schlingensief's preoccupation with his artistic predecessors, their legacy or what remains of it (demystified to the condition of a campsite toilet), their status as acclaimed pioneers of the avant-garde and, primarily, the bearing of such a legacy on art and radical art practice given the social and political climate of the time. The climate in question was the build-up to the 2003 war on Iraq, following the 9/11 attacks on US landmarks and the initial retaliatory bombing campaign on Afghanistan. The thematic concerns of *Atta-Atta* circumscribed art, terrorism and a questioning of the methods employed by both parties to achieve their ends, which, inevitably, require spectators and/or witnesses. The production raised questions such as: Are art and terrorism diametrically opposed? Is today's martyr the answer to the failed avant-garde artist (as Schlingensief proclaimed onstage)? Does art possess any weapons of its own?[1] While attempting neither to put critical distance from its subject matter nor to offer linear or causal explanations of recent events, the performance did not avoid the megalomaniacal delusions of grandeur shared by both 'camps'.

The campsite dwellers and their melancholy citations of avant-garde performances reveal the dilemma of the artist, as Schlingensief perceived it, in the post-9/11 era. The work queries whether attempts at uninhibited artistic expression – uninterpellated by political ideologies, free of instrumentalization or even a liberal humanistic purpose – are now completely redundant or even still possible after the morbid spectacle of airliners flying into skyscrapers. A performer in *Atta-Atta* asks plaintively: 'How can one react when a few Saudi Arabian video artists lead 1:0?', thereby provocatively highlighting the anxiety of the 'great artist' who cannot bear to be trumped. The very idea that the terrorist pilots could be viewed as being engaged in a media performance was introduced – albeit unintentionally – by the composer Karlheinz Stockhausen during a press conference he gave after 9/11. The frequent misquoting of Stockhausen's comment in the media, which engendered a public furore, had him declaring 9/11 to be 'the greatest work of art there has ever been' (quoted in Virilio 2002: 45).

However, the televised attacks were quickly transposed from their initial occurrence in real time into a carefully edited slow-motion, before-and-after sequence, broadcast in synch with the hauntingly sad voice of the singer Enya. This transposition of a 'real' event follows the definition of 'remediation' as that which improves upon and 'refashion[s] other forms of media "in the name of the real"' (Bolter & Grusin 1999: 65). The same principle is, I argue, what informed the dramaturgy of *Atta-Atta*, with its aesthetic transpositions and investigations of avant-gardism and terrorism which provided the impulse for Schlingensief's subsequent desire to intervene in, and remediate, public perceptions of fear at the beginning of the war on Iraq.

Schlingensief's interest in replaying the radical gestures of the historical avant-garde raise the diagnosis of its end either before World War Two or, at the latest, by the end of the Sixties after the Cold War avant-gardes of Happenings and Fluxus. Its demise has been frequently considered, not least by Peter Bürger (*Theory of the Avant-Garde*, 1984) and Paul Mann (*The Theory-Death of the Avant-Garde*, 1991). But both appear to have left ajar a small window of opportunity, just in case, perhaps, the notion of a post Cold-War avant-garde was not finally and forever interred. In a later work, Bürger qualified his previously dismissive approach to the neo-avant-garde:

> Instead of trying to isolate the avant-garde impulse, we should ask ourselves whether it might contain a potential which could still be developed, if art is to be more than an institution that compensates for problems arising from the process of social modernization. (1992: 152)

It seems that a regenerative or palingenetic avant-garde 'potential' may still be dormant, in converse fashion to the scholarly desire to 'isolate', historizise and categorize its subversive qualities. Mann, in contrast to the 'death' his book discusses, makes a curious statement that infers an ongoing 'liveliness': 'If art sometimes operates through tacit collusion with discourse and sometimes through futile resistance, sometimes it also pursues a kind of resistance by collusion, a seizure of the means of discourse production' (Mann 1991: 25). The 'actions' implied by the language he uses invite comparisons with the concerns and aesthetics of Schlingensief's theatre praxis.

With the frequent incursions of his work into public spaces, Schlingensief perpetuated a longstanding dialogue with the aims of the historical avant-garde to forcibly close the gap between art and daily life. However, he also inserted politics into the mix and drew on their attempts to create his own models of 'unpredictable fields of action' that can be characterized by 'improvisation and the participation of the audience' (Berghaus 2005: 23). While it cannot be claimed that the repercussions of Schlingensief's work have brought about political change in either Germany or Austria, they did nonetheless cause irritation at many levels. Works such as *Chance 2000* (1998) and the well-documented project *Bitte Liebt Österreich* (Please Love Austria) in 2000 reached an audience via mass-media coverage that included national newspaper features, internet postings and radio and television broadcasts, thus providing the sort of attention for Schlingensief's projects more commonly reserved for politicians themselves, who in many instances reluctantly became protagonists in absentia (see Poet 2002; Varney 2010). Schlingensief achieved this most notoriously with *Bitte Liebt Österreich*, which directly targeted the 'absent' right-wing populist Jörg Haider and called attention to his xenophobic politics.

The sombre, pessimistic tone of *Atta-Atta* was underscored by the approaching Iraq war. In response to the question of whether – in view of its inevitability – he was afraid, Schlingensief said: 'I haven't bought a campervan for nothing. A helpless attempt to escape. We are all entering the Church of Fear' (quoted in Laudenbach 2003). Despite his pensive musings on the status of art and the vestiges of avant-gardism, Schlingensief's next project abandoned the prescribed art space of the theatre building in favour of public spaces – including cyberspace, in this case, as a website was dedicated to the project – to once again explore the dialectic between art and non-art, and experiment with avant-gardist ambitions to subvert the boundaries between art and life.

## The Antecedents of the *Church of Fear*

Schlingensief's founding of the *Church of Fear* (CoF) on 20 March 2003 coincided with the day the second war on Iraq began (Koegel & König 2005: 7). A website in both German and English was set up to inform potential members of its activities. The site featured a 'Barometer of Fear' – with stages ranging from 'Apocalypse' to 'Peace of Mind' – and, as an introduction to virtual visitors, a video trailer could be viewed. It begins with an audio collage of religious chanting, which becomes louder as the sound of a woman's screams can be heard. An image of an airport runway appears onscreen. Ominously dramatic music precedes a flash cut sequence of images of war zones, bombings, religious icons, political protests and prisoners, which abruptly cease as a calm, clearly British voice announces:

Welcome to the Church of Fear. [...] The Church of Fear is a community of non-believers. [...] The aim of the CoF is the achievement of an individual worldview. [...] The Church of Fear is only the launching platform for your very own missile of fear. The Church of Fear says: Fear is Power, Have Fear. Terror your own world.

The text on the website elaborates:

Let us fight the politicians' MONOPOLY ON TERROR!
They have taken our faith, but they will not take our fear!
The Church of Fear is a secular church and not a political party,
not an industry, not an institution and not beholden to any theatre! Just like you!
(Church of Fear, s.d.)

The deeply ironic notion of a secular church, its non-identification with political ide-ologies and the implicit assumption of autonomy on the part of the reader signal its in-terest in attracting free thinkers and maintaining its independence. The activist fervour of both texts seems to indicate an interest in creating a popular, grassroots social move-ment, welded together by the desire of its members to publicly acknowledge fear as a weapon and to oppose those institutions that, according to the CoF, were deliberately manipulating political and social fears. The targets of its critique extended to theatre, identified, in line with the other institutions listed, as a site of oppression to which one need not feel obliged or 'beholden'.

The Church's radical aims suggest that the impetus behind its founding was Schlin-gensief's desire to intervene – in both aesthetic and political terms – in what has been termed the 'politics of fear' (Füredi 2005; Altheide 2006). This phrase has often been used in regard to the mode of public discourse employed by the neo-liberal Bush ad-ministration and its Western allies following the 9/11 terrorist attacks in the US. Specif-ically, it denotes the implicit manipulation of the populace by the ruling government to hinder public dissent. Yet the political stance taken by the US also had direct implica-tions for those beyond its jurisdiction. The relative security that Germany had enjoyed throughout the past two decades had been shaken due to the fact that the attacks had been partially planned in Hamburg. As a result, and in line with countries including the US, UK and France, Germany sent troops to Afghanistan and drafted new anti-terrorist legislation aimed at increasing surveillance and enabling closer cooperation between police and international intelligence agencies (Safferling 2006: 1152). Capitalizing on the new measures deemed necessary for public safety, the German mainstream media networks were, as elsewhere, abuzz with talk of further 'terror', and potential 'sleeper-s'. With the impending war on Iraq, 'weapons of mass destruction' provided a new di-version from political issues at home, as images of military personnel seeking chemi-cal weapons in Iraq flashed on television screens around the world with increasing regularity.

In his book *Creating Fear. News and the Construction of Crisis* (2002), David Altheide has incisively argued that mainstream media networks are inextricably linked not only with 'spectacle and surveillance' but also with the military industrial complex, the framing of critical social issues and with agents of social control. In terms of the media coverage of the war(s) in Iraq, and pre-empting Schlingensief's project in remarkably prescient fashion, Altheide states:

> the news media are the main source and tool used to 'soften up' the audience, to prepare them to accept the justificatory account of the coming action. Fear in a democratic society requires the mass media. If these media are perpetuating claims about the 'other' – the likely targets of future state action – then this fear-generating endeavor becomes an act of *mass media terrorism* on the 'public body', if not the individuals who subsequently suffer from state actions. (2002: 12, emphasis added)

However, as Frank Furedi has pointed out, the rhetoric of fear has also been utilized successfully by the political left as well as by a wide assortment of interest groups ranging from pharmaceutical companies to green campaigners warning against the dangers of climate change. Thus, he asserts, 'the politics of fear captures a sensibility towards life in general' and 'tends to express a diffuse sense of powerlessness' (Furedi 2005: 130). This powerlessness is, in turn, reflected by the preference of transnational news formats for worst-case scenarios that typically offer no in-depth analysis or background contextualization to comprehend the complex issues they claim to 'cover'.

The all-pervasive spectacle of fear that proliferated in 2003 – accompanied by political, religious and paranoid rhetoric and the media's excesses of morbid imagery – was the territory Schlingensief's project explicitly sought to engage with. Drawing on the technologies of video, surveillance and computers, the CoF encompassed installation, performance and activism, combining a media campaign with an internet presence to insert its ambiguous messages into public spaces. It intentionally blurred conventional borders between art, political dissent, social critique and reality to engage a heterogeneous public in the urban locations it traversed.

## 50th Venice Biennale: Preaching Fear to the Art World

The first public manifestation of the CoF was at the Venice Biennale, where it was initially unveiled in June 2003 as an art project in the opening week. A daily report that summarized the *Church*'s daily activities was circulated to visitors. For 14 June, it read:

> Venice in fear. [...] Confused by various sorts of empty art, more and more people have lost their faith in art's power to change the world. The *Church of Fear* gives even those non-believers a new home. So far more than 800 visitors have entered their names in the CoF subscription lists. [...] The internet jackpot rise up (*sic*) to

over 30,000 Euro. More than 4,500 holy pictures have been sold. (Van der Horst 2005, unpaginated 'Daily Report' section)

The bizarre features of the report – a church for non-believers, an internet jackpot, references to empty art, fear and holy pictures – created a semiotic jumble that I will attempt to unravel in this section.

In the Arsenale grounds, Schlingensief had installed a small, white wooden church from which a muezzin's call to prayer was audible. A large sign with the imperative 'Have Fear' stood outside the entrance. The interior featured a confessional booth with the phrases 'Look out behind you!' and 'Look up!' scrawled in white chalk along with childishly executed voodoo masks, an image of a rotting hare and a pug dog's anus (Koegel & König 2005: 20, 24). Visitors to the site were welcomed by CoF members who distributed printed material and explained how one's own 'congregation of fear' could be established. Interested parties were told that the church would promise nothing and make no demands on its members. There would be no pressure to subscribe to any particular dogma nor, they emphasized, would the CoF offer any solutions to the personal fears of its members.

In the Giardini nearby, the church held its first ritual, an international pole-sitting competition. The practice of pole-sitting dates back to AD 423 when the Stylites, a group of early Christian ascetics, spent days and nights atop pillars as a ritual of purification. In Venice, the poles used were constructed from roughly hewn tree trunks, approximately 2.5 metres high, with a small canopy providing limited shade and a backrest with a seat that could be supported with cushions. Atop their poles, seven contestants (from Russia, Switzerland, Mexico, Italy and Germany) were required to spend seven days, with a fifteen-minute break every three hours, meditating on their

Fig. 1    Pole-sitting at the 50ᵗʰ Venice Biennale, 2003 © Patrick Hilss, 2003.

fears. Whoever remained on his or her pole for the longest period of time would be declared the winner. Sitting scores for each participant were recorded on a blackboard, and visitors were permitted to pole-sit with their favourite competitor, thereby increasing the total time accrued by the sitter. Through the purchase of 'holy pictures' or by placing bets via the CoF website, spectators could enter the 'fun' and bet on the contestants.

The pole-sitting event was filmed and streamed back live to the church, where visitors were required to kneel in order to view the sitters via a computer screen visible through a low-cut slit in the wall. The conditions of viewing were a sardonic comment on the status of surveillance technology in the global city. Gabriella Giannachi has accurately identified that, with the increased monitoring of citizens both in the workplace and in urban spaces, 'Surveillance is not simply reducible to the act of putting someone under surveillance. It implies their commercial and political exploitation' (2007: 44). This act was inverted by having visitors kneel to observe those 'performing'. It was further commented upon by a sign adjacent to the pole-sitting area that read 'Win With Your Losers', which was both an encouragement to place bets and ironically extrapolated upon by the CoF website: 'Thus everybody may be in a position to profit from people degraded to a profitless position' (*Church of Fear*, s.d.). The slogan pointed to the 'degraded' status of those who live in fear without the possibility of profiting from it. Degradation in this context refers to the conditions of subjects in late capitalism, who see their private capital – for Schlingensief's purposes, fear – misappropriated by industries such as the national security sector, correctional facilities, surveillance firms, pharmaceutical and private healthcare companies and defence contractors. These industries successfully manipulate social fears to increase revenue, desirous of an anxious public that is then vulnerable to whatever solutions they propose. Degradation through fear also refers to the citizens of countries marked by war and poverty who have little or no capital and whose fears do not register as fully as those of the citizens of Western democracies.

The CoF website regularly updated photographs of the pole-sitting event and duly noted the sitting scores of the contestants. On day seven of the competition, Ralf Baumgarten of Germany – a former priest – was declared the winner and announced by the CoF to be the new 'Pillar Saint of Modernity'. The pole-sitters dismounted in ceremonial fashion and a prize cheque was handed over, while at a reception held later all the participants were appointed 'Ambassadors of Fear'. Later, on the Piazza San Marco, 350 Biennale visitors arrived to collect on their bets, and the competition was declared to be over.

## Fear and Fundamentalism

In order to understand the paradoxes of the CoF's activities, it may be useful to examine the etymology of the word 'church'. The Greek word *ekklesia* is a compound of the preposition '*ek*', meaning 'out', and the noun '*klesis*' which means 'summons' or 'invitation'. The origins of the word generally identified an assembly or gathering of people for any purpose, with no direct relation to those specially chosen by God (Ferguson 1996: 129-130). According to this definition, the idea of a secular church becomes less a contradiction in terms than a statement of intention, implying that the CoF was in fact a group of people who had come together to examine and consider fear in a variety of contexts, rather than a movement that aimed to denigrate all religious beliefs.

The modest white wooden church installed at the Biennale recalled those often seen in rural areas of the United States in the so-called 'Bible Belt' associated with the neo-conservative religious right and its alliances with the military. The sound of the muezzin broadcast from the church was incongruous with its appearance, but it created a linkage with the concepts of an influential book by Samuel P. Huntington *The Clash Of Civilizations and the Remaking of World Order* (1998). The 'clash' of the title refers to the so-called conflict between 'Islam' and 'the West' that Huntington predicted would be an inevitable part of the post Cold War world. For Schlingensief, it also alluded to religious fear as practised by both the Christian right and Islamic fundamentalists. Fundamentalism stresses strict and literal adherence to a set of basic principles and, in their attempts to impose their views on the rest of the world, religious fundamentalists are hostile to anything that does not concur with their beliefs. The common denominator of both fundamentalist groups is their use of fear as a driving force and their belief in binary constructions of good and evil, believers and unbelievers, heaven and hell and God and Satan. Both groups have extolled the approaching end of the world while making exorbitant claims of salvation for their followers. The fanatical belief they share in a controlling deity with the power to exterminate wrongdoers with his wrath relies heavily on fear as the governing principle of their faiths.

Fig. 2    The small white church at the Venice Biennale, 2003 © Etzard Piltz, 2003.

Fear as a tool to shore up the authority of religious institutions has been in use for centuries. It is a central component of religious pedagogy promoted by Christian fundamentalists and adherents of the apocalyptic 'Rapture' movement who believe that Christ will return to earth to save his followers and then proceed to execute non-believers in a period known as 'the Tribulation' (Kagin 2003: 38). However, the conviction that politics has a moral obligation to carry out God's work was also underscored by the Bush administration and its Manichean world view. The discourse of the 'War on Terror' was validated with the unambiguously religious rhetoric of George W. Bush, whose jeremiad-style speeches on good and evil including references to the war as a 'crusade' (Kradel 2004) encroached on the religious terrain of a battle between the 'righteous' and the 'unrighteous'. While Schlingensief's project was not constructed as a direct attack on the Bush administration or its policies, its imagery exposed and exaggerated the narrative of fear underpinning both conservative neo-liberal foreign policy and Christian nationalism.

## Mediatized Terror, Counter-Images and a Counterpublic

In his book *Liquid Fear* (2006), which deals specifically with rising fear in contemporary Western societies, Zygmunt Bauman discusses insecurity in relation to a wide range of concerns: the instability of a world post 9/11, global warming, the increasing precariousness of working life, the dismantling of the welfare state and the disintegration of social security as previously constructed by family, neighbourhoods and other communities. Ironically, he points out, the technological progress made in developed countries over the past fifty years has led neither to a greater sense of security, nor to a renewed sense of agency over the powers that inform and affect our lives (Bauman 2006: 157). Passive viewing of the daily news exacerbates a sense of helplessness while the promises made by mainstream media to keep us 'informed' encourage a sense of perpetual and anxious vigilance. The politics of neo-liberalism and unlimited globalization have, as Bauman postulates, created docile populations easily manipulated by fear and willing to surrender democratic principles in the attempt to guarantee security within and around their national borders. Politicians vow to protect national borders, fight 'terror', increase public safety, secure natural resources and defend economic prosperity on the condition that the public shows support for their political agendas, or 'belief in them', by means of the ballot box.

By employing one of the expedient features of cyberspace in terms of its capacity to extend beyond national borders, the CoF constructed a unified, global identity for itself – clearly in excess of its actual, active membership – in order to demand 'non-belief' in the political discourses circulating in regard to fear and terrorism. In its radical calls for 'non-believers' to take action, the CoF appeared to construct itself as a *counterpublic* in opposition to institutionalized power. Here, the term 'counterpublic' describes a group that sees its discourse as excluded by the broader, more dominant political and public spheres and which seeks to mobilize communication networks to advance its interests via 'parallel discursive arenas' (Fraser 1992: 123). Schlingensief's attempt to gain control over the meaning of words such as 'sleepers' and 'terror', misappropriated by political agendas, as well as the re-appropriation and spread of terms such as 'terrorist' and 'explosive' by an active cyber-community forum, were central to the CoF project. The populist tone of the English flash text on the website reveals the subversively political ground of the project:

> You sleepers of the world! Wake up now! Are you planning a terrorist action? Stand up for your right to personal terror! Become a member of the CHURCH OF FEAR and take part in our actions worldwide!
> Fear is power
> Fear is our explosive
> Confess your fear
> Terror Your World!!!
> (Church of Fear, s.d.)

Staking its claim to fear as private property, the CoF used a form of rhetoric more common to tabloid media and cheap advertising techniques that use rhetorical questions and exhortations to 'Buy Now!' The linguistic component of the work co-opts the notion of the 'vox populi', or 'the people's voice', drawing attention to the use of language as political currency while simultaneously co-opting it for itself (Rectanus 2004: 243). By associating Christian iconography and language with the images of terror seen on the nightly news, it attempted to question both what a 'terrorist' actually is and how the use of the word 'terrorism' has been employed to create political leverage (ibid.). The deployment of 'holy pictures' on the website in relation to texts on fear composed by CoF members, or 'Saints of Fear', ridiculed the idea of religious martyrdom and 'salvation rhetoric' as an antidote to contemporary anxieties. Through the bizarre juxtaposition of images and language related to 'terrorism', both the website and the CoF's physical manifestations sought to intervene in the dominant production of fear discourses and imagery by inserting Schlingensief's own subversive readings of socio-political events. Schlingensief's intentional clashing of images, context and language recall his reference to the container event in Vienna as a 'Bilderstörungsmaschine' (in Poet 2002). This self-coined term describes a machine that functions as a disturbance or produces malfunction or breakdown in the 'Bilder' or images it is connected with. The intermedial strategies of the CoF project were similarly designed to 'scramble' the connections usually made in terms of the graphics, images and text that served the interests of those propagating the dominant fear discourses of 2003.

Thus, the slogan 'Fear is the Answer' that featured on CoF publicity material was, according to Schlingensief, 'the call to see things from another perspective' (Koegel & König 2005: 20). Such a perspective would embrace the idea of public admission to private fear as a solution to social insecurity in the form of a common bond shared by all communities, not as a problem for politicians to manipulate. The pole-sitting events encouraged individuals to publicly display their readiness to embrace their own fears and test their endurance while admitting that they had lost the ability or desire to believe in the kind of 'fear management' offered by political and religious institutions. Fears of death, poverty, aging, terrorism or illness would, in the Church's view, become the property or – to put it in financial terms – the capital of the church member and not of a political or evangelical organization. The CoF's call to fear was a call to *publicly* fear such organizations and their political alliances, while valorizing private fear as a valuable commodity – one that diverse institutions sought to exploit yet with no intention of providing solutions to the underlying causes of fear such as poverty, unemployment and social injustices.

## Moving Corpus: A Social Sculpture?

*Actually, I want to get back into the picture and I can't do that without movement. So what should I do?*
Christoph Schlingensief (quoted in Heineke & Umathum 2002: 5)

In contrast, however, to the privacy entailed by the contemplation of one's personal fears, the CoF sought external witnesses for its group activities. After gathering in Cologne, Schlingensief and CoF members walked to Frankfurt, Germany's financial capital, in a five-day procession entitled *Moving Corpus*. Images of the march show a group of people holding banners with the words 'Terror' and 'Have Fear' – people who seem, in fact, to be promoting fear. That this was indeed what they were doing does not detract from the Church's vision of a community that was made mobile through fear rather than passive and invisible, each isolated in their homes. When asked by a journalist during the *Moving Corpus* procession, 'What does it all mean?' Schlingensief responded, 'Meaning is always a problem for television. We don't have that, we are simply on the move' (Uphoff 2003: 74). His refusal to give a ready-made interpretation of his project for unreflective consumption by a TV audience or a snappy sound bite for the media accentuates his reluctance to foreclose or categorize his work as politics, art or even political art. In this view, one could say that, while the CoF is not resisting hegemonic powers, it is participating in a newly configured protest movement, with the emphasis on 'movement' rather than on old ideologies and fixed binary positions.

By maintaining a deliberate ambiguity about his intentions, Schlingensief sought to avoid the dismissal that usually accompanies protest movements with 'resistance' as their core methodology. It can indeed be argued that resistance movements are all too easily absorbed by the rhetoric of freedom our democracies permit. And should that fail, their activities can be criminalized or outlawed by legislation such as the Patriot Act passed in the US in 2001, which found its counterpart in Germany's 'security package', albeit in a more moderate form (Safferling 2006: 1152). Schlingensief has claimed that generating 'contradiction not resistance' (quoted in Poet 2002) is his preferred modus operandi, and by choosing to operate within mainstream media discourses – as op-

Fig. 3    Schlingensief on the pilgrimage to Germany's financial capital © Patrick Hilss, 2003.

posed to distancing himself from them – his work provides an alternative to the weaknesses inherent in binary protest modes that focus on being *against* something.

The implication that the process is in fact the goal stands at the heart of Schlingensief's interventionist and performative cultural actions. Once a project has been conceived and set up in its raw form, it is 'exposed' in public, where unpredictable elements determine the course of action and spectators become participants critically engaging with the content, as we shall see happened in Frankfurt.

But, firstly, in view of contemporary debates on aesthetics and politics (see, for example, Rancière 2006), it is relevant to compare Schlingensief with one of his predecessors, with whom he is – in German criticism – most often equated.

While perhaps not immediately apparent, the work of Joseph Beuys (1921-1986) and his engagement with the diverse mediums of sculpture, drawing, installation, performance and political activism influenced Schlingensief primarily with regard to the latter. Like Beuys, he consistently sought to merge art, politics and daily life in his projects. References to Beuys and his works have frequently appeared in Schlingensief's numerous political *aktionen*, or 'actions,' to borrow Beuys's term for activities he distinguished from 'performance'. The title of Schlingensief's 1997 Kassel Documenta project, *My Felt, My Fat, My Hare: 48 Hours of Survival for Germany*, clearly reveals itself as a quotation of iconographic motifs belonging to the work of Beuys. In the German federal election year of 1998, he founded his own political/art party called *Chance 2000* and borrowed Beuys's slogans 'Vote for Yourself' and 'Active Neutrality' as part of its media campaign (Schlingensief & Hegemann 1998: 18).

As an activist, Beuys demanded the increased participation of citizens in politics, defining his vision of *soziale plastik* or social sculpture as 'how we mould and shape the world in which we live' (quoted in Harlan 2007: 9). Beuys's endeavours to merge his artistic practice with his political goals are evident in his founding of the *Organization for Direct Democracy by Referendum* in 1971, and his *Information Office* at the Kassel Documenta exhibition in 1972, where he discussed and debated issues on current society, politics and the arts with gallery visitors for one hundred days, to cite only two such examples (Stachelhaus 1991: 108-9). A passionate advocate of the integration of art into education and life, Beuys believed it could ultimately bring about social change and political transformation.

Schlingensief's attempts to break through the social inertia produced by the proliferation of fear discourses recall the efforts of Beuys to stimulate social change through the energy created by movement or *Bewegung*. Beuys considered post-war 1970s humanity 'in its present psychological configuration' to be in a state of 'deep torpor' that could only be overcome via the principle of *Bewegung* aligned with 'provocation' (Bunge 1996: 265). In a Beuysian context, provocation refers to the artist's attempts to create environments or performances that would effect a change of perspective on the part of the spectators or audience, encouraging them, in a sense, to revision their modes of seeing, perceiving and responding to art and its broader role in the cultural landscape.

Schlingensief's project differed quite considerably from Beuys's, however, who has been heavily criticized for casting himself in the role of shaman or social healer. Schlingensief rejected the latter's esoteric endowment of his *objets d'art* and public performance activities and was sceptical of Beuys's assertions of the healing powers of art to achieve social transformation. Whilst clearly foregrounding his own presence in his work, as did Beuys, and professing a non-cynical commitment to what he espoused, Schlingensief tried to avoid the accusation levelled at Beuys by art historian Benjamin Buchloh, who claimed he was 'in favour of a renewed foregrounding of the artist as a privileged being, a seer that provides deeper knowledge [...] to an audience that is in deep dependence and in need of epiphanic revelations' (Buchloh 2001: 82).

This critique has been tempered by a more recent analysis that sees Beuys's presence in his works not as a means of self-promotion but as being 'part of a process which is varied and shifting' and engaged in 'a work which is open and subject to contestation by those who enter into its space' (Nicholson 2007: 119) – a description that applies equally well to Schlingensief's activities. Nevertheless, I would suggest that the CoF presented a platform for Schlingensief to lampoon the construction of the artist as a messianic figure and 'seer'. The Beuysian dead hare was indeed one of the 'totem' figures in the small white church, but it was shown in juxtaposition to a pug dog's anus, a symbol that is unlikely to engender any significant esoteric connotations. In contrast to the mythical status that Beuys attributed to certain events in his personal history, Schlingensief insisted upon the bourgeois ordinariness of his background as the only son of a pharmacist and a nurse from Oberhausen in West Germany. Thus, there remains a playful inconclusiveness about Schlingensief's position as artist and spokesman of his own church, aware perhaps of his tendency toward 'compulsive self-exposure', as Buchloh (2001: 210) would have it, while undermining his own messianic grandiosity by having a shabby plush donkey on wheels as the mascot or 'totem' accompanying the CoF's perambulations. While Schlingensief played with the notion of the artist as a godlike figure, he disavowed it by affirming himself as part of an autonomous collective (Koegel & König 2005: 44). Members of the CoF were at liberty to carry out their own actions, post reports and photographs on the website forum and influence the transmission of the church's activities, thereby undermining the concept of the artist as sole leader, visionary or high priest.

## Self-Marginalization in Frankfurt

Upon the CoF's arrival in Frankfurt, a 'Last Supper' event was organized for the public in the Bockenheimer Depot. Over 800 people gathered to welcome the Moving Corpus procession, take part in the supper and witness the preparations for the next pole-sitting event to take place at the Hauptwache, Frankfurt's most famous square. A key difference from the Venice Biennale environment was that a public casting situation was set up for the socially marginalized, 'unemployed, homeless and/or hopeless' who would then become the centrepiece of the event. Once again passers-by were encouraged to place bets on their favourite sitter, in order to 'make visible how unemployment can be turned into consumer goods when it has entertainment value' (Görres Kulturbetrieb 2003). This statement underpins the difference between the historical avant-gardes' attack on the institutions of art, which those institutions were relatively quickly capable of subsuming, and Schlingensief's critique of commodity relations, which acknowledges that there is no outside position from which to take an objective stance. Schlingensief's self-reflexivity in regard to the socio-cultural contexts in which his work took place complies with Auslander's assertion that 'postmodernist political art must position itself within postmodern culture, it must use the same representational means as all other cultural expression yet remain permanently suspicious of them' (1994: 23). The problem remains, however, that Schlingensief's body of work concurs neither with 'postmodernist political' nor 'postmodern art'. Rather, his performance events reveal a motivation similar to that of the Fluxus movement, and Beuys, by relating to socio-political activism, playfulness, artistic aspirations and the intentional blurring of the boundaries between them all.

In Frankfurt, the status of the CoF as an art project was not foregrounded as was the case at the Venice Biennale, and members of the public, unaware of other contexts, perceived it more as a 'real' event that was extending an invitation to participate. Outside an obvious art context, the project found a new audience consisting not only of unemployed and homeless but also of 'punks gathering to support one of their own who was participating, bankers who came to poke fun, Christians who wanted to argue, culture

Fig. 4    Pole-sitters victory in Frankfurt © Patrick Hilss, 2003.

vultures to have a laugh and anti-fascists who enquired about a possible collaboration' (Malzacher 2003: 21).

For all the aforementioned interest groups, an open microphone was available to communicate with the spectators, and over the course of the contest, opinions and grievances were aired, providing an interactive dimension for this public work. Thus, in Frankfurt, the CoF became a social project, with the socially underprivileged or 'outsiders' in the position of looking down on the spectators, lending them an aura of holiness while the city went about its financial business. In essence, the pole-sitters were performing a practice of 'self-marginalization' by revealing their inability to believe in established religious and/or political doctrines. This contrasts with other public assemblies where people come together to demonstrate their 'belief' in something, be it a religious faith, a political party or social cause. The CoF's public activities draw on 'the society of the spectacle' – as conceptualized by Guy Debord – to turn performance into spectacle, utilizing its visibility and ostension to draw attention, not away from the political context (as in Roman bread and circus spectacles) but back to it. Using the methods of mass spectacle, the project subverted the principles of commodification and consumption that usually accompany it – there being nothing concrete to purchase or consume. Participation in the event, either active or passive, meant contributing to the spectacle while not necessarily being entertained by it. The spectacle of 'pole-sitting' became a public admission of personal fear and, as such, used public space more commonly dominated by consumer transactions as a site to reclaim the autonomy of one's own emotions from political manipulation.

## Conclusion: A Church with no Walls

The CoF was a short-lived movement of no fixed location, building or diocese, crossing borders from art installation and cyber-community network to public activities and media event. The counter-images and fear discourses it created, in opposition to the dominant flow of images and rhetoric produced by the media and political leaders, constitute one feature of the political aspect of the work. Within the ambiguity of the Church's goals, the intention was not to dwell in a private world but to create a widespread social movement. And, according to website updates, the Church had a total of nine hundred communities with over twenty-one thousand members on six continents. However, in terms of its employment of virtual space, some criticism of its exaggeratedly colourful claims is in order. The membership numbers as stated on the website cannot be verified nor can the alleged participation of groups in La Paz, Bombay, Lüderitz or Port-au-Prince. Given that the CoF's activities took place exclusively in wealthy areas of Europe such as Venice, Cologne and Frankfurt, can predominantly white subjects with full access to technologies stand in for the bodies and the fears of those whose countries usually make the news when disaster strikes or when military measures are deemed necessary against them? Is fear the great leveller? Despite the prevailing tendency to consider the internet as having a global reach, David Lieberman (1999: 1A) has pointed out that 'the Internet revolution is largely bypassing the poor, minorities and those who live in rural communities.' Had the website been accessible in different languages, the claims to a diverse global movement may have been justified. Pole-sitting events did not take place in London or the US as announced, which, due to Schlingensief's mostly unknown status there, would have facilitated a new perspective and even expanded the CoF community in curiously interesting ways.

Although the CoF has not been active since the end of 2003, neither has it been acknowledged as 'finished', and elements of its iconography were incorporated or 'remediated' into the stage design of Schlingensief's *Parsifal* at the Bayreuth Festival in 2004, itself a bastion of bourgeois, 'high-brow' culture (Schlingensief quoted in Koegel & König 2005: 39).[2] The website contains no updates and the discussion forum is closed, but details of the pole-sitting events and other pages remain accessible for 'members and sympathisers'. Its main function now seems to be as a document of what *did* happen and to promote, in typically hyperbolic fashion, Schlingensief's solo CoF-related ventures. These include the publication of Museum Ludwig's *AC. Christoph Schlingensief: Church of Fear* catalogue in 2005, and the installation of the wooden church at the museum in the same year that Pope Benedict XVI visited Cologne for World Youth Day. Although Schlingensief had been invited to install the small white church as part of an exhibition, he emphasized that it was only one component of the entire work. Making it clear that the CoF did not belong in its entirety to a museum, which had only a relic of it, Schlingensief underlined its autonomy and its connections to Beuys's concept of social sculpture (quoted in Koegel & König 2005: 37-38).

The CoF's flexibility as art event, ritual procession, public intervention and cyber-movement make it an example of socially engaged art that can operate in the form of a counterpublic for a brief period before morphing into a new form. This is perhaps in keeping with the temporal, campsite location of the avant-garde in Schlingensief's *Atta-Atta* production and its 'potential' (Bürger 1992), which would appear to be a fleeting phenomenon in response to the demands of its times. The various manifestations of the *CoF* – in the co-optation of public spaces and the invitation to participate – raise again the possibility of art encroaching on political arenas to create a counterflow of images and turn public reflection back on itself to examine the contradictions between perception of supposedly responsible politics and irresponsible art.

**Anna Scheer** is a contributor to and co-editor (with Tara Forrest) of the book *Christoph Schlingensief: Art without Borders* (Intellect, 2010). She is currently writing her doctoral thesis on Schlingensief's theatre practice at the University of Melbourne and lectures at the Centre for Theatre and Performance at Monash University.

**NOTES**

1   Schlingensief raised this question in a seminar series held at the Volksbühne from 2-20 December 2002 on the thematics of art, terrorism, politics and crime.
2   In 2009, Schlingensief's production *Ein Kirche der Angst vor der Fremden in Mir* (A Church of Fear for the Stranger in Me) was invited to the Berlin Theatertreffen. However, this work was related to his sudden diagnosis with cancer in 2008 and, as such, was an expression of his subjective fear and was not linked to the activities of the *CoF* per se. In contrast to the latter, no English title was given for the work.

**REFERENCES**

Altheide, D., *Creating Fear. News and the Construction of Crisis*. New York, 2002.

Auslander, P., *Presence and Resistance. Postmodernism and Cultural Politics in Contemporary American Performance*. Ann Arbor, 1994.

Bauman, Z., *Liquid Fear*. Cambridge, 2006.

Berghaus, G., *Avant-Garde Performance, Live Events and Electronic Technologies*. London/New York, 2005.

Bolter, J. D. and R. Grusin, *Remediation. Understanding New Media*. Cambridge/London, 1999.

Buchloh, B. H., 'Beuys: Twilight of the Idol, Preliminary Notes for a Critique'. In: G. Ray, (ed.), *Joseph Beuys. Mapping the Legacy*. New York, 2001.

Bunge, M., *Zwischen Intuition und Ratio. Pole des bildnerischen Denkens bei Kandinsky, Klee und Beuys*. Stuttgart, 1996.

Bürger, P., 'Everydayness, Allegory and the Avant-garde. Some Reflections on the Work of Joseph Beuys'. In: P. Bürger, *The Decline of Modernism*. Cambridge, 1992.

Carlson, M., 'Has Video Killed the Theatre Star? Some German Responses'. In: *Contemporary Theatre Review*, 18,1, p. 20-29. London, 2008.

Chapple, F. and C. Kattenbelt (eds.), *Intermediality in Theatre and Performance*. Amsterdam, 2006.

Church of Fear, 'Right for Personal Terror', 'Pole-sitting conditions in Venice', and 'Media Gallery'. In: *Church of Fear*. s.l., s.d. Web. < http://www.church-of-fear.net >

Ferguson, E., *The Church of Christ. A Biblical Ecclesiology for Today*. Grand Rapids, 1996.

Fraser, N., 'Rethinking the Public Sphere. A Contribution to the Critique of Actually Existing Democracy'. In: C. Calhoun (ed.), *Habermas and the Public Sphere*. Cambridge, 1992.

Furedi, F., *Politics of Fear. Beyond Left and Right*. London/New York, 2005.

Giannachi, G., *The Politics of New Media Theatre. Life®™*. London/New York, 2007.

Harlan, V. (ed.), *What is Art? Conversations with Joseph Beuys*. London, 2007.

Heineke, T. and S. Umathum (eds.), *Christoph Schlingensiefs Nazis rein, Nazis raus*. Frankfurt, 2002.

Kagin, E. F., 'The Gathering Storm'. In: K. Blaker (ed.), *The Fundamentals of Extremism. The Christian Right in America*. Michigan, 2003.

Koegel, A. and K. König (eds.), *AC. Christoph Schlingensief: Church of Fear*. Köln, 2005.

Kradel, A., 'God on Our Side. The Religious Rhetoric of Recent U.S. Presidents'. Paper presented at the annual meeting of the American Political Science Association, Hilton Chicago and the Palmer House Hilton, Chicago, Illinois, 16 May 2004. <http://www.allacademic.com/meta/p60644_index.html>

Laudenbach, P., 'Wer Kunst macht wird so leicht kein Terrorist'. In: *Tagesspiegel*, 23 January 2003.

Lieberman, D., 'Internet Gap Widening'. In: *USA Today*, 9-11 July 1999.

Malzacher, F., 'Die Kirche Lebt'. In: *Frankfurter Rundschau*, 18 September 2003.

Mann, P., *The Theory-Death of the Avant-Garde*. Bloomington, 1991.

Nicholson, T. J., *Actions towards the Image. On Traces, Images and Memory in the Work of Joseph Beuys*. PhD thesis, University of Melbourne, School of Culture and Communication, 2007.

Poet, P., *Ausländer Raus, Schlingensief's Container* (DVD). Monitorpop Entertainment, 2002.

Rancière, J., *The Politics of Aesthetics*. London/New York, 2006.

Rectanus, M. W., 'Populism, Performance, and Postmodern Aesthetics. Christoph Schlingensief's Politics of Social Intervention'. In: *Gegenwartsliteratur*, 3, p. 225-249. Tübingen, 2004.

Safferling, C. J. M., 'Terror and Law. German Responses to 9/11'. In: *Journal of International Criminal Justice*, 4, 5, p. 1152-1165. Oxford, 2006.

Schlingensief, C. and C. Hegemann., *Chance 2000. Wähle Dich Selbst*. Cologne, 1998.

Stachelhaus, H., *Joseph Beuys*. New York, 1991.

Stockhausen, K., 'Message from Professor Karlheinz Stockhausen'. In: *Karlheinz Stock-hausen*. s.l., 2001. Web. <http://www.stockhausen.org/message_from_karlheinz.html>

Uphoff, H., 'Fadenscheinigkeit mit Fadenscheinigkeit bekämpfen. Schlingensief und die Church of Fear'. In: *Novo Magazin*, 67/68, p. 72-75. Frankfurt/Main, 2003.

Van der Horst, J., 'Daily Report, June 14, 2003'. In: A. Koegel and K. König (eds.), *AC. Christoph Schlingensief: Church of Fear*. Köln, 2005.

Varney, D., '"Right now Austria looks ridiculous": *Please Love Austria! – Reforging the Interaction between Art and Politics'*. In: T. Forrest and A. T. Scheer (eds.), *Christoph Schlingensief. Art Without Borders*. Bristol, 2010.

Virilio, P., *Ground Zero*. London/New York, 2002.

Görres Kulturbetrieb, 'Church of Fear Pfahlsitzwettbewerb "WIN WITH YOUR LOSER!".' In: *Görres Kulturbetrieb*, s.l., 2003. Web. <http://www.kulturbetrieb.com/gkmain_de/projekte/church_of_fear.html>

# Echoes from the Animist Past

## Abattoir Fermé's Dark Backward and Abysm of Time

Evelien Jonckheere

> When I was little I used to make robots out of wallpaper my father brought from work. At a certain moment I could barely enter my room. The place was filled with robots.
> Stef Lernous[1]

Children like to play. They animate lifeless objects, often with grotesque gestures. When they get bruised by bumping into a table, the table is to blame: it's a 'bad table'. A childish environment seems to be filled with demons, both good and bad. It was Jean Piaget, the cognitive psychologist, who in 1929 considered 'animism' a typical feature of the development of children (Looft & Bartz 1969: 1). Already in 1906, Ernst Jentsch had made a similar observation in his essay 'On the Psychology of the Uncanny'.

The most 'uncanny' theatre spectacles in Flanders by far are made by Abattoir Fermé, a theatre company founded in 1991 in Mechelen, with a core group consisting of director Stef Lernous and actors Tine Van den Wyngaert, Nick Kaldunski, Kirsten Pieters, Chiel Van Berkel and Pepijn Coudron. Since the performance *Bloetverlies* ('Blood loss') in 2003, they have obtained a firm position in the Flemish theatre landscape and abroad: in 2006, Romeo Castellucci invited them to Cesena, and they also performed at the 2010 Avignon Festival.

To be certain, their performances are not in the least childish but rather illustrations of a frightening and despicable world of violence and sex. Inspired by media such as exploitation movies, comic books and fairytales, Abattoir Fermé displays detached characters in a ritualistic atmosphere with animistic roots. Breaking down one taboo after another, they present subversive spectacle that is as amusing as it is touching.

In this chapter I will interpret Abattoir Fermé's spectacle as an answer to the contemporary urge for transgression or 'liminal experience' that is closely connected with concepts like the uncanny, the grotesque, the carnivalesque and the marvellous. Even in a modern rational world, people look for thrills that confront them with the limits of life and take them into an illusionary world. Abattoir Fermé illustrates and answers both the urge and the thrills with transgressive content and forms. The latter results in mutating media: their theatrical vocabulary is mixed with film, television, games, painting, photography, etc. Before examining the formal transgressions of these mutating media, however, I will discuss the concept of liminality and its traces in performances by Abattoir Fermé.

## I. From the Rabbit Hole towards the Garden of Eden

### Betwixt and Between

The concept of liminality – a word that derives from *limen*, Latin for 'threshold' – implies all manner of 'interstitiality', of being 'betwixt and between', and is connected with the work of Victor Turner. It elaborates on the ideas of Arnold van Gennep who declared that the life of an individual in any society is a series of passages marking changes of place, state, social position and age. This rite of passage is generally divided into three distinct phases. First, there is a 'separation phase' in which the old identity, status or frame of mind is sloughed off. This is followed by the 'liminal phase' in which the protagonist undergoes the change, and is concluded by the 'rite of incorporation', or aggregation of the new identity (Rapport & Overing 2007: 262-268).

Zones of transgression characterize the spectacles of Abattoir Fermé. In *Bloetverlies*, for example, the protagonists evolve from childhood to adulthood in the course of one performance. Rites of passage are staged by making references to phenomena like menstruation, for example when Kirsten Pieters conjures up a long red ribbon from between her labia in *Hardboiled* (2007). The ultimate human rite of passage – death – is illustrated almost literally when Tine Van den Wyngaert is buried under a heap of soil in *Moe maar op en dolend* ('Tired but beat and astray', 2005). But the transformation never stops. The burial scene quickly transforms into a childish game of planting little trees in the soil and playing with toy cars around it. During the liminal phase, the initiate is literally 'neither here nor there', he is beyond the normal everyday social and cultural categories, beyond normal conceptions of routine identity, also beyond conceptions of behaviour, law, time and space (ibid.). The protagonists of the ritual, the initiates here transformed into actors, are in an imaginative universe between life and death, like animated objects.

References to the story of *Alice in Wonderland* were clearly displayed in the performance *Testament* (2006). Lewis Carroll's story is often interpreted as Alice's rite of passage (Shere 1996) and features several playful animistic occurrences such as speaking animals, play cards and teacups. The story was of great influence on Stef Lernous's imagination due to a biographical event: while watching a pornographic version of Carroll's success story on television as a child he 'underwent his *rite de passage* towards manhood' (Lernous 2010).

### Carnivalesque/Grotesque

The liminal phase often was a celebration of liberated social structures and both subversive and reversive elements (Turner 1982: 27). It forced the participants to think about their individuality, society, cosmos and the powers generated between these elements (Turner & Turner 1982: 204). A striking example of such a liminal phase was the annual carnival, a festivity that celebrated the days preceding the Lenten period of fasting. Although a Christian feast, the carnival alluded to another, older festive agricultural tradition, namely, the celebration of Spring: the rebirth of nature. This festivity gave birth to an upside-down world, with carnivalesque features like wildmen and fools (Kinser 1999). Ritual participants often represented bizarre and monstrous configurations in a direct, spontaneous and egalitarian mode of social relationship (Turner & Turner 1982: 202). Their game was akin to the animistic play of children.

The liminal play dealt with many expressions of the grotesque in which the incompatible come together: the comical and the shocking, often showing a strong affinity with the physically abnormal (Thomson 1972: 3, 8). In 1957, German critic Wolfgang Kayser defined the grotesque as an expression of the estranged or alienated world, created by an artist half laughing, half horrified with the deep absurdities of existence (ibid. 11).

Monsters can be seen as typical examples of the grotesque. No surprise then, perhaps, that one of Abattoir Fermé's latest projects was called *Monster!*.[2] In this grotesque television series, viewers could see Tine van de Wyngaert transform from an adorable innocent young girl into a horrifying monster. On the stage as well, many examples of the grotesque can be found, as the Abattoir Fermé actors are well trained in the art of mutating. Kirsten Pieters, a former top model, knows how to transform from a longlegged beauty into a freak by pushing her eyes forward: her beauty fades in a split second into a terrifying creature thanks to this unique physical ability.

Fig. 1    Kirsten Pieters in *Phantasmapolis* © Abattoir Fermé.

Next to expressions of the grotesque, 'sacra' appeared during the liminal festivities. These symbolic objects and actions represented religious mysteries and often referred to the origins and foundations of both cosmic order and infinite space (Turner & Turner 1982: 202). Abattoir Fermé tries to re-enact this cosmic order through liminal expressions and by bringing together all history in a time- and space-less continuum. In *Tourniquet* (2006), exorcism is the central theme, entailing an accusation of both barbarism and Catholicism. The title refers to the French word for a turnstile and at the same time to the form of a Saint Andrew's cross, on which this saint was tortured. So it is simultaneously a symbol of the sacred and of horror. *Phantasmapolis* (2009) contains sacra as well, in the form of giant halos referring to sainthood, but at the same time to the representation of Da Vinci's Homo Universalis. Titles of performances such as *Mythobarbital/Val der Titanen* ('Mythobarbital/Fall of the Titans', 2007) point to a trans-historical approach. Spectators could witness the transformation of three vacuum cleaners in a living room into a three-headed dragon, followed by a bloody scene mutating into an orgiastic ritual with grape juice referring to Dionysus. As Lernous says, 'the epic, myths, the urge for heroes and gods: that too is universal.'

The performances often showcase a trans-historical approach. In *Tourniquet*, Aztecs, Renaissance figures, Germans and neo-Nazis pass in review and blend into one another. The aim of such historical associations, according to Lernous, is the uniting of history into one universal moment and space: 'My biggest dream is to stop time. I long for some rest. I want to create a taxidermist paradise where clocks no longer tick. Travels through time and courses of life dissolve into unities in our performances. We want to stage timeless life.'

'I'm a man of the extreme,' says Lernous, and on the stage '*les extrèmes se touchent*':

Fig. 2    Dionysos on stage in *Mythobarbital/Val der Titanen* (Chiel Van Berkel, Kirsten Pieters and Tine Van Den Wyngaert) © Abattoir Fermé.

reality/illusion, visible/invisible, true/false, light/dark, laughter/tears, noise/silence, monsters/heroes, life/death. These extremes transform into each other and create the perfect twilight zone. Dynamic and associative transformations of characters and scenography illustrate the urge for continuity or 'unity' on the stage of Abattoir Fermé, a characteristic of the liminal experience.

The liminal experience creates a strangeness of borders or framing. Sigmund Freud called this experience '*unheimlich*' or 'uncanny' (Royle 2003: vii). The basis for Freud's analysis of the concept of the uncanny was Jentsch's text about animism (1906). The uncanny can be described as ghostly and concerned with a flickering sense of something supernatural (ibid. 1). It is a game of knowing and unknowing. Objects like teacups look familiar, but when they start to speak, as they do in *Alice in Wonderland*, they create an unfamiliar, uncanny feeling. Lernous's robots look familiar as well, like human beings, but create an uncanny feeling because of the absence of expression. The uncanny and its ambivalence that links it to the liminal experience take us back to the Garden of Eden, a time when animals could speak and lived together with people in a harmonious unity. Abattoir Fermé travels through the history of spectacle and reconnects with the animistic echoes from the Garden of Eden. Not surprisingly, their logo is an anthropoid...

## Marvellous Spectacle

Since the Enlightenment the spectacle has developed towards performances of the 'marvellous' or '*merveilleux*' – from the Latin '*mirabilis*' and '*mirabilia*'; things or people that inspire admiration (Christout 1965: 8). Curiosity cabinets with grotesque and uncanny exotic species, magicians with illusionist tricks and gymnasts with extraordinary physical exercises replaced religious and ritual sacra and elicited 'wonder' because of their 'unknowingness'. The shadow zone of the 'wonder' between knowing and unknowing escapes every form of rational logical thinking and confronts the spectator with something bigger: the universe and its irrational reality (ibid.). The marvel confronts the spectator with 'insignificant' spectacle: no rational meaning can be attached to it, only a physical feeling of admiration or, as the Oxford English Dictionary defines 'spectacle':

1. A specially prepared or arranged display of a more or less public nature (esp. one on a large scale), forming an impressive or interesting show or entertainment for those viewing it.
2. A person or thing exhibited to, or set before, the public gaze as an object either (a) of curiosity or contempt, or (b) of marvel or admiration.
   (Oxford English Dictionary online)

As such, the 'spectacle' appeals to the senses rather than to the mind of the spectator, but its secular character is still connected to the liminal experience. Spectacular attractions like the clown and illusionist have inherited their techniques from health rituals and *rites de passage* and can be compared to activities of primitive cultures like the Evenk in Siberia or the Yoruba Egungun in Nigeria (Kirby 1974). Spectacular attractions can also be associated with myths, like gymnasts, ropewalkers and trapeze artists that recall Icarus, automatons and marionettes referring to the animism of Pygmalion's story and the fire artist to Prometheus (Christout 1965: 111). In an increasingly capitalist society, spectacle became institutionalized in formats like the nineteenth-century variety theatre, where names like 'Eden-Théâtre' echo the liminal experience and an animist past (Jonckheere 2009: 7-9). These were places where spectators were thrilled by seeing acrobats flirting with death and fakirs executing dangerous tricks with hypnotized subjects.

'Appealing to the senses rather than the mind' is also one of Abattoir Fermé's mission statements. Lernous asserts: 'I'm proud of the variety of our performances but that makes them also hard to define. Actually our work needs no other label than "a good show".' Grotesque or horrifying passages alternate with attractions of a 'lighter' genre, such as white rabbits coming out of a hat or burlesque pantomimes with lots of confetti (see, for instance, *Hardboiled*). Contemporary counterparts to the modern, liminal-experience spectacle such as variety theatre can be found in television and games. These illustrate the 'marvellous' of today with fantasy, horror, etc., absorbing us in the twilight zones between reality and fiction, the rational and the irrational.

Fig. 3     Coffee on stage in *Mythobarbital/Val der Titanen* (Kirsten Pieters) © Abattoir Fermé.

Fig. 4
Red Bull and cigarettes on stage in *Mythobarbital/Val der Titanen* (Chiel Van Berkel and Tine Van Den Wyngaert) © Abattoir Fermé.

Also in everyday life, people look for liminal activities. Luxurious shopping malls immerse the consumer in an idealistic life full of light, music and the latest attractive novelties resulting in a feeling of astonishment, giving the individual the opportunity to change his social status and identity (Moss 2007: 1-30). Alcohol, coffee, energy drinks and nicotine, all of which boost the heartbeat and stimulate the mind, can be seen as a light version of the liminal experience. The coffee machine is, in fact, an often-returning element in Abattoir Fermé performances, even acquiring a central position in *Tinseltown* (2006). The urge for liminal experiences is indeed still very much alive.

### Dark Pleasure

Sometimes the urge for liminal experiences results in more extreme activities than shopping or drinking coffee. In *Galapagos* (2003), people are walking around in the microcosm of a hotel, searching for an experience that brings them closer to the twilight zone of death. Through all kinds of extreme activities ranging from SM to religion, they hope to feel 'one' again, closer to the original nature of their being, and feeling confronted with life and death.

In almost every performance by Abattoir Fermé, the characters seem to be balancing between life and death. According to Lernous, 'Death plays a major role in our plays: it happens to everyone. It is so universal and at the same time the ultimate mystery that nobody can explain.' The protagonists' death drive is part of a quest for a more powerful liminal experience in the form of thrills. In facing death, the point where time stands still, one feels the ultimate pleasure: it reminds you of the fact that you are still alive. This is almost literally the subject of *Testament*, in which the transitional stage between life and death after a car crash is illustrated. A similar topic can be traced in *Phantasmapolis*, where murderers bear witness to their cruel actions.

In *L'Erotisme*, Georges Bataille claims that our fascination with moments of self-denial, as in death but sex as well, originates from a feeling of nostalgia for a lost continuity. According to Bataille, reality used to be excessively violent, with life and death being closely connected to each other. Since man lives in a structured world, with labour and leisure, life has become much more peaceful and rational. Still, sometimes the urge to go back to the chaotic and violent life, close to death, less rational but more universal, returns.

Crossing the safe border means breaking down prohibitions and taboos. Abattoir Fermé constantly play with these borders and consequently create the liminal experience. Therefore they connect with the hidden though all too available content of exploitation movies: B-films, slasher films, horror, pornography, ... 'Such genres are very direct. They tap into your body. They give evidence of very human and clear desires but still they are very much taboo,' according to Lernous. Intertextual references to masters of transgressive film such as Fellini and Visconti abound in Abattoir Fermé's performances. David Lynch with his mise-en-scène of liminal spaces and protagonists is never far away either. The trilogy consisting of *Tinseltown*, *Indie* (2006) and *Lalaland* (2006) was inspired by the faded glory of Hollywood, as the names indicate.[3] Chopped-off pig heads and drinking urine were part of the transgressive nature of *Indie*. More alternative than Hollywood was the inspiration for the performance *Phantasmapolis*: the giallo film *All the Colors of the Dark* (Sergio Martino, 1972).

The transgressive genre *par excellence* in a secularized society – the gothic – is always present in the performances of Abattoir Fermé. Empiricist John Locke described the gothic as the result of the fear of insensibility, of not being able to follow the new rational attitude towards existence and consciousness (Cohen 1995: 896). Lernous seems to share this feeling: 'Everything has been explained, everything is cleared up. We know so much and therefore we need to go back in time so that things become magical again. We need miracles. Giant halos, crosses, mysticism and horror.' Extremely rational and formalized genres like seventeenth-century classicism provoked reactions such as gothic literature that dealt with liminal experiences connected to objects and phenomena like the veil, hysteria and madness (Kosofsky Sedgwick 1981). *Phantasmapolis* stages a hysteric, a psychopath and a vampire. In *Testament*, a dark transparent veil separates the audience from the stage. Still, Abattoir Fermé's horror is always covered with a touch of romance or humour, giving the spectacle a touch of the burlesque or grotesque.

## II. Ultimate Unity: Mutating Media

### Dead Media

Some media bring the twilight zone between life and death very close to the spectator: the absence of motion gives the medium a 'death feature'. For example, painting, drawing and photography can be regarded as snapshots of the past. Bringing features of these 'dead media' alive on stage creates an uncanny atmosphere. Lernous explains: 'I don't want to make a literal painting on stage but I want to adapt the idea of painting to the stage, by its grain, texture, features like the trompe l'oeil of famous masterpieces. Combining such elements with other media creates one idea. That's the result of my urge for unity.' In Snuff (2008), the central theme was painting adapted to the stage. The performance took the spectator on a trip through art history spiced with lots of grotesque subversive elements.

It may seem paradoxical, but the animation of dead media still results from an urge to put time and image in one stable unity. Every scene is a balancing act between animation and death, one of the basic liminal experiences. Lernous: 'How long can you freeze a scene? For every performance, I make 2000 to 5000 pictures on average. I really love photographs a lot. With every performance again, I ask myself whether I'm making a performance in order to make nice pictures or if I am making a picture that can last forever in life.' On stage, this idea results in tableaux vivants giving evidence of little associative movements.

### Never-Ending Novelty

Despite a passion for the timeless, 'slowly moving images' also frequently return in the performances of Abattoir Fermé. The filmic genre can be seen as an uncanny extension of the dead medium when, for example, photographs start to move and consequently create a strange feeling. Its montage technique, moreover, is a prime feature for staging associative transformations that may help to install the timeless unity. Moe maar op en dolend was a theatre adaptation of the television series Twin Peaks (David Lynch and Mark Frost, 1990-1991), where the soundscape was partly based on audio fragments from the series. 'We push film, television and theatre beyond their limits, treating them as toys,' elaborates Lernous. 'By putting film on stage you can avoid the seams that are so typical for theatre and create a way to blend the scenes into each other in an associative way.' A nice example of the ongoing metamorphosis was Tourniquet, running before the eyes of the spectator like a movie.

Lernous blends theatrical elements with all different kinds of media. In the television series 'Monster!', theatre was mutated through the mix with other media. Characters shuffle on screen in front of 2D props and respect the theatrical foreground, centre and background. Next to pushing media beyond its borders, all theatrical genres are also mixed together: monologues (in Phantasmapolis and Lalaland), stand-up comedy (in

*Tines Routine*, 2004), youth theatre (in *Nimmermeer* or 'Nevermore', in cooperation with De Maan, 2008) and even opera (in *L'Intruse*, 2011, with De Vlaamse Opera). This endless search for the new on a formal level originates from a specific way of thinking about theatre: 'We look at the theatre field, what others create, and subsequently we search for a unique place. New formats mixed with original genres like pulp, fantasy, detective, science fiction, comics, occultism, etc.'

The quest for new, original ways of dealing with performances, both in form and in content, is a preoccupation shared with modern spectacle. Just like in fashion, a never-ending renewal is demanded in order to safeguard the experience of liminality. This made spectacle dependent on a continuing evolution of machinery and new media, as only the 'unknown' brings the spectator into the twilight zone. For, as Lernous puts it, 'If one knows already halfway through the performance where things are going, then things are going wrong.'

## Immersion

'I used to be a passionate gamer, I was called the "dungeon master".'[4] Lernous is fascinated not only by spectacle entailing self-denial but also by media that create this experience. The activity of gaming is a very clear example. Lernous adapts not only the thematic content of popular games and its monsters, heroes and violence to the stage, but also its formal structure: 'Levels, kill screens, pixels, the possibility to zoom in... These are interesting features with its own specific vocabulary.'

In order to be able to lose oneself, the spectator has to be immersed in the spectacle. Experiencing the unity of the associative dream state is only possible with the right 'stimmung'. The importance of the appropriate soundscape is evidenced by the presence of a 'home composer', Pepijn Coudron, alias Kreng, who belongs to the hard core of actors as well. His soundscapes boost the atmosphere of, for example, horror genres: they terrify the subject into momentary speechlessness or loss of consciousness (Cohen 1995: 884). In many scenes the words are subordinate to the atmosphere, and no place is left for any rational sign. At this moment, spectators look into the dark abyss of time and space, beyond the taboo where no words fit.

This speechlessness was witnessed in *Bloetverlies*, *Tourniquet*, *Moe maar op en dolend* and *Mythobarbital/Val der Titanen*. These silent performances leave no place for words, only for the soundscape and the sounds created by the actors and the audience. Now and then, monologues are staged, as in *Phantasmapolis* or *Lalaland*. But these are still closer to silent performances because of how words seem to mutate into flesh, as one journalist described it (Hillaert 2010). Lernous explains, 'The spectator needs to be in the story, not just stare at it. But don't push people to come into your world. They have to step into it.' The subconscious dreamlike character of these performances makes one lose oneself and step into another, irrational, world.

## III.  Conclusion: *Solve et Coagula*

For a long time, roughly from ancient Egypt until the seventeenth century, religion and science were closely connected in the realm of alchemy that was, in the West at least, ultimately replaced by chemistry and pharmacology. In its methods, Abattoir Fermé adheres to the legacy of this historical pseudoscience. *Solve et Coagula*: take things apart and put them back together in a changed formation (Guiley 2006: 8). Abattoir Fermé shares this method with Antonin Artaud, who claimed that 'what connects alchemy and theatre is a mysterious necessary identity: the reality of the imagination and the dreams that appear on equal foot with life' (quoted in Christout 1965: 374).

The analogy with Artaud is no coincidence. The dynamic association leads to the endless transformation on the level of content and form that is necessary to create a dream state in which also cruelty can be present. 'To surprise is our final goal. There I find a connection with Artaud: we do not want to shock but try to mystify with the use of masks and without the use of words. Just those things that disappeared from cinema and television.' Through transgression, the spectator goes beyond reason and consciousness and safely returns to reality afterwards. Stef Lernous's ultimate dream is to bring the audience under hypnosis, the ultimate liminal experience, in order to experiment with them and let them watch their own show afterwards.

Surprise or 'marvel', curiosity and animism characterize the childish game, but in growing up, our rational consciousness represses exactly these things. Spectacle originated from the rational human being's urge to come home once again in the animistic Garden of Eden where the animals speak, but in the dreadful Apocalypse as well, where

Fig. 5    A grotesque show full of curiosities in *Tourniquet* © Abattoir Fermé.

tempting heroines transform into monsters. Present, past and future melt into one. Abattoir Fermé likes to take their audiences on a neo-shamanistic trip into the world of spectacle within the setting, the sound and the image of the endless mutation of the 'dark backward and abysm of time'.[5]


**Evelien Jonckheere**'s thesis on 'Variety Theatre in Ghent' was honoured with the 2007 Vlaamse Scriptieprijs, an award for the best thesis in Flanders. Since January 2008 she has been working on a PhD about the spectacular in the nineteenth-century modern industrial city at Ghent University. In 2009, her book *Kijklust en Sensatiezucht. Een geschiedenis van revue en variété* was published by Manteau/Meulenhoff.

**NOTES**

1  All quotes from Stef Lernous in this article are taken from an interview with him in Mechelen, 16 December 2010.
2  *Monster!* was directed by Jonas Govaerts. Six instalments aired on the digital channel Acht, starting 26 December 2010.
3  'Indie' refers to independent films; 'Tinseltown' is a nickname for Hollywood; and 'Lalaland' refers to Los Angeles or 'LA'.
4  'The dungeon master' is a reference to the series of computer games called *Dungeons and Dragons*, based on the role-playing game of the same name first developed by Gary Gygax and David Cook in 1974.
5  Prospero in Shakespeare's *The Tempest*, act 1, scene 2.


**REFERENCES**

Bataille, G., *L'Erotisme*. Paris, 1957.
Christout, M.-F., *Le Merveilleux et le 'théâtre du silence' en France à partir du XVIIe siècle*. La Haye/Paris, 1965.
Cohen, E. J., 'Museums of the Mind. The Gothic and the Art of Memory'. In: *ELH*, 62, 4, p. 883-905. Baltimore, 1995.
Guiley, R., *The Encyclopedia of Magic and Alchemy*. New York, 2006.
Hillaert, W., 'Wegsoezen bij Abattoir Fermé'. In: *De Standaard*, 28 April 2010.
Jentsch, E., 'Zur Psychologie des Unheimlichen'. In: *Psychiatrisch-Neurologische Wochenschrift*, 8, 22, p.195-198 (part 1) and 8, 23, p. 203-205. Halle a/S., 1906.
–. 'On the Psychology of the Uncanny'. Trans. Roy Sellars. In: *Angelaki*, 2, 1, p. 7-21. Oxford, 1996.
Jonckheere, E., *Kijklust en Sensatiezucht. Een geschiedenis van revue en variété*. Antwerpen/Amsterdam, 2009.
Kinser, S., 'Why is Carnival So Wild?'. In: K. Eisenbichler and W. Hüsken (eds.), *Carni-*

val and the Carnivalesque. The Fool, the Reformer, the Wildman, and Others in Early Modern Theatre. Amsterdam/Atlanta, 1999.

Kirby, E. T., 'The Shamanistic Origins of Popular Entertainments'. In: *The Drama Review*, 18, 1, p. 5-15. Cambridge, 1974.

Kosofsky Sedgwick, E., 'The Character in the Veil. Imagery of the Surface in the Gothic Novel'. In: *PMLA*, 96, 2, p. 255-270. New York, 1981.

Lernous, S., 'Kasklezing'. Lecture held at KASK, University College Ghent, 7 December 2010.

Looft, W. R.. and W. H. Bartz, 'Animism Revived'. In: *Psychological Bulletin*, 71, 1, p. 1-19. Washington, 1969.

Moss, M., *Shopping as an Entertainment Experience*. Lanham, 2007.

Rapport, N. and J. Overing, 'Liminality'. In: Rapport and Overing, *Social and Cultural Anthropology. The Key Concepts*. London/New York, 2007.

Royle, N., *The Uncanny*. Manchester, 2003.

Shere, S., 'Secrecy and Autonomy in Lewis Carroll'. In: *Philosophy and Literature*, 20, 1, p. 1-16. Baltimore, 1996.

Thomson, P., *The Grotesque*. Methuen Critical Idiom Series nr. 24. London, 1972.

Turner, V., 'Introduction'. In: V. Turner (ed.), *Celebration. Studies in Festivity and Ritual*. Washington, 1982.

Turner, V. and E. Turner, 'Religious Celebrations'. In: V. Turner (ed.), *Celebration. Studies in Festivity and Ritual*. Washington, 1982.

# Folding Mutants or Crumbling Hybrids?

## Of Looking Baroque in Contemporary Theatre and Performance

Jeroen Coppens

In recent years, due mainly to technological and digital advancement, there has been a revolution in representational practices that is pushing towards the merging of different media into one another. Nowadays, one can watch TV shows on the internet, enact movie characters in 3D game environments and even enjoy an opera performance from another continent in the movie theatre via live internet streaming technology.

The introduction of new media in the theatre is in itself nothing new – it happened during the historical avant-garde (e.g. Erwin Piscator's experiments with documentary footage or the futurist multimedia happenings), in the 1960s with mixed-media performances and since the 1990s with experiments to connect the digital to the theatrical (Dixon 2007: 87). This evolution has been the direct cause of hybrid forms of theatre and performance that combine many different artistic disciplines, media and visual codes.

In this regard, I would like to propose the baroque as a productive interpretative tool to approach this multimedia richness. The current neo-baroque discourse and vocabulary focus mainly on general formal analogies between seventeenth-century representational practices and contemporary visual culture, favouring concepts like seriality, polycentrism, eclecticism, instability, virtuosity and illusionism.[1] A fundamental critique on this account of the baroque is that the detected analogies of forms do not pay respect to the diverse cultural and artistic manifestations of the baroque throughout Europe, with outreaches from Italy (Caravaggio and Bernini) and Spain (Velázquez) to the Northern and Southern Netherlands (Jan Vermeer and Peter Paul Rubens, respectively). In this respect, the baroque has been imbued with a remarkable undefinability and unlocalizability, illustrated by Gilles Deleuze's notion of the baroque as a pure concept that exists through no other means than its expression. Therefore, 'it is easy to render the Baroque non-existent; one only has to stop proposing its concept' (Deleuze 1993: 33).

One could even extend this critique by asking why historicizing contemporary art through the baroque can be helpful, as it involves old theories that at first glance do not seem to be relevant to analysing the contemporary revolution in representational practices. In this chapter, I will argue that through an actualization of the baroque – no longer based on formal analogies but rather on the perspective that baroque art produces – an interesting framework emerges to specifically think about the engagement and activation of the spectator that can be recognized in many hybrid theatre practices. In concentrating on the baroque perspective rather than on mere baroque forms, I follow in the footsteps of art historians and contemporary thinkers like Martin Jay, Christine Buci-Glucksmann and Mieke Bal, who discern the baroque from other representational practices based upon the perspective or vision it installs. I will argue that in the instability and the multiplicity of frames that is introduced in many contemporary hybrid theatre performances we may trace reverberations of the baroque experiments with the *bel composto* – the beautiful union of multiple media – by analyzing the different media and the baroque perspective they activate at the Cornaro Chapel with its central sculpture *Ecstasy of Saint Teresa*, designed by Gianlorenzo Bernini. I will argue that the contemporary hybrid theatre installs a baroque account of vision that emphasizes the active engagement of the spectator in a fictional world of which the borders and the meaning are not always perfectly delineated. This blurring of the borders of reality and illusion has often been associated with a seductive strategy that results in instability and chaos. Instead, through an analysis of the baroque vision that is installed in the hybrid theatre work of Romeo Castellucci, I will show that this blurring of the borders and of meaning opens up the space for an active and critical viewer. But to eliminate the threat of the baroque as an empty concept mentioned above, I will first demarcate the baroque and its perspective.

In 'Scopic Regimes of Modernity', Martin Jay proposes a baroque scopic regime[2] that counteracts other modern models of vision as well as Cartesian perspectivalism, which favours 'a "natural" experience of sight valorized by the scientific world view' (Jay 1988: 5) and what Svetlana Alpers has called *The Art of Describing*, a visual mode that 'casts its attentive eye on the fragmentary, detailed and richly articulated surface of a world it is content to describe rather than explain' (ibid. 13). Obviously, one has to be cautious when introducing ideal typical characterizations (Jay is indeed very aware of this), but the account of baroque vision as 'a permanent, if often repressed, visual possibility throughout the entire modern era' (ibid. 16) remains particularly interesting. In close dialogue with Christine Buci-Glucksmann, Jay explores this visual regime that aims to represent the unrepresentable and is fascinated by opacity, unreadability and indecipherability. It is caught up in what Buci-Glucksmann calls '*folie du voir*' (madness of vision), as it 'self-consciously revels in the contradictions between surface and depth, disparaging as a result any attempt to reduce the multiplicity of visual spaces into any one coherent essence' (ibid. 17).[3] In this overloading of the visual apparatus, the body of the spectator returns, to be enthralled, manipulated, moved and distanced again. In this respect, Mieke Bal mentions 'a vision that can be characterized as a vacillation between the subject and the object of that vision and which changes the status of both' (Bal 2001: 7).

Let us now turn our gaze to the Cornaro chapel in the Santa Maria della Vittoria church in Rome, designed by Gianlorenzo Bernini, to examine this specific account of baroque vision. The chapel was built between 1647 and 1652 and centres around the *Ecstasy of Saint Teresa*, a white marble sculpture encapsulated by a polychromatic marble shrine, with, in the background, stucco rays of light that seem to shine downwards. The whole is illuminated by a window in the ceiling that is concealed behind the enormous architectural framing around the sculpture.

This dramatic reworking of the light, the framing of the shrine and the spectacular portrayal of enthralment have frequently triggered a comparison to the theatre, as Bernini theatricalizes his figures in order to seduce the senses of the spectator. This approach, however, focuses mainly on the enthralment that the *bel composto*, the beautiful merging of different art forms, brings about. This montage of different media – sculpture, architecture and painting – is, however, not to be reduced to a mere pleasure and seduction of the beholder, but instead offers an active role to the spectator. At this point, it is interesting to take up the comparison with Gilles Deleuze's aesthetics of intensities, which is 'not a mere aesthetics of sensory stimulation and emotion' (*plaisir-décharge*) (Stalpaert 2007: 6; translation JC) but rather opens up a space for creative and critical thinking for the spectator (Stalpaert 2004: 19). The *bel composto* offers an active role to the spectator in that it offers a montage in which 'each *composto* induces the spectator to reassemble its disparate elements into a whole through a diverse "free play of the faculties"'(Careri 1995: 3). In other words, the theatrical paradigm ignores the distinct function fulfilled by each of the respective components of the *composto*, which, according to Giovanni Careri, activate the spectator to participate 'by applying a specific form of contemplation to the act of reassembling the heterogeneous elements of the *composto* into a whole' (ibid.). For Careri, the *bel composto* functions as a montage that mobilizes heterogeneous elements into a whole, which is to be taken apart and recomposed by the viewer himself, who is in the end its true material (cf. Damisch 1995: ix). Here, vision is thought of as a mobilization that tries to bridge the gaps between the different art forms that were lost in the beautiful union that engages the senses through sensational spectacle.

Mieke Bal, on the other hand, localizes the mobility in the work of Bernini on another level, arguing that the spatial relations of the spectator constantly change during the act of observing, thereby recalling Martin Jay's renunciation of any totalizing vision from above: 'The way you see it, is never quite adequate. You have to walk around it, and in doing so, you change it. And when you come back, you see something different than when you started' (Bal 2009). The Cornaro chapel is, indeed, to be understood as a whole, not as merely its central focal point of the sculpture of Saint Teresa, but also taking into account the mural decorations, the illusionistic frescos on the vault of the chapel and the sculptural group of witnesses portraying some members of the Cornaro family. The whole combines different layers of reality and representation, which is overwhelming in its visual exuberance and can only be appropriated by a moving gaze that, after the initial enthralment, casts its light on the different components of the chapel. As a consequence, one fixed perspective on the artwork is no longer possible.

Another trope of mobility can be discerned in the figure of the fold that the French post-structuralist philosopher Gilles Deleuze uses as a central metaphor to describe the baroque and that is overtly present in Bernini's rendering of the ecstasy of Saint Teresa. The innumerable folds in the drapery of Saint Teresa fold inwards and outwards, unfold to the surface and enfold in the deep, partly extracting the drapery from the spectator's gaze but at the same time suggesting a movement and voluminosity beyond the frame, beyond the marble and beyond the visible. As the baroque is imbued with a tendency to represent the unrepresentable, the figure of the fold functions as a directive towards the infinite. The spectator is initially caught by a fold and sucked into the imaginary, and is in a later instance activated to creative thinking. Although heavily loaded with Leibnizian philosophy, the concept of the baroque fold in Deleuze's work points to that endless movement into infinity:

> The Baroque refers not to an essence but rather to an operative function, to a trait. It endlessly produces folds. It does not invent things: there are all kinds of folds coming from the East, Greek, Roman, Romanesque, Gothic, Classical folds. Yet the Baroque trait twists and turns its folds, pushing them to infinity, fold over fold, one upon the other. The Baroque fold unfurls all the way to infinity. (Deleuze 1993: 3)

The baroque scopic regime can thus be thought of as a set of visual strategies to actively engage (the senses of) the spectator, thereby mobilizing the gaze in a threefold manner. After the initial usurpation by baroque spectacle, a dismantling gaze works actively to reconstruct the components of the *bel composto*, thereby jumping from one medium to another. In this process, the bodily movement that Mieke Bal quotes provides an essential spatial mobility of the gaze (in which the other senses are also actively involved), necessary to grasp the different layers of representation and reality that are integrated in the artwork as a whole. This process is initiated by the baroque taking beyond its limit the viewpoint, vanishing point and distance of traditional perspectivalism (cf. Calabrese 1992: 50) as a consequence of 'its refusal to respect the limits of the frame that contains the illusion' (Ndalianis 2004: 25).

This complex dynamic between being lost and finding a way out has been conceptualized by the Italian semiologist Omar Calabrese, who argues that the figures of the labyrinth and the knot were pre-eminently baroque because of the different intellectual registers they trigger: 'the pleasure of becoming lost when confronted by its inextricability (followed by fear) and the taste for solving something by the concentrated use of reason' (Calabrese 1992: 131).

Baroque representation therefore organizes a constructed *undecidedness* that transforms the spectator into an actor who is involved in a constantly shifting relationship towards the artwork, being seduced by and being lost in the baroque spectacle of exuberance, desire and infinity, but at the same time activating the faculty of reason in order to find a way out of the visual, spatial and conceptual labyrinth that is at work in the baroque scopic regime.

In contemporary postdramatic theatre practice, one can recognize a similar interest in the playing with (theatrical) codes, with spectacle and constructed undecidedness. I will concentrate on the theatre practice of Romeo Castellucci, whose theatre language has often been described as theatrical, grotesque and excessive. Castellucci's *Tragedia Endogonidia* cycle is a fundamentally hybrid theatre project in which mutant technologies literally take their space on stage. The grand project consisted of a total of eleven performances, each performed in a different city throughout Europe, the first premiering in January 2002 and the last in October 2004. Each episode carried as a title the initial of the respective city and the serial number of the episode in the whole cycle.

Thematically, *Tragedia Endogonidia* engages with the (possibility of) tragedy today. The title combines an epic notion (*Tragedia*) with one from microbiology (*Endogonidia*). For Castellucci, these two poles constitute the contemporary possibility of tragedy as a clash between life and death. In the tragedy, the hero has to die, but *endogonidia* – microscopic organisms that are able to procreate eternally as they have both male and female reproductive organs – conceptualize the idea of reproduction *ad infinitum*, of immortality and thus of eternal life.

The theatre language of Castellucci's company is extremely visual, as dialogues practically never occur throughout the whole cycle. The different subsequent scenes have neither narrative nor logical context (cf. Castellucci in Kelleher & Ridout 2007: 3) but are instead strong visual montages, often accompanied by electronic music by composer Scott Gibbons and further enhanced by highly technological sculptures, installations and mechanisms. This hybrid mixture takes on quite different forms throughout the cycle. As Castelluci explains:

> The technology I use is very diverse and ranges from being very primitive to very sophisticated: video technology, endoscopes which reconnoiter the insides of the actor and upset the traditional relationship that the audience has with the actor, in the sense that it's possible to see the actor's interior [...]. Pneumatic, hydraulic, oleic dynamic or oil-pressure machines, taxidermy, automaton mechanics, microscopes, organic chemistry, chemiluminescence, techniques for breeding certain animals, acoustical physics, robotic components, but also little pieces of sacred wood that have been badly nailed together [...] in short, whatever. (Valentini & Marranca 2002)

In *Tragedia Endogonidia*, the spectator is confronted with (often returning) bizarre machineries firing darts into the wall, airport announcement boards, mechanical sound installations, intense colour effects, mechanically driven streaming flags and advanced video technology. This army of mutant technologies combines theatre with other disciplines like video and installation art, serving the goal of creating another layer of reality on stage that enthrals the spectator in such a way that (s)he initially feels overwhelmed. As such, the events on stage present themselves as a visual riddle and, as a consequence, they cannot be placed exactly, but at the same time they spark an urge to be interpreted (cf. Crombez 2006: 4). Castellucci works very actively with this trope of uncertainty, declaring: 'all I can say is that I sincerely believe in the power of "not saying". The audience will soon realise that this does not necessarily mean "silence"' (quoted in Sociètas Raffaello Sanzio 2007: 71). The non-narrative and illogical sequence of visual scenes does not implicate in any way a non-committal or irrational relation towards dramaturgy or structure. On the contrary, the different scenes and images are rigidly structured and imbued with an organization in extreme detail and for that reason, the heterogeneity and non-narrativity at work in Tragedia Endogonidia is fundamentally not surreal:

> But every time there is the presence of logic because there is always the enigma. The enigma contains a logical core. The enigma is exact. The enigma is as a sword that is capable of penetrating itself. Tragedy is the art of the enigma. (Castellucci in: Crombez, Colson & Tratsaert 2005: 11; translation JC)

Tragedy is the art of opening up questions rather than providing closed answers, and therefore the picture as enigma serves as the perfect visual strategy for the project behind Tragedia Endogonidia. One specific way of doing this is to focus excessively on the detail as a result of which the macrostructure becomes blurred. Castellucci compares this effect with reading a book too closely, with the consequence of a very clear look at specific words, surrounded by a blur (cf. Castellucci in: Crombez & Hillaert 2004: 5).

> Our theatre is full of signs – I don't know if 'signs' is the right word, of figures, then – and with care for the detail, the figure flourishes, in the sense that there is an excess of figure in the detail. In this excess of the experience of vision, we have a whole host of perceptions. At a certain point, and this is really a question of montage, of dramaturgy, it is as if everything else had vanished, as if everything else had been annihilated and the concentration is fixed on a single hand, the attention rests on a hand moving or on a face that makes movements [...]. (Chiara Guidi in Castellucci et al. 2007a: 224)

This style has been characterized as 'hypericonographical', in the sense that the fundamental enigmatic quality of the abundance of signs functions as an emersive alienation strategy aiming at seducing the spectator into an immersive experience of spectacle (Vanderbeeken 2009: 49). At the same time, however, this alienation strategy of offering 'an abundance of hermeneutic signs and symbols that do not contain any direct or gradual reference to any coordinating narrative' (ibid. 48; translation JC) obliges the spectator to relate to the presented enigmatic visual language in a hyperindividual way.

*Tragedia Endogonidia* is a cycle that is incomprehensible, even unreadable, confronting the spectator with a visual labyrinth with no way out but a personal one. For that reason, Castellucci talks about the spectator having to search for a personal access to enter into the spectacle, a personal way to approach, interpret and appropriate the events on stage (Crombez, Colson & Tratsaert 2005: 12). As a consequence, the spectator can only find a personal way out, trying to make sense out of the bits and pieces, searching for a personal way to deal with the highly suggestive images at hand. In this way, the enigma confronts the spectator with the dangerous task of personally acting upon the spectacle, neutralizing it, much like defusing a bomb (Castellucci et al. 2007b: 255). In that sense, talking about *Tragedia Endogonidia* always becomes a highly personal – and therefore precarious and non-objective – interpretation of the performances.

This art of 'not saying' and the silence it invokes are of course situated at the level of interpretation. The events on stage are, on the contrary, exuberant and highly spectacular; in *P#06 Paris*, three cars fall violently onto the stage, throughout the cycle different animals (rabbits, apes, horses, etc.) are put on stage, and in *S#08 Strassbourg*, a real war tank rolls onto the stage. But *Tragedia Endogonidia* is not only spectacular in the sense of sensational because of these extraordinary events unfolding on stage; it presents a visual spectacle that exuberantly appeals to the senses (*plaisir-décharge*) in which 'the whole body [of the spectator] is affected by the scene on stage' (Sociètas Raffaello Sanzio 2007: 72). The theatricalization of spectacle bedazzles and overwhelms the spectator, who is being immersed in the 'parallel reality' that is opened up through the spectacle (cf. Castellucci in Crombez & Hillaert 2003: 2). To a certain extent, this process comes down to an erasure of the clear boundaries between fiction and reality, transforming theatre into a hybrid organism that stuns the senses, much in the same way as the baroque theatrical machines were designed to make the fictitious world of the theatre present itself as real as possible (cf. Castellucci et al. 2007a: 222).

In this sense, *Tragedia Endogonidia* can be seen as a continuous visual attempt to organize and trigger amazement, thereby withholding the spectator of any definitive clue about the (or even: a) meaning of the unfolding spectacle. At this point, it is interesting to take up the comparison with the baroque *Wunderkammer*.[4] The cabinet of wonders is a pre-modern collection of rare objects (like exotic animals, stones and leaves but also books, weapons and jewellery) that are displayed in a seemingly haphazard and chaotic manner. This specific arrangement of the objects drew attention to the wonderful diversity of nature, thereby seducing the spectator from one amazement to the other. This early museal collecting practice was of course also a scientific endeavour – although radically different from modern science, in that it amasses 'the history of nature as anecdote, and in its tendency to revel in the bizarre and unnatural as it was concerned with demonstrating the presence of the underlying laws of the world' (Munster 2006: 67). On the other hand, the labyrinthine method of displaying enabled the spectator to jump from one object to the other, thus also associating freely in the abundance of displayed objects.

*Tragedia Endogonidia* offers the same experience as the baroque *Wunderkammer* in that it aims to amaze the spectator in a heterogeneity of images, scenes and experiences. Furthermore, this amazement is extremely organized up to the smallest detail, but at the same time opens up an active part for the spectator, who must associate freely in making sense of the initial total enthralment of spectacle. Although tragedy, according to Castellucci, is a universal structure that encompasses the entire Western world (cf. Crombez & Hillaert 2003: 1), his visual language is, however, a spectacle that can only be approached in a hyperindividual process of recreation.[5]

The images Castellucci creates surpass any definitive rational analysis and thereby reject any totalizing vision or interpretation. Rather, the spectator finds himself

> touched by the imprint that this flight makes upon [him], the imprint of an image which [he] make[s] for [himself], as [he is] drawn into a language where thought and feeling are – as it were – brought to life, but with an emotion devoid of pathos. (Kelleher & Ridout 2007: 12)

As a consequence, this theatre is founded on the intimate and individual experience of each spectator. *Tragedia Endogonidia* is theatre that speaks to the senses, that wants to offer an overwhelming spectacle, an awareness of an opening (cf. Kelleher & Ridout 2007: 4), and in this sense deploys an aesthetics of haptic seeing, directly and overtly engaging the spectator.

In this sense, the individual gaze becomes crucial to the *Tragedia Endogonidia* – and, by extension, to the visual strategy employed by the Socìetas Raffaello Sanzio. In the case of the *Tragedia*, the possibility for tragedy is located in the gaze itself. In this regard, Romeo Castellucci himself talks about the tragic gaze of the spectacle:

> I don't go to the theatre to watch the spectacle, but to be watched by the spectacle. That gaze of the spectacle transforms something into a tragic object. It is the movement of the gaze that creates the tragic. There are no tragic objects as such! (Crombez, Colson & Tratsaert 2005: 12; translation JC)

Much as in the *bel composto*, the hybrid and excessive visuality of the *Tragedia Endogonidia* presents a challenge for the spectator, as it installs a performative (postdramatic) madness of vision through the figure of visual enigma. Through an overload of the visual apparatus and the seeming lack of logic and narrativity behind it, the spectator is thrown – almost violently – upon his/her own resources, initially being lost and only able to find a way out through a hyperindividual – and consequently non-objective and unstable – process of interpreting and generating personal meaning. This process can be understood as retrospective and retroactive; as a reconstruction that is temporally situated after the usurpation of the spectacle and actively transforms this experience through the act of reading, interpreting and recreating it. In other words, it requires a temporal mobilization of vision that can conceptually be compared to Mieke Bal's spatial mobility at work in the visual arts, but that also recalls Hans-Thies Lehmann's concept of the 'evenly hovering attention' (*gleichschwebende Aufmerksamkeit*) that refers to the category of 'not understanding immediately':

> Rather one's perception has to remain open for connections, correspondences and clues at completely unexpected moments, perhaps casting what was said earlier in a completely new light. Thus, meaning remains in principle postponed. (Lehmann 2006: 87)

As such, the spectator becomes an active creative force who, in wandering through the spectacle, appropriates it on a personal level. And precisely this process constitutes the future of theatre, according to Castellucci:

> For me, the future of the theatre is that of the spectator. Perhaps this project, Tragedia, was an attempt to go in this direction. In all probability, it is an incomplete attempt, and only a step, towards this dimension of the art of the spectator, and no longer of the artist. (Castellucci et al. 2007b: 259)

Furthermore, the typically baroque staged uncertainty that is at work in Tragedia Endogonidia through the figure of the spectacular enigma functions in the same way as the baroque fold conceptualized by Gilles Deleuze. Through the presentation of a fundamental openness on stage, an infinite interpretative space is opened, an inexhaustible process of unfolding and enfolding (different layers of) meaning is started, or – to put it in Deleuzian terms – the spectator is touched by a fold toward an infinite interpretation.

Tragedia Endogonidia thus at the same time destabilizes and confirms its spectator through an instalment of baroque vision in which the hybrid spectacle cannot only be brought to a coherent essence anymore, as Christine Buci-Gluckmann argues, but goes even further in opening up to an endless stream of possible – individual – meaning.

This way of 'looking baroque' faces us with new challenges in performance studies involving documentation and archiving. How can a performance that pivots around the individual spectator be reviewed without lapsing into a central vantage point (of a camera, a witness, a discourse)? And how can the interpretative openness installed in Tragedia Endogonidia oxymoronically be 'captured' with respect for the labyrinthine quality of the visual language? In the experimental recordings of Tragedia Endogonidia by video artists Cristiano Carloni and Stefano Franceschetti, we can find a preliminary answer in their attempt to let documentation come as close as possible to the performance through inventive montage and deformation of the filmic medium, thereby refuting its status of evidence.

Yet, the answers to these questions depend on a more fundamental epistemological question. As is shown in the museal practice of the *Wunderkammer*, baroque vision also involves a baroque way of knowing – a knowledge that centres around the individual spectator, individual associations and personal anecdotes. In other words, in refuting the vantage point as a certain and fixed position to seize upon the visual, the epistemological status of both the observer and the observed radically alter. Both become transitional, dynamic and even unstable in their constant vacillation between one another. In this view, spectacle is no longer sheer affective seduction nor totalizing enthralment; instead, it presents a critical adventure for the beholder, as a two-way mirror that casts both a reflection and a projection of the spectator.

**Jeroen Coppens** (1986) holds a bachelor's degree in Philosophy and a master's degree in Theatre and Film Studies from the University of Antwerp. In 2009, he completed his studies at the Free University of Berlin. Since September 2009, Jeroen has been a doctoral assistant for Prof. Pewny at the Department of Theatre, Performance and Media Studies at Ghent University. His current research concerns contemporary scopic regimes, concentrating particularly on the baroque mobilized vision in present-day theatre. As a freelance dramaturge, Jeroen collaborates with video artist Ariane Loze.

## NOTES

1 See Calabrese (1992) and, based on Calabrese, Ndalianis (2004).

2 Jay borrows the term 'scopic regime' from the French film theorist Christian Metz, who introduced it in his 1975 study *The Imaginary Signifier* to distinguish between the cinematic scopic regime and the theatrical.

3 Christine Buci-Glucksmann develops these notions of the baroque gaze and the madness of vision it installs in close dialogue with the phenomenological tradition of Maurice Merleau-Ponty. See Buci-Glucksmann (2010: 140-156).

4 See also Hillaert & Crombez (2005: 6).

5 In the DVD documentary about the *Tragedia Endogonidia*, video artists Cristiano Carloni and Stefano Franceschetti tried to achieve the same interplay between the spectacle and its hyperindividual perception that is at work in the live performances, mainly through meticulous montage and filmic deformation. For an extensive account of that transformation, see Von Brinken (2010).

## REFERENCES

Bal, M., 'Contemporary Baroque and Preposterous History'. Lecture held at the New Perspectives on Baroque Art and Culture conference in Rome, 4-5 June 2009. Podcast. <http://www.einarpetterson.org/New_Perspectives_on_Baroque_Art_and_

Culture/Podcasts/Entries/2009/6/8_Mieke_Bal__Contemporary_Baroque_and_Pr
eposterous_History._Part_1_%26_2.html>

–. *Quoting Caravaggio. Contemporary Art, Preposterous History.* Chicago/London, 2001.

Buci-Glucksmann, C., 'The Work of the Gaze'. In: L. P. Zamora and M. Kaup (eds.),
*Baroque New Worlds. Representation, Transculturation, Counterconquest.* Durham, 2010.

Calabrese, O., *Neo-Baroque. A Sign of the Times.* Princeton, 1992.

Careri, G., *Bernini. Flights of Love, the Art of Devotion.* Chicago, 1995.

Castellucci, C. *et al.*, 'A Conversation about Pretence and Illusion'. In: C. Castellucci, R.
Castellucci, C. Guidi, J. Kelleher and N. Ridout (eds.), *The Theatre of Socìetas Raffaello
Sanzio.* New York, 2007a.

Castellucci, C. *et al.*, 'A Conversation about the Future'. In: C. Castellucci, R. Castellucci, C. Guidi, J. Kelleher and N. Ridout (eds.), *The Theatre of Socìetas Raffaello Sanzio.*
New York, 2007b.

Crombez, T., 'Transgressie in de Tragedia Endogonidia door Socìetas Raffaello
Sanzio'. In: *Zombrec.* s.l., 2006. Web. <http://www.zombrec.be/srs/srstransgressie.
pdf>

Crombez, T., S. Colson and H. Tratsaert, 'Interview de Romeo Castellucci, 15 avril
2005'. In: *Zombrec.* s.l., 2005. Web. <http://www.zombrec.be/srs/interviewsfr.pdf>

Crombez, T. and W. Hillaert, 'Interview de Romeo Castellucci, conduite par Thomas
Crombez et Wouter Hillaert, 1er mai 2003'. In: *Zombrec.* s.l., 2003. Web. <http://
www.zombrec.be/srs/interviewsfr.pdf>

–. 'Interview de Romeo Castellucci, 19 déc. 2004'. In: *Zombrec.* s.l., 2004. Web. <http://
www.zombrec.be/srs/interviewsfr.pdf>

Damisch, H., 'Foreword'. In: G. Careri, *Bernini. Flights of Love, the Art of Devotion.* Chicago, 1995.

Deleuze, G., *The Fold. Leibniz and the Baroque.* Minneapolis, 1993.

Dixon, S., *Digital Performance. A History of New Media in Theater, Dance, Performance Art and
Installation.* Cambridge/London, 2007.

Hillaert, W. and T. Crombez, 'Cruelty in the Theatre of The Socìetas Raffaello Sanzio'.
s.l., 2005. Web. <http://homepages.ulb.ac.be/ffirgeerts/inlthewet/castelluci.pdf>

Jay, M., 'Scopic Regimes of Modernity'. In: H. Foster (ed.), *Vision and Visuality.* New
York, 1988.

Kelleher, J. and N. Ridout, 'Introduction. The Spectators and the Archive'. In: C. Castellucci, R. Castellucci, C. Guidi, J. Kelleher and N. Ridout (eds.), *The Theatre of Socìetas
Raffaello Sanzio.* New York, 2007.

Lehmann, H.-T., *Postdramatic Theatre.* London/New York, 2006.

Munster, A., *Materializing New Media. Embodiment in Information Aesthetics.* Hanover,
2006.

Ndalianis, A., *Neo-Baroque Aesthetics and Contemporary Entertainment.* Cambridge/London,
2004.

Purgar, K., *The Neo-Baroque Subject.* Zagreb, 2006.

Socìetas Raffaello Sanzio, *Tragedia Endogonidia di/by Romeo Castellucci. Memoria video* di/memory video by Cristiano Carloni, Stefano Franceschetti. Musica originale di/original music by Scott Gibbons. Rome, 2007. DVD and booklet.

Stalpaert, C., 'De kunst van het falen. De participerende toeschouwer met stomheid geslagen'. In: R. Vanderbeeken (ed.), Kritische metafysica. Gilles Deleuze. Brussels, 2007. In-text references refer to the online version of this article, available at <http://dx.doi.org/1854/7692>

–. 'Donnez-moi donc un corps. Deleuze's aesthetics of intensities and the possibilities of queer postrepresentations'. In: K. Deufert, J. Peeters and T. Plischke (eds.), B-Book. A Project by Frankfurter Kueche (FK) and Vooruit after B-Visible, Ghent, 2004.

Valentini, V. and B. Marranca, Interview with Romeo Castellucci, June 2002. <http://www.zombrec.be/srs/valentini-marranca.html>

Vanderbeeken, R., 'Immersie in de schouwburg door emersie op scène'. In: M. Bleeker, L. van Heteren, C. Kattenbelt and R. van der Zalm (eds.), Theater Topics. Concepten en Objecten. Amsterdam, 2009.

Von Brinken, J., 'DVDeformazione. Zur ästhetischen Transformation der Tragedia Endogonidia im digitalen Videoformat'. In: K. Pewny, S. Tigges and E. Deutsch-Schreiner (eds.), Zwischenspiele. Neue Texte, Wahrnehmungs und Fiktionsräume in Theater, Tanz und Performance. Bielenfeld, 2010.

# Making *UNMAKEABLELOVE*

## The Relocation of Theatre

Sarah Kenderdine and Jeffrey Shaw

### Introduction

*We need machines that suffer from the burden of their memory.*
Jean-François Lyotard (1991: 22)

This paper addresses the histories of liveness and performance and the life of machines by articulating theoretical positions on Samuel Beckett's prose work *The Lost Ones* in relation to a recent new media work UNMAKEABLELOVE (Kenderdine & Shaw 2008). UN-MAKEABLELOVE is a revisioning of Beckett's initial investigation, which focuses and makes interactively tangible a state of confrontation and interpolation between ourselves and another society that is operating in a severe state of physical and psychological entropy. This interactive theatre advances the practices of algorithmic agency, artificial life, virtual communities, human-computer interaction, augmented virtuality, mixed reality and multimedia performance to engage 'the body's primordial inscriptions' (Schwab 2000: 73). Its mixed reality strategies of embodied simulation intricately engage the presence and agency of the viewers and impel them to experience the anomalies of a perceptual disequilibrium that directly implicates them in an alienated and claustrophobic situation. Beckett's prose has been interpreted by a number of leading scholars, including Lyotard in *The Inhuman* who speaks of 'systematic madness' (Lyotard 1991: 186), Porush who describes Beckett's 'cybernetic machine' and Schwab who interprets *The Lost Ones* as a kind of 'soul-making' (Schwab 2000: 73) and envisions the texts' narrative agency as 'a disembodied artificial intelligence' (ibid. 64) exploring the boundaries between the human and posthuman.

As such, UNMAKEABLELOVE calls upon a long history of fascination with automatic theatre. This essay touches on automaton history and looks to key transformations in more recent times using new technologies. We also look at the 'computer as performer' and the notions of the human embodiment in relation to machines to make more explicit the entanglement in the theatre of the human-computer interface. Embedded within contemporary artistic practice, the role of the viewers and the theatrical concept of the spectacle are central concerns. Jonathan Crary in *Suspension of Perception* describes the spectacle as a set of techniques for the management of bodies and the regulation of attention (Crary 1999: 9). And in *The Society of the Spectacle*, Guy Debord wrote '[T]he spectacle is not a collection of images, but a social relation among people, mediated by images' (Debord 1999: chapter 1.4). The masses subjected to the society of spectacle have traditionally been seen as aesthetically and politically passive – in response, both artists and thinkers have sought to transform the spectator into an active agent and the spectacle into a performance. In *Eclipse of the Spectacle*, Jonathan Crary suggests that the society of spectacle is no longer a fruitful paradigm because in a world characterized by 'digitized flows of data', the dominant society is no longer characterized by passive contemplation but rather by new investments of desire and new forms of representation (1984: 287). In understanding the transformations in theatre, philosopher and visual theorist Jacques Rancière observes new qualities:

> a new scene of equality where heterogeneous performances are translated into one another [...] For in all these performances what is involved is linking what one knows with what one does not know; being at once a performer deploying her skills and a spectator observing what these skills might produce in a new context among other spectators (Rancière 2009: 22)

UNMAKEABLELOVE locates Beckett's society of 'lost ones' in a virtual space that represents a severe state of physical confinement, evoking perhaps a prison, an asylum, a detention camp or a dystopia of a 'reality' TV show. As Beckett describes, 'The effect of this climate on the soul is not to be underestimated' (1972: 52). Viewers of this installation engage with the work through a hexagonal panoptic display system called Re-Actor. Wearing polarizing 3D glasses, up to six audience members are able to interrogate the world of stereographic virtual humans using interactive torches. Each torch casts real-time light beams onto the inhabitants confined within virtual space of Re-Actor. A technical description of the making of the work can be found in UNMAKEABLELOVE. *Gaming Technologies for the Cybernetic Theatre Re-Actor* (Kenderdine & Shaw 2009). The discussion in this essay examines the roles of human and virtual agents in the performance of the work. Interaction with the installation engenders participants complicit in the revealing of this world both for themselves and for other audience members who gather in front of the screens. Indeed, the active torch users are essential co-performers in the work, elemental to the endless play of an artificially intelligent world of machine agents, casting the only visible light into this world, revealing it at their will. Through augmented reality techniques, these 'performers' of the work also become embedded 'actors', visible to each other in the virtual world (in the real world they cannot see each other), albeit explicitly ignored by the community of virtual co-inhabitants.

The adventure of theatre and technological (re)construction provides context for some of these fresh relationships between the audience/spectator/performer and the virtual. Rancière offers us further insights in this context:

Like researchers, artists construct the stages where the manifestation and effect of their skills are exhibited, rendered uncertain in the terms of the new idiom that conveys a new intellectual adventure. The effect of the idiom cannot be anticipated. It requires the spectators who play the active role of interpreters, who develop their own translation in order to 'appropriate' the story and make it their own story. (Rancière 2009: 22)

## I. Automaton Theatres

Figurines were amongst the earliest signs of human culture. In thinking about the history of the life of machines, it may well be that the first figurines imbued with agency (automatons) were the Egyptian shabti depicting servants engaged in different tasks, equipped with hoes, grain baskets and other necessary tools, who would continue to work for the wealthy and powerful in the netherworld. During the period of the Alexandrian school, Heron of Alexandria produced a number of manuscripts, including *The Automaton Theater*, that describes a puppet theatre controlled by strings, drums and weights. Mechanical, hydraulic and pneumatic automatons continued to be developed in medieval times in Europe and the Indian subcontinent.[1] In the notebooks of Villard de Honnecourt we encounter an enduring theme associated with the entire history of automata – the notion of a perpetual motion machine, a machine that could run itself for an infinite period. Hydraulics, magnetism and alchemy were variously considered as the likely source of such an inexhaustible and/or renewable energy source (Nocks 2007: 4-19).

Fig. 1    Ancient Egyptian shabti figurines from the Musée du Louvre, Paris.
Source, photo: Hans Ollermann, 2008, online at Flickr.

THEATER TOPICS

Fig. 2

'Abu'l Izz Ismail al-Jazari and Farkh ibn Abd al-Latif: The Elephant Clock: Leaf from The Book of Knowledge of Ingenious Mechanical Devices by al-Jazari (57.51.23)'. In: *Heilbrunn Timeline of Art History*. New York: The Metropolitan Museum of Art, 2000.

*It is chance that is infinite, not god.*
Antonin Artaud (quoted in Derrida 2004: 46)

With the invention of computing machines, a new kind of virtual perpetual motion apparatus came into existence with the capacity to render an 'automaton theatre' that is artificially enlivened by software algorithms, imbuing its virtual fabrications with agency. This circumstance allowed UNMAKEABLELOVE² to undertake a reconsideration of the nature of automatic theatre and of the existential dilemmas that can be entertained within its realms of simulations and human interaction. Computers also redefined the nature of interactivity between humans and machines, and works like Jeffrey Shaw's POINTS OF VIEW (1983)³ demonstrated how the artist is able to convert that into a means of theatrical expression.

## POINTS OF VIEW

POINTS OF VIEW was an experiment in computational theatre that espoused real-time three-dimensional computer graphics and the extended space of real-time flight simu-

Fig. 3    *UNMAKEABLELOVE* © Kenderdine & Shaw, 2008.

lation as a dramatic and appropriate domain for artistic formulations and theatrical expression. In the late 1970s, Bruce Artwick developed the Flight Simulator, one of the first popular game engines that has become the longest running PC game series of all time (Artwick 1975). Early on, this game engine only permitted about one hundred low-resolution straight monochrome lines to be drawn, yet, by engaging its potentialities and constraints, *POINTS OF VIEW* could configure an interactive audiovisual three-dimensional virtual world that the viewer was able to freely navigate in real time.

Fig. 4
*POINTS OF VIEW*
© Jeffrey Shaw, 1983.

In his 1905 essay *The Actor and the Über-Marionette*, Edward Gordon Craig called for 'a new form of acting, consisting for the main part of symbolic gesture' (quoted in Baugh 2005: 104). In POINTS OF VIEW, Egyptian hieroglyphics function as three-dimensional stick figures, constituting a theatre of linguistic symbols that is video-projected onto a large screen in front of a seated audience. One member of the audience using two specially designed joysticks can control the action of the work, moving his virtual point of view within a hemispherical space that contains the visual setting: 360 degrees around the stage, 90 degrees up and down from ground level to aerial view, and forwards and backwards from the centre of the stage. In this work the dramatic scenography has little to do with the movement of the hieroglyphic figurines but everything to do with the movement of the viewer's point of view with respect to those actors, and it is the viewer's virtual movement that constructs the temporal expression of this work's dramaturgy. This is also explicit in the sound design of POINTS OF VIEW, where it is not the linguistic symbols on stage that are audible but rather the commentators who are virtually located in the space that surrounds the stage and whose voices are heard by the viewers depending on their proximity to those commentators' positions in the virtual space. These sound tracks are interactively linked to the image via the same joystick that controls the user's visual navigation – it modulates the various voices in relation to the different spatial positions that the user is taking with respect to the stage scene. The mix of sound tracks thus generates an extemporary conjunction of spoken information that is directed at the shifting visual/conceptual juxtapositions of the hieroglyphic figures.

POINTS OF VIEW construes a navigable virtual theatrical space populated by its virtual figurines whose novel theatrical expression and temporal dramaturgical articulation is precipitated by the actions of the viewer. The notion of a miniature theatre of figurines is also the central dramaturgical construct in Mabou Mines' interpretation of *The Lost Ones*, while UNMAKEABLELOVE takes this paradigm further by extending the viewers' modalities of navigation and examination, by enlivening the synthetic actors' space with autonomous agency, and by translating viewer interactivity into viewer complicity.

## Mabou Mines' The Lost Ones

The New York theatre company Mabou Mines is considered one of the foremost interpreters of Samuel Beckett's works. It premiered *The Lost Ones* in 1975, directed by Lee Breuer, designed by Thom Cathcart, performed by David Warrilow and with music by Philip Glass. Richard Gottlieb in the *Soho Weekly News* remarked, 'I've seen many Beckett Hells, but this is the first one I've experienced' (quoted in Mabou Mines, s.d.). Beckett's prose piece opens with stage directions for an eerie scene, evoking, in postmodern abstraction, a space resonating with Dante's Purgatorio: 'Abode where lost bodies roam, each searching for its lost one. Vast enough for search to be in vain. Narrow enough for light to be in vain. Inside a flattened cylinder fifty metres round and sixteen high for the sake of harmony' (Beckett 1972: 7).

Like works by Kafka, *The Lost Ones* creates a fictional and somewhat fantastic circum-

Fig. 5    *The Lost Ones* by Mabou Mines © Richard Landry, 1977.

stance of constraint and deprivation. It describes a community of about two hundred people who are incarcerated inside a confined space and the resulting existential tension of these inhabitants' lives. Minutely constructed according to geometrical shapes and measurements, *The Lost Ones* is populated by an abject and languishing people whose culture seems to be organized according to an elusive order, if not an unfamiliar harmony, the principles of which have yet to be discovered (ibid. 7-8).

The Mabou Mines' rendition of *The Lost Ones* has become an avant-garde legend, and there are certain aspects that demonstrate strategies of theatrical representation and viewer engagement that, albeit without its new media underpinnings, are synchronous with conceptual and operational methodologies in UNMAKEABLELOVE. Cathcart's stage design encompasses the entire theatre and is a specially constructed cylindrical amphitheatre in which the audience members sit, so that they are led to focus on their own circumstance and compare their own state of incarceration with that of Beckett's protagonists. This interpolation of real and fictional space that is a feature of UNMAKE-ABLELOVE's mixed reality is a tactic that 'puts us in (the play's) own state of ontological estrangement' (Kalb 1989: 139). Mabou Mines' production also follows the traditions of the theatre of automatons by articulating its representation of *The Lost Ones*' environment and characters as a small architectural model inhabited by tiny centimetre-high stick figures. These figures are manipulated by the production's single actor/narrator who dramatizes his narrative telling of their predicament. In anticipation of the optical immersion afforded by virtual reality technologies, the audience members are each given opera glasses so that they can peer into this micro-world and lose themselves in its estranged imaginary. But like UNMAKEABLELOVE, immersive engagement is directly accompanied by techniques that shift the symmetry of real and virtual ontologies into a theatrical condition of paradoxical confrontation that implies the complicity of the viewer. For example, both productions exploit lighting to this effect. UNMAKE-ABLELOVE's totally darkened space only becomes perceptible via the torch beams that are directed by the viewers, while at one point in the Mabou Mines' production, the single hanging lamp that illuminates the performance suddenly switches off and plunges everything, including the audience, into a shared state of pitch darkness. Then, as the actor 'speaks his final anecdote to a toy figure balanced on his knee, illuminating it with a penlight, apparently dispending with distinctions amongst contexts, questions arise to threaten to throw all mimetic readings into confusion' (ibid. 138). These 'vacillations of identities and contexts' (ibid.) are key to both undertakings.

## II. Re-Actor

The history of the cinematic experience is a rich chronicle of viewing and projection machines. Before Hollywood imposed its set of ubiquitous formats, there were a myriad of extraordinary devices, like the Lumière Brothers' Photodrama, the Cyclorama, Cosmorama, Kineorama, Neorama, Uranorama and many more. Tom Gunning, in his writings on the visual regimes of magic performance and early cinema, reveals how in this 'cinema of attractions', the viewer's interest is solicited by means of overt display that is 'willing to rupture a self-enclosed fictional world' (Gunning 1990: 57). The Kaiserpanorama – a stereoscopic cylindrical peepshow – is an especially relevant forerunner of a newly configured display system, Re-Actor.

Fig. 6    Kaiserpanorama circa 1880-1910.

In 1911, Franz Kafka saw a Kaiserpanorama and wrote:

> the scenes [are] more alive than in the cinematograph [...] because they allow the eye the stillness of reality. The cinematograph lends the observed objects the agitation of their movements, the stillness of the gaze seems more important. Smooth floors of the cathedrals in front of our tongue. (quoted in Zischler 2003: 25)

David Trotter, media theorist, takes note of Kafka's appreciation of the scene's qualities of 'tactility'. The images are indeed tactile in the specific ways found only in immersive architectures and through stereographic materials.

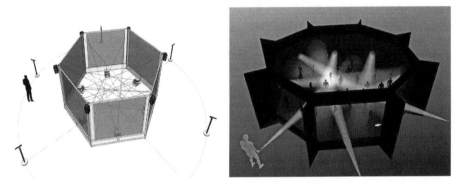

Fig. 7 and 8   Axonometric plan view and schematic diagram of Re-Actor © Kenderdine & Shaw, 2008.

Re-Actor evolved from Museum Victoria's highly successful Virtual Room (Kenderdine & Hart 2003), and the uniqueness of this system was its ability to conjure a persuasive and coherent three-dimensional virtual reality within an architectonic enclosure that the audience could freely circulate around and gaze into. Re-Actor's six rear-projected screens use twelve projectors, passive Polaroid filters and glasses for stereoscopic three-dimensional viewing. It is operated by six workstations that are connected to six pairs of 1050 x 1400 pixel Projectiondesign DLP projectors. The UNMAKEABLELOVE installation also has six custom-made torch interfaces that are positioned in front of each screen, and six infrared video cameras are positioned above each screen. These torches enable the visitors to peer into the virtual world; their virtual light beams intersect and illuminate the computer-generated figures that inhabit its virtually represented interior.

UNMAKEABLELOVE in Re-Actor offers a physically immersive three-dimensional space of representation that constitutes an augmentation and amalgamation of real and virtual realities. It is a hybrid location-based manifestation that operates both as an individual and socially shared experience, and its interactive modalities of operation incorporate the kinaesthetic dimensions of human apprehension to establish a congruence of human and machine agency. To explicitly articulate the conjunction be-

Fig. 9    Interactive torches and augmented reality interface in UNMAKEABLELOVE
© Kenderdine & Shaw, 2008.

tween the real and virtual spaces in this work, the viewer's virtual torch beams penetrate
through the container and illuminate other viewers who are standing opposite them on
other sides of the installation. This augmented reality is achieved using infrared cameras that are positioned on each screen pointing at its respective torch operators, and
the video images are rendered in real time onto each viewer's screen so as to create the
semblance of illuminating the persons opposite them. The resulting ambiguity experienced between the actual and rendered reality of the viewers' presences in this installation reinforces the perceptual and psychological tensions between 'self' and 'other'. In
'Deconstructing the Machine. Beckett's *The Lost Ones*', David Porush perceives the cylinder as an enormous cybernetic machine controlled from some outside source (1985:
157-171). In UNMAKEABLELOVE, 'control' is both illusive and made more explicit. Participants operate through the sensorium of interaction with Re-Actor, its inhabitants
and each other. The space that opens 'facilitates the emergence of hitherto unimagined
visions and sensations that exert a unique appeal to the senses and generate an intense
cathexis' (Schwab 2000: 73).

    Virtual space is distinguished by the paradoxical relationships it can configure with
real space – its multi-dimensional environments and temporal warps are like funhouse
mirrors that deform (and reform) our everyday perceptions. Yet these digital manipulations of the world are not so far removed from the traditional activities of art and science
that also reinterpret the world through various modalities of representation. In that
sense it is the interplay between reality and virtuality that is the crux of the undertaking,
and this interplay is also at work within the engine of UNMAKEABLELOVE. Samuel Beckett's 'lost ones' constitute what can be understood as a terminal community, and UN-

MAKEABLELOVE expresses this exigency as a living theatre of human performativity that has mutated into a virtual theatre of machine agents whose code heralds their extinction. On many levels, real and virtual, life and death are interpolated and concurrent in this mutant realm. UNMAKEABLELOVES's citizens are animated by the motion-captured recordings of real performers, but these now constitute a database (a fragmented memory bank) of behaviours that are conscripted by the computerized codes of their virtual representation. Fragments of memory, fragments of the real, still operate at this intersection of presence and absence, which multiplies again as a new kind of 'theatre and its double' by incorporating the presence of living viewers as witnesses and inhabitants of this liminal zone. The operational correlation (and confusion) between what is real and what is represented dictates the design of Re-Actor. The overtly physical architecture of its visualization system differentiates it from VR head-mounted displays (HMD).[4] While an HMD enables an effective conjunction of real and virtual elements, it embeds the real with an encompassing virtual frame whereas Re-Actor embeds the virtual within the surrounding real-world frame. The latter strategy is more suited to a theatrical enterprise that wants to locate the shocking immediacy of this capsule of 'lost ones' as an entity (inhabitation) that is 'living' in our actual midst (thereby reminding us for example of the proximity of those many other enclosures of human deprivation and degradation that are in operation worldwide).

## Cybernetic Systems and Performing Perception

New media theories of performance and spectatorship tend to emphasize interaction between human and machine as an embodied theatre of participation. From the perspective of the social interaction and individual/group interaction within UNMAKE-ABLELOVE, it is worthwhile to explore the dynamic series of relationships as performance in this cybernetic theatre. As this essay infers, digital technologies can be contextualized within the historical frameworks of human experience and immersion in all types of media, and interactive and immersive cinema has clear links to performance, ritual, theatre, the circus and painting (Burnett 2005: 129).

Recognizing the performative qualities of the human-computer interface, Brenda Laurel (1993) wrote a seminal work on 'computers as theatres' that set the stage for the discussions that followed.[5] McKenzie went on to suggest that 'one might invent the computer as performance' (1994: 90). Media theorist Gabriella Gianacchi, in her analysis of the virtual theatre, describes it as 'one which through its virtuality is able not only to include the viewers within the art but also to distribute their presence globally in both the real and simulated virtual world' (2004: 10).

It is useful to emphasize here the difference between (virtual) theatres and cinema to distinguish once again the different modalities and affordances of new media installations from the cinematic. Performance theorist Gay McAuley writes:

Actors are energized by the presence of the spectators, and the live presence of the actors means that the spectators' relationship to them is very different from the relationship between spectator and dramatic fiction in the cinema. In the theatre, due to the live presence of both spectators and performers, the energy circulates from performer to spectator and back again, from spectator to performer and back again [...] the live presence of both performers and spectators creates complex flows of energy between both groups [...]. (quoted in The Presence Project, 2007)

The theoretical discussion of performative qualities of the cybernetic theatres often neglects the primary communication that occurs between people in the real-world space as they perform the act of spectatorship or user participation. The aesthetics of interaction are 'rooted in the user's experience of herself performing her perception' (Dalsgaard & Koefoed Hansen 2008: 1). Both performance theory and sociology, when considering how a Human-Computer Interface (HCI) works, suggest that the user is simultaneously the operator of the system, the performer of the system and the spectator.

Interactivity has been a seminal feature of media art research over the last decades, and it proliferates because the digital technologies open a broad new range of interaction-design possibilities that were not available in the analogue world. While interactivity exists during a theatre performance inasmuch as each member of the audience reconstructs its meaning and expression as a personal experience, in the 1960s, happenings and 'expanded cinema' performances enlarged this interactivity by offering members of the audience opportunities to physically intervene in and modulate the outcome (Shaw 2003: 19). In the digital domain, Jeffrey Shaw's art practice over the last forty years has researched numerous computerized forms of interactivity that articulate an interaction paradigm whereby the viewer becomes an explorer of virtual spaces and discoverer of combinatory narratives (Duguet et al. 1997). The interactivity offered by the authors of UNMAKEABLOVE is a hybrid of these theatrical and digital modalities. Its six physical torches ('search lights') allow viewers to individually illuminate and explore the virtual scene, and these moving, intersecting torch beams constitute a significant aspect of its dramaturgical aesthetic. But at the same time the viewers cannot intervene in the computer-coded behaviour of the denizens of UNMAKEABLELOVE – these self-absorbed 'lost ones' follow Samuel Beckett's algorithmic prescription and are oblivious to the viewer's presences or actions. We interact in this world via those intangible theatrical strategies of confrontation, identification and complicity.

In multi-participatory works, which embody a single or multiple operators/users and multiple spectators (as in UNMAKEABLELOVE), numerous bonds exist between the user and the spectators, and the user and the system. Between the user and the system, the concept of embodiment is of primary concern. Embodiment is a 'participatory' status and a foundation for exploring interaction in context (Dourish 2001). In terms of the trichotomy of system-user-spectators, embodiment implies a reciprocal relationship with the context, encompassing users, interactive systems, spectators, co-users, physical surroundings and the meanings ascribed to these entities (Dalsgaard & Koefoed Hansen 2008: 5; Dourish 2001). Four researchers of computer-human interaction – Stuart Reeves, Steve Benford, Claire O'Malley and Mike Fraser – address the issue of how a spectator should experience a user's interaction with the computer (2005: 48).[6] Borrowing from performance theory, the user is the inter-actor with the system and the interaction between the user and the system is the performance. While this relationship is what is mostly described in media art and HCI, it is the spectators' relation to and experience of the performance that is also of interest here. As Dalsgaard and Koefoed Hansen describe:

> It is the ways in which the user perceives and experiences the act of interacting with the system under the potential scrutiny of spectators that greatly influences the interaction as a whole [...] it is precisely this awareness of the (potentiality of a) spectator that transforms the user into a performer. (2008: 6)

The key to this relationship is the 'awareness' of others, which provides the context for individual activity. The tension that occurs is between the spectators watching the user and the user's awareness of being the centre of the spectators' gaze. The user not only acts in relation to the system but is propelled by the knowledge that her perception of the system is a performance for others. Dalsgaard and Koefoed Hansen call this 'performing perception' (ibid. 31). The user simultaneously engages in three actions: the act of interacting with the system; the act of perceiving himself/herself in relation to the system and her surroundings; and the act of performing (ibid.).

Fig. 10   Motion capture for UNMAKEABLELOVE © Kenderdine & Shaw, 2008.

Fig. 11    Characters in UNMAKEABLELOVE revealed by interactive torches of viewers
© Kenderdine & Shaw, 2008.

## III.  Making UNMAKEABLELOVE

The Lost Ones describes a community of about 200 people who inhabit a cylinder that is 50 metres in diameter and 18 metres high. In UNMAKEABLELOVE this is scaled down to 30 characters that inhabit Re-Actor's hexagonally shaped room that is 5.5 metres wide and 3.5 metres high. To reflect the body-to-space ratio that Beckett proposes, its characters are reduced to approximately half life-size. Three actors performed over 300 motion-captured sequences that became the primary resources for the real-time behaviours of the characters in UNMAKEABLELOVE. Each character is a 12,000 triangle polygonal model with a 1024 x 1024 pixel texture and is animated by a 53-bone skeleton. Real-time rendering of the characters using the Microsoft XNA game engine allows for dynamic lighting, controlled by the viewers. Six volumetric light beams, casting shadows onto each other and the environment, light the characters.

### Coding UNMAKEABLELOVE

The almost scientific exactitude of Beckett's text enables it to be analysed and coded into software algorithms that can then computationally animate virtual representations of his characters. In UNMAKEABLELOVE, these virtual representations then become the seemingly self-motivated narrative agents of Beckett's scenario.

The world of UNMAKEABLELOVE consists of the Searchers who are always active and searching in vain, the Sedentary who no longer move around and are only occasionally roused from their lethargy, and the Defeated for whom all hope is gone and who are slumped and vaguely stirring in the perimeter of the enclosure. Each group with their specific behaviours is largely confined to particular zones inside the hexagonal space and permitted occasional interactions, moving between zones. Violence sporadically breaks out, and now and then they collide in a frenzied sexual encounter. The narrative agency in The Lost Ones has been described as a 'disembodied artificial intelligence' (Schwab 2000: 61). One can imagine its denizens as inhabiting a posthuman space, the last humans secluded in a capsule that is, like a nautilus, organized according to a 'self-sufficient cosmogony, which has its own categories, its own time, space, fulfilment and even existential principle' (Barthes 1972: 65).

UNMAKEABLELOVE advances the practices of algorithmic agency, artificial life, virtual communities, human-computer interaction, augmented virtuality, mixed reality and multimedia performance in a 'polyaesthetic' experience to 'engage the body's primordial inscriptions' (Schwab 2000: 73). It locates Beckett's society of 'lost ones' in a virtual space that represents a severe state of physical and psychological entropy, evoking perhaps a prison, an asylum, a detention camp, or a dystopian Big Brother show; 'the condition of the human at its ultimate vanishing point' (ibid. 63). The inhabitants of Beckett's cylindrical space are oblivious to their condition, and we, the viewers of their world, with our probing torch lights and prying gaze, are positioned as the 'other' and forced to experience the anomalies of a perceptual disequilibrium that implicates us in this alienated narrative. The resulting ambiguity reinforces a perceptual and psychological tension between 'self' and 'other' generated by the works' mixed reality strategies of embodied simulation that intricately engage the presence, agency and complicity of the viewer.

UNMAKEABLELOVE takes motion-captured, human-performed actions and then re-embodies and codifies them in a post-theatrical space of virtual representation. The Australian artist Stelarc is a researcher who also explores mediated ways to engage the complicity of the viewer in theatrical expressions. His MOVATAR, which he calls an 'inverse motion capture system' (Stelarc, s.d.), maintains his tangible on-stage presence where he is transformed into a posthuman machine agent being remote-controlled by people acting on his body over the internet. Despite the dissimilar aesthetic and technological approaches in UNMAKEABLELOVE and MOVATAR, both achieve the viewer's identification with a 'suffering object' (Stelarc's Involuntary Body, see Fernandes 2002). Yet the latter presents a narrative that is entirely played out within its interaction paradigm, while UNMAKEABLELOVE plays across a human imaginary as it has been plotted in Samuel Beckett's The Lost Ones.

There must be no let up, no vacuum in the audience's mind or sensitivity...
Antonin Artaud (quoted in Derrida 2004: 47)

Following on from Artaud, Marinetti and Brecht, UNMAKEABLELOVE reframes the central role of the audience in theatrical experimentation. But rather than the convivial participations described in Relational Aesthetics (Bourriaud 2002), UNMAKEABLELOVE alludes to more troubled evidence of audience behaviour, such as the violence that it perpetrated in the Living Theatre's *Paradise Now!* (Avignon Festival 1968) and Marina Abramovic's *Rhythm 0* (Studio Morra, Naples, 1974). Facing up to this latent pathology, Terry O'Connor, an actor in Forced Entertainment's *Showtime* (Alsager Arts Centre, Stoke-on-Trent 1996) suddenly shouts at the audience: 'What the fuck are you looking at? What the fuck is your problem? Fuck off! Voyeurs! There's a fucking line and you've just crossed it. Where's your human decency?' (in Freshwater 2009: 52; cf. Etchells 1999).

UNMAKEABLELOVE interpolates two scenarios for this loss of 'human decency' – one that is evoked in Beckett's existential endgame *The Lost Ones*, and the other that confronts the viewer/voyeur with the explicit experience that they are complicit in both the origin and outcome of this endgame. It is a spectrum that ranges from interpersonal sadism and refugee brutality to environmental defilement. Conjoined in the narrative extremity of Beckett's *The Lost Ones*, UNMAKEABLELOVE's computational scenography exposes that 'What is tragic is not the impossibility, but the necessity of repetition' (Derrida 2004: 44). UNMAKEABLELOVE's torch-lit metaverse correlates with Susan Sontag's observations on Artuad's view of shadows and spectacles:

> Artaud thinks that modern consciousness suffers from a lack of shadows. The remedy is not to remain in (Plato's) cave but devise better spectacles. The theatre that Artaud proposes will serve consciousness by 'naming and directing shadows' and destroying the 'false shadows' to 'prepare the way for a new generation of shadows' around which will assemble 'the true spectacle of life'. It will be a stage of extreme austerity dominated by the 'physics of the absolute gesture, which is itself idea'. (2004: 88)

Here, the rigour of an algorithmically defined and simulated universe of prescribed emergent behaviours aligns with Artaud's contempt for dramatic performativity: 'the uselessness of the action, which, once done, is not to be done, and the superior use of the state unused by the action, and which restored produces a purification' (1958: 82). UNMAKEABLELOVE's actors do not strike poses or construct gestures, they respond to events out of computational necessity. As in Dante's *Purgatorio*, gloominess and indifference periodically lead to 'zeal and fervent affection' (*Purgatorio Canto* XVIII), and now and then Beckett's vanquished resurrect to perform vain attempts at copulation. In UNMAKEABLELOVE, lovers are caught in desiccated bodies whose 'hampering effect on the work of love' condemns them to perform a grotesque spectacle of 'making unmakeable love' (Beckett 1972: 37). Understood as a 'glittering' space of 'cryptic incorporation' (Perniola 2003: 69), UNMAKEABLELOVE's forever-automated posthuman universe is driven by a 'gratuitous and baseless necessity' (Derrida 2004: 46).

> To think the closure of representation is to think the tragic: not as the representation of fate, but as the fate of representation. And it is to think why it is fatal that, in its closure, representation continues. (ibid.)

**Sarah Kenderdine** holds a lifelong position at Museum Victoria as head of Special Projects and works at the forefront of immersive and interactive systems in cultural heritage and art. Dr Kenderdine is currently Visiting Associate Professor at the City University of Hong Kong and Director of Research at ALiVE (Applied Laboratory of Interactive Visualization and Embodiment).

**Jeffrey Shaw** has been a leading figure in new media art since the 1960s. He was the founding director of the ZKM Institute for Visual Media Karlsruhe (1991-2002), and since 2009 is Chair Professor of Media Art and Dean of the School of Creative Media at the City University of Hong Kong.

NOTES

1   An excellent article about the history of al-Jazari's automata can be found in Nadarajan (2007).
2   UNMAKEABLELOVE is an interactive artwork by Sarah Kenderdine and Jeffrey Shaw first launched for the eArts Festival, Shanghai 2008. Since then it has toured worldwide. Most recently, it premiered in Hong Kong at the HK Arts Fair 2011. See <http://unmakeablelove.org>.
3   For POINTS OF VIEW by Jeffrey Shaw (Mickery Theatre, Amsterdam 1983), see <http://www.jeffrey-shaw.net/html_main/show_work.php3?record_id=67>.
4   Head Mounted Display, see<http://en.wikipedia.org/wiki/Head-mounted_display>.
5   Other seminal figures include Philip Auslander.
6   Steve Benford and his associates at Collaborative Computing in the Mixed Reality Laboratory at the University of Nottingham extend the user-spectator relation through a series of locative media interactive game/performances (Bell et al. 2006).

REFERENCES

Artaud, A., 'Fragmentations'. In: J. Hirschman (ed)., *Antonin Artaud Anthology*. San Francisco, 1965.
Artaud, A., *The Theatre and Its Double*. New York, 1958.
Artwick, B. A., 'A Versatile Computer-Generated Dynamic Flight Display'. PhD Thesis. Urbana-Champaign, 1975.
Barthes, R., 'The Nautilus and the Drunken Boat'. In: R. Barthes, *Mythologies*. New York, 1972.
Baugh, C., *Theatre, Performance and Technology*. New York, 2005.
Beckett, S., *The Lost Ones*. New York, 1972.
Bell, M., M. Chalmers, L. Barkhuus, M. Hall, S. Sherwood, P. Tennent, B. Brown, D. Rowland and S. Benford, 'Interweaving Mobile Games with Everyday Life'. In: R. Grinter et al. (eds.), *Proceedings of the SIGCHI Conference on Human Factors in Computing Systems (CHI '06)*. London, 2006.

Bourriaud, N., *Relational Aesthetics*. Dijon, 2002.

Burnett R., *How Images Think*. Cambridge/London, 2005.

Crary, J., *Suspensions of Perception*. Cambridge, 1999.

Crary, J., 'Eclipse of Spectacle'. In: B. Wallis (ed.), *Art After Modernism: Rethinking Representation*. New York, 1984.

Dalsgaard, P. and L. Koefoed Hansen, 'Performing Perception. Staging Aesthetics of Interaction'. In: *ACM Transactions on Computer-Human Interaction*, 15, 3, p. 13:1-33. New York, 2008.

Debord, G. *The Society of the Spectacle*. New York, 1999.

Derrida, J., 'The Theater of Cruelty and the Closure of Representation'. In: E. Scheer (ed.), *Antonin Artaud. A Critical Reader*. London, 2004.

Dourish, P., 'Seeking a Foundation for Context-Aware Computing'. In: *Human-Computer Interaction*, 16, 2, p. 229-241. London, 2001.

Duguet, A.M., A. M. Weibel, H. Klotz, *Jeffrey Shaw. A User's Manual from Expanded Cinema to Virtual Reality*. Ostfildern, 1997.

Etchells, T., *Certain Fragments. Contemporary Performance and Forced Entertainment*. London, 1999.

Fernandes, M., 'The Body Without Memory: An Interview with Stelarc'. In: *CTheory*. Victoria, 2002. Web. <http://www.ctheory.net/articles.aspx?id=354>

Freshwater, H., *Theatre and Audience*. Hampshire, 2009.

Gianacchi, G., *Virtual theatres. An Introduction*. London, 2004.

Gunning, T., 'The Cinema of Attractions. Early Film, Its Spectator and the Avant-Garde'. In: T. Elsaesser (ed.), *Early Cinema. Space, Frame, Narrative*. London, 1990.

Kalb, J., *Beckett in Performance*. Cambridge, 1989.

Kenderine, S. and T. Hart, 'This is Not a Peep Show! The Virtual Room at the Melbourne Museum'. In: *Proceedings of International Committee on Hypermedia and Interactivity, Paris, September 2003*. CD-ROM. Pittsburgh, 2003. <http://www.archimuse.com/publishing/ichim03/003C.pdf>.

Kenderine, S. and J. Shaw, 'UNMAKEABLELOVE. Gaming Technologies for the Cybernetic Theatre Re-Actor'. In: *Proceedings of DIMEA/ACE Conference (5th Advances in Computer Entertainment Technology Conference and 3rd Digital Interactive Media Entertainment and Arts Conference), Athens, November 2009*. ACM International Conference Proceeding Series, 422, p. 362–367. New York, 2009.

Laurel B., *Computers as Theatre*. Boston, 1993.

Lyotard, J.-F., 'Can Thought Go on without a Body?'. In: J.-F. Lyotard, *The Inhuman. Reflections on Time*. California, 1991.

Mabou Mines, 'Productions: *The Lost Ones*'. In: *MabouMines.org*. New York, s.d. Web. <http://maboumines.org/productions/lost-ones>

McKenzie J., 'Virtual Reality. Performance, Immersion, and the Thaw'. In: *The Drama Review*, 38, 4, p. 83-106. New York, 1994.

Nadarajan, G., 'Automation and Robotics in Muslim Heritage. The Cultural Roots of al-Jazari's Mechanical Systems'. In: G. Nadarajan, *Islamic Automation. A reading of al-*

Jazari's *The Book of Knowledge of Ingenious Devices* (1206). Manchester, 2007. <http://www.muslimheritage.com/uploads/Automation_Robotics_in_Muslim Heritage. pdf>

Nocks, L., *The Robot. The Life Story of a Technology*. Westport, 2007.

Perniola, M., *Art and its Shadow*. New York, 2003.

Porush, D., *The Soft Machine. Cybernetic Fiction*. New York, 1985.

The Presence Project, 'Audience and Presence'. In: *The Presence Project*. Stanford, 2007. Web. <http://presence.stanford.edu:3455/Collaboratory/643>

Rancière, J., *The Emancipated Spectator*. London/New York, 2009.

Reeves, S., S. Benford, C. O'Malley and M. Fraser, 'Designing the Spectator Experience'. In: *Proceedings of the Conference of Human factors in Computer Systems (CHI05)*. New York, 2005.

Schwab, G., 'Cosmographical Meditations on the In/Human. Beckett's *The Lost Ones* and Lyotard's "Scapeland"'. In: *Parallax*, 6, 4, p. 58-75. London, 2000.

Shaw, J., 'Introduction'. In Weibel, P. and Shaw, J. (eds), *Future Cinema. The Cinematic Imaginary After Film*. Cambridge, 2003.

Sontag, S., 'Approaching Artaud'. In E. Scheer (ed.), *Antonin Artaud. A Critical Reader*. London, 2004.

Stelarc, 'Movatar'. In: *Stelarc.org*. s.l, s.d. Web. < http://stelarc.org/?catID=20225 >

Zischler, H., *Kafka Goes to the Movies*. Chicago, 2003.

ACKNOWLEDGEMENTS

UNMAKEABLELOVE © Sarah Kenderdine & Jeffrey Shaw 2008, with Scott Ashton, Yossi Landesman and Conor O'Kane. Re-Actor © Sarah Kenderdine & Jeffrey Shaw 2008. Projectors generously sponsored by Projectiondesign, Norway. This project was developed with the support of the UNSW iCinema Centre, Museum Victoria, and EPIDEMIC. A version of this paper was first presented at *Re-Live 09*: media art history conference, Melbourne, Australia 2009.

unmakeablelove.org

# Witness Protection?

## Surveillance Technologies in Theatrical Performance

Elise Morrison

In the spring of 2008, the Lyric Hammersmith Theatre in London summoned audiences for the Shunt Collective's *Contains Violence* with a peculiar request: arrive at dusk, wear gloves, and get ready for an evening of rooftop espionage. Upon arrival, audience members were ushered onto the rooftop terrace of the Lyric Hammersmith, seated under the darkening sky on the edge of the balcony, and outfitted with a set of in-ear microphones and high-power binoculars. A uniform-clad officer brusquely ordered audience members to use their individually issued surveillance equipment to follow a drama that would take place several hundred yards away, across a busy commercial street, in a newly built five-story glass-fronted office building.

As the office-world drama across the street unfolded, the lighted rooms revealed a disillusioned office worker typing his letter of resignation, a bubbly male co-worker watering ornamental plants, and, several floors below, a woman in a neck brace and polka-dot dress sashaying around a photocopier and talking heatedly on her mobile phone. Over the hour-plus performance, the audience had to piece together the suspenseful Hitchcockian narrative through the clues they gathered via their zoom lens binoculars and specially calibrated earphones, drawing connections between a fragmented series of sounds and gestures that included obscene and threatening phone calls, a passionate embrace and choice inner thoughts narrated by the characters, all of which were underscored by environmental sounds of typing, phones ringing, paper crackling, water pouring, and mundane office conversation. Finally, much as the title of the show promises, the audience members were witnesses to an act of theatrical violence, a dramatically bloody murder worthy of any televised crime thriller.

The Shunt Collective's *Contains Violence* (2008) is illustrative of an emergent genre of mixed media performance that I am calling 'surveillance theatre'. Surveillance theatre pieces are characterized by the significant integration of technologies of surveillance into the form and content of live theatre works, as surveillance theatre artists explore aesthetic and theatrical as well as disciplinary capabilities of surveillance technologies. *Contains Violence* joins a growing number of surveillance theatre works that include Edit Kaldor's *Point Blank* (2007), Juggernaut Theatre's *Oh What War* (2008), The Builders Association's *Super Vision* (2005-6), Big Picture Group's *True + False* (2007), the WaxFactory's *Quartet* (v4.0, 2010), theatre two point oh #'s *Surveillance* (2008), Rebecca Schneider's The Blind (2007), Simon McBurney's Measure for Measure (2004), and the Living Theatre in collaboration with Surveillance Camera Players' Not in My Name (2000), as well as a wide range of surveillance artworks installed and performed in art galleries, at political protests, academic and corporate conferences, quotidian urban spaces and on online websites around the world.[1]

Artists such as these employ theatre as a medium through which to represent historical and contemporary surveillance practices as well as to reflect upon attendant issues of control, discipline, evidence and freedom. In Simon McBurney's Measure for Measure and The Builders Association's Super Vision, surveillance technologies functioned as part of the theatrical mise-en-scène for the purposes of representing sociopolitical conditions of contemporary surveillance. McBurney employed live feed and recorded video on the stage of the Royal National Theatre to infuse the Shakespearean drama with contemporary politics of postmodern, mediatized London (Hopkins & Orr 2005), while The Builders Association overlaid various systems of contemporary digital surveillance to trace the 'data trails' of three characters caught in the changing conditions of a 'post-private' society (Builders Association, s.d.). In a more conceptual turn, Edit Kaldor's Point Blank featured a young woman's search for the secret of a happy life through the high-power zoom lens of her camera, a surveillant tool that she had used to amass a sprawling collection of thousands of surreptitious photographs taken of strangers from around the world. Audiences of Point Blank were enlisted to help the young woman analyse the thousands of surreptitious photographs, a difficult and troubling task that prompted participants to critically reflect upon the status of surveillance data as stable 'evidence'.

In these productions, surveillance technologies emerge as effective theatrical tools to foreground, reformulate and challenge practices of watching and being watched. By bringing surveillance technologies into traditional theatre spaces, surveillance theatre artists not only ask their audiences to reflect upon disciplinary aspects of surveillance society, they also bring questions of watching and being watched to bear on habitual processes of representation and reception in theatre. This is to say that by theatricalizing surveillance-based practices, surveillance theatre artists simultaneously interrogate paradigms of theatre and of surveillance, as well as the ways in which each paradigm has materially and symbolically shaped the other. As such, surveillance theatre productions reveal the productive capacity of surveillance and theatre to mutate, reflect and challenge fundamental practices of representation and reception in each other.

Contains Violence, described above, provides a particularly innovative case study of the significant interventions that surveillance theatre can stage. In building this murder mystery cum peepshow, director and Shunt Collective member David Rosenberg employed surveillance technologies not only as representational objects of socio-political surveillance, summoning images of Jimmy Stewart as the classic Rear Window vigilante voyeur, but also as tools with which to defamiliarize and challenge habitual modes of theatre spectatorship.[2] Rosenberg actively reframed his audience's reception and perception of the theatrical event by requiring them to access the performance through the mediating devices of binoculars and earpieces. These conditions served to accentuate and alienate the naturalized behaviour of watching and overhearing that is so habitual and familiar to theatre that it generally escapes recognition.

In particular, Rosenberg's use of surveillant media challenges and unsettles long-running habits of passive spectatorship induced by theatrical histories of realism. Traditions of representation and reception in realist theatre such as the 'fourth wall' and darkened auditoriums date back to the influential writings of encyclopedist Denis Diderot in the eighteenth century.[3] Conventions of seeing and being seen in dramatic realism came into common practice at the end of the nineteenth and beginning of the twentieth century under directors and writers such as Konstantin Stanislavski, Anton Chekhov and Henrik Ibsen, and such practices continue to be familiar to audiences of mainstream commercial theatres such as the Lyric Hammersmith. These deeply ingrained behavioural habits entail quiet attention from a largely invisible and passive audience, a shared understanding of the imaginary fourth wall that sets the audience outside of the narrative frame, and the 'suspension of disbelief' that marks the borders between the everyday 'real world' and the fictional theatrical space.[4]

As I explore at more length in the second half of this article, the performance conditions of *Contains Violence* challenged many of these ingrained habits of spectatorship in mainstream realist theatre. By supplying his audience with surveillant media (earpieces and binoculars), Rosenberg insisted that his audience become viscerally aware of their own habits of spectatorship and theatre-going as well as their embedded assumptions about popular representations of surveillance. He did so using three central strategies: firstly, by outfitting audience members with familiar symbols of surveillance, he recast habitually passive theatre spectators into the role of rooftop spies, activating their dramatic participation within the fictional narrative of surveillance and violence he had staged. Secondly, he destabilized his audience's relationship to the fictional realm of theatre by placing them on the blurry border between the theatrical and the everyday. Thirdly, he disoriented their visual and aural intake of the theatrical event itself with powerful zoom lenses and specially calibrated earphones. These subtle but powerful modifications reframed and defamiliarized expectations and habits of theatre spectatorship, making them re-emerge as new and strange to themselves.

## Remediating Evidence and Spectatorship in Surveillance Theatre

In elucidating the unique provocations offered by surveillance theatre pieces such as *Contains Violence*, 'remediation' – a term coined by cultural theorists Jay David Bolter and Richard Grusin – serves as a particularly useful concept. Simply defined, remediation is 'the representation of one medium in another', the practice of which is a primary characteristic of new digital media, such as virtual reality, computer games, and the internet, as well as longer standing forms of visual representation, such as theatre, linear-perspective painting, photography, film and television (Bolter & Grusin 1996: 345). Given the common social usage of the term 'remediate' to refer to the process or act of re-educating a deficient or misbehaving student, it is not altogether surprising that Bolter and Grusin tend to align remediation with techno-social progress, improvement and reform. As they put it, 'new media [present] themselves as refashioned and improved versions of other media' (1999: 14-15). This is because 'the assumption of reform is so strong that a new medium is now expected to justify itself by improving on a predecessor' (ibid. 59). Bolter and Grusin extend this cultural expectation for 'reform' beyond contemporary digital media, noting that 'photography was seen as the reform of illusionistic painting and the cinema as the reform of the theater' (ibid. 60).

However, by investing in developmental genealogies of reform, Bolter and Grusin overlook significant ways in which existing 'older' media such as theatre have integrated and critically reframed newer forms of media. In contrast, performance and media theorists such as Steve Dixon and Greg Geisekam have persuasively argued that theatre, throughout its rich and varied history, has functioned as a malleable platform for artists and audiences to experiment with and reflect upon new technologies of representation, communication and information exchange.[5] In *Digital Performance* (2007), Dixon chronicles a genealogical history of 'digital performance', citing early theatrical devices of the Greek *deus ex machina*, and moving through Wagner's concept of the total artwork (*Gesamtkunstwerk*) to early dance and technology experiments by Loïe Fuller in the late nineteenth century and by the Bauhaus artist Oskar Schlemmer in the 1920s. Greg Geisekam's *Staging the Screen* (2007) importantly counters formulations of remediation that posit new media as distinct from theatre or theatricality, as he argues that theatre has substantially shaped film, video and television since the mid-nineteenth century:

> recent alarms over theatre remediating film, television, and video are ironic, given that these media themselves originally borrowed considerably from the theatre, before they developed more distinctive conventions and concerns. As the newer media evolved, critics attempted to demarcate their specific qualities and conventions, often rejecting work that seemed too 'theatrical' for failing to acknowledge the distinctiveness of the particular medium [...]. (2007: 5-6)

These less 'progress-based' or 'corrective' understandings of remediation articulated by Dixon and Geisekam show that surveillance theatre pieces such as *Contains Violence* do not necessarily aim to *improve* upon historical or contemporary practices of watching and being watched. Such productions do not reform social systems of surveillance or radically advance techniques of theatrical production, as the main thrust of Bolter and Grusin's concept might suggest. Instead, surveillance theatre pieces provide valuable opportunities for audience members and practitioners to reflect upon and physically respond to prescient questions about discipline and performance within the theatrical and surveillant media themselves. Moreover, in interfacing with these representational media, audiences of surveillance theatre have the opportunity to critically consider aspects of contemporary culture and daily life that these media represent.

A brief look at an earlier moment in the history of surveillance theatre shows that theatre has long been a site of remediation in which audiences and practitioners could critically reflect upon emergent regimes of visibility. In 'Performing Remediation: Minstrelsy, Photography, and the Octoroon', Adam Sonstegard uses Dion Boucicault's The Octoroon (1859) to look at the process by which 'one medium, a stage performance [...] participated in constructing another medium, photography' (Sonstegard 2006: 375). Sonstegard contextualizes the overlapping media of stage performance and photography in the particular historical moment of the production's debut, arguing that the remediation of photography in theatre was a means by which Boucicault instructed his nineteenth-century audiences in the surveillant and evidentiary capabilities of photography:

> The play represents an important historical moment, at which Americans first moved toward naturalizing photography's role in surveillance; an analysis of the play today dramatizes, as it were, the extent to which Americans have accepted – indeed, have become saturated with – that very culture of photographic surveillance. (ibid. 376)

For Sonstegard, surveillance theatre functioned as an instructive device that disciplined and instructed early audiences of The Octoroon in the use and ideology of new technologies of vision. In a similar, though less overtly disciplinary, fashion, contemporary surveillance theatre pieces such as Contains Violence facilitate critical reflections about surveillance techniques and technologies of the twentieth and early twenty-first centuries. In building Contains Violence, Rosenberg employed a simple but powerful model of remediation, putting two familiar modes of watching in dialogue with each other. On the one hand, the individually issued surveillance equipment gestured to familiar cultural representations of surveillance that the audience eagerly re-enacted, as the rooftop setting, binoculars and wiretapping invoked films such as Hitchcock's Rear Window or televised crime shows such as The Wire. On the other hand, the Lyric Hammersmith's status as an internationally renowned theatre invoked long-standing traditions and expectations of theatre-spectatorship. Rosenberg employed popular representations of surveillance to defamiliarize habitual processes of theatre spectatorship, while at the same time using a theatrical context to provide a conceptual frame through which audience members could critically consider applications of surveillance techniques to contemporary everyday life.

Importantly, the cultural conditions portrayed in Contains Violence and The Octoroon demonstrate that remediation is a radically contingent process, intrinsically tied to the temporally specific conceptions of surveillance that contemporary audiences bring to surveillance theatre productions. Just as The Octoroon functioned as a cultural instruction manual that used theatrical representation to 'coach' mid-nineteenth-century audiences in the evidentiary function of photography, so too do contemporary surveillance theatre productions stage familiar and emergent surveillance techniques and technologies in order to reflect, and reflect upon, sociopolitical uses of surveillance.[6] As I discuss in the following section, late twentieth- and early twenty-first-century surveillance systems depend upon new and old modes of discipline and interpellation. Contemporary social subjects encounter surveillance technologies in everyday 'user-friendly' social, economic and cultural forms (ATMs, online shopping, GPS, Facebook, etc), as well as in more traditional disciplinary encounters with police officers and surveillance cameras. As a result, just as they have been conditioned to behave according to conventions of theatre spectatorship, contemporary theatre audiences are primed to interact with surveillance technologies in a variety of culturally determined ways.

## Policing the Intersection: Key Issues in Surveillance and Theatre

At this juncture, a brief, investigative detour into surveillance and theatre as visual media with distinct – as well as shared – traditions of representation and reception will help to lay the groundwork for a deeper analysis of the intersections of contemporary surveillance and theatre in *Contains Violence*. There are notable similarities between the histories of surveillance and theatre, as each medium has been shaped around practices of watching and being watched, carefully calibrated visibilities and invisibilities, and the power dynamics that attend each of these arrangements. At the same time, recent changes in surveillance society continue to significantly shape the ways in which audiences and practitioners approach contemporary surveillance theatre.

Surveillance, not unlike theatre, can be understood according to a foundational question: 'Who is watching whom?'. This question implies a unidirectional, disciplinary gaze in surveillance, a gaze that has been most famously theorized by cultural theorist Michel Foucault in his analysis of Jeremy Bentham's 1791 prison design known as the Panopticon. According to Foucault, Bentham's panoptic principle produces an efficient and sustainable form of discipline based on a visible yet unverifiable site/sight of power:

> Bentham laid down the principle that power should be visible and unverifiable. Visible: the inmate will constantly have before his eyes the tall outline of the central tower from which he is spied upon. Unverifiable: the inmate must never know whether he is being looked at any one moment; but he must be sure that he may always be so. (Foucault 1995: 201)

The inmate of the Panopticon, realizing that any infraction might be punished if observed by the visible but unverifiable surveilling gaze, begins to discipline him- or herself, thus internalizing the aims and ideology of the presumed authoritarian gaze.

In the panoptic principle, which has been heralded as the dominant model for modern surveillance systems, the hierarchy of 'who is watching whom' is expressed through a matrix of *visibility* and *invisibility*, as processes of watching/being watched are strategically made visible or invisible, and certain bodies are socially constructed as either given to be seen or given to see. The panoptic guard tower (analogous to contemporary closed-circuit television or CCTV surveillance systems in urban streets and shops), placed prominently in the centre of the complex, could be viewed from anywhere within the prison, thus displaying the site/sight of power without ever showing the actual embodied presence of the surveillance guard. In contrast to the distinctly visible bodies of the surveilled inmates, the actual gaze of surveillance was designed to be hidden and never verifiable at any one point in time. As such, certain symbols of surveillance were (and still are) strategically displayed so that the subjects of surveillance – be they inmates in a panoptic prison or contemporary shoppers in a store with CCTV cameras – are always aware of the disciplinary systems in place around them, even while they are never sure if they are being watched in 'real time'.

Even while the Foucauldian analysis of a disciplinary society continues to elucidate aspects of contemporary surveillance systems (such as nearly ubiquitous CCTV cameras in urban centres), the panoptic principle as a political and cultural model has been stretched and revised to a great degree in recent decades. In place of the visually monitored institutions and individuals that defined Foucault's disciplinary society, cultural theorist Gilles Deleuze coined the term 'societies of control' to describe contemporary surveillance society and the rapid rise of interconnected computer databases in which personal information rather than material bodies are visualized, tracked and monitored (1990: 3). In 'societies of control', the human body has been destabilized as a corporeal entity, represented not as a recognizable individual but instead as bits of personal data that are abstracted from distinct locales and bodies and sorted into a series of discrete informational flows (ibid. 4-5). These flows of personal data coalesce into distinct 'data doubles', correlating to individual subjects that are tracked and targeted by state and corporate entities (Haggerty & Erikson 2006: 606).

Such radical shifts in representations of bodies and places in contemporary information-based surveillance complicate the question of 'who is watching whom'. The power dynamics of contemporary surveillance are still closely linked to who has access to these flows of information and who can observe and effect the subjects of surveillance through their 'data doubles'. However, recent scholarship on surveillance reveals an added concern regarding which bodies, processes and data networks are made *visible* and which are kept *invisible* in the processes of contemporary, information-based surveillance. Personal information gathered through a range of software interfaces is often quickly dissociated from the contingent time, place and techno-human interface of its gathering, as software systems translate personal data into virtually invisible flows of information (Gandy 1993: 15-18). The relative invisibility of dispersed and digitized flows of personal information gives rise to easily obscured links between state and corporate entities that access these networks. Surveillance theorists David Lyon, Oscar Gandy, Wendy Chun, David Murakami Wood and Stephen Graham have described these processes within contemporary surveillance as productive of a less visible and thus more insidious mode of discipline.[7] Thus, in addition to the question 'who is watching whom', surveillance theory and practice are shaped by the critical question of 'what is visible and what is invisible in techniques and technologies of contemporary surveillance?'.

Moreover, surveillance as a practice and concept has itself been progressively remediated through techno-cultural changes in digital media, visual culture, communication networks and popular entertainment. No longer is surveillance only a top-down process of discipline in which an unseen body of power polices its subjects (even as this aspect of surveillance has also intensified in response to major terrorist activities, especially in the last decade). Surveillance has also come to be foundational to a range of social media of communication, entertainment and commerce through which social subjects are encouraged and even rewarded to actively participate in the work of watching and being watched. Through social software systems such as Facebook, Twitter and Foursquare, and the proliferation of reality TV programmes, contemporary social subjects have become increasingly facile user-consumers of digital surveillance technologies, encountering them not only in overtly disciplinary exchanges (with surveillance cameras or policemen), but also in a multitude of quotidian transactions and forms of entertainment. Cell phones, ATMs, and social and commercial software programmes such as Facebook and Amazon.com are all functionally undergirded by technologies of surveillance. These 'user-friendly' social software systems offer interfaces through which user-consumers can be more easily and comprehensively tracked, monitored and controlled (through individualized accounts, special offers and limited access). However, these risks are tempered or even eclipsed by the increasingly familiar benefits of online shopping, ATMs, locating old high school friends via Facebook or following the latest reality TV show.

In other words, in the individualized, dispersed and networked operations of contemporary surveillance society, a different kind of discipline has emerged. Deleuze, Lyon and Chun, among other cultural theorists writing about surveillance, have noted that the shift towards subjects *using* surveillance technologies constitutes a shift in Althusserian and Foucauldian models of discipline and interpellation associated with modern systems of surveillance. In contrast to more overtly disciplinary models of surveillance – such as Jeremy Bentham's Panopticon or Louis Althusser's 'Repressive State Apparatuses' – social subjects are hailed by contemporary technologies of surveillance into user-consumer-subject positions. Chun has argued that digital software interfaces used in everyday surveillance constitute a new kind of discipline, suggesting that the software interfaces of digital surveillance technologies function as updated Althusserian 'Ideological State Apparatuses' subtly conditioning the user's behaviour, choices and socio-economic outcomes (Chun 2006: 44). Despite being active and even well-informed user-consumers of digital surveillance technologies and systems, contemporary social subjects are conditioned through these software interfaces to see and interact with certain bodies and events in certain ways.

In addition to carefully designed software interfaces that condition users to properly interact with personal digital technologies in prescribed ways, social subjects are trained to view everyday situations according to certain ideological sightlines. This has been most memorably and visibly represented in the United States through the post-9/11 campaign, 'If You See Something, Say Something'. The campaign posters plastered in urban centres aim to democratize surveillance, suggesting that all patriotic citizens are (or should be) in concert with the police in their efforts to report any suspicious persons, packages or activities. The campaign asks everyday commuters and passers-by to act as surveillance cameras, urging them to become as attentive but also as invisible as surveillance cameras. And yet, within this sociopolitical campaign of hyper-vigilance, contemporary social subjects are not necessarily 'given to see' what is there in front of them. Althusser's former colleague Jacques Rancière has reformulated and updated Althusser's famous model of interpellation, arguing that sites/sights of discipline in late capitalism are predicated not only on what is made hyper-visible – advertising, monuments, walkways – but, more importantly, on what is *not* given to be seen, or what is given to be *not seen*. If there actually *is* something to see – something out of the ordinary, something politically subversive – the phrase, 'move along, nothing to see here', is mouthed by police or other authorities on the scene (Rancière 2001: 5). It is implicit in the 'If You See Something' campaign that if one has seen *something that should not be*, one is obligated to alert authorities. To *say something* is to *say it to the police* so that the offending person or action – that which should not have appeared – can be addressed within a police-dominated logic of vision; that is, rendered invisible again.

These modes of discipline-by-participation have conditioned user-consumer-subjects to accept certain cultural blind spots in contemporary surveillance society. Mainstream sociopolitical campaigns such as 'If You See Something' attempt to interpellate social subjects into a police-dominated logic of vision in which subversive social elements are repeatedly reinscribed as not visible or permissible. In this ideology, politically subversive events or bodies should be passed by rather than critically reflected upon. As Rancière puts it, 'The police say there is nothing to see, nothing happening, nothing to be done, but to keep moving, circulating; they say that the space of circulation is nothing but the space of circulation' (ibid.). Similarly, disciplinary models embedded within social software systems reward users for taking social and economic risks with their personal information by granting greater and faster access to digital systems of communication, entertainment and commerce. In contemporary surveillance systems, then, gaining access to technologies of vision and participating in the work of watching distracts from, but does not erase, the risks and consequences involved in political and economic strategies of visibility and invisibility.

In theatrical practice, intersecting matrices of power, knowledge, representation and reception are likewise tied to the questions of 'who is watching whom' and 'what is visible and what is invisible?'. Performance theorist and career theatre director John McGrath has gone so far as to describe theatre directing as a form of surveillance, suggesting that the two practices have come to share a great deal of cultural common ground. In *Loving Big Brother*, McGrath astutely links director-dominated avant-garde theatre groups in the twentieth century to a growing cultural acceptance of sociopolitical surveillance. Citing artists such as Bertolt Brecht, Robert Wilson, Jerzy Grotowski, Tadeusz Kantor, Anne Bogart, Liz LeCompte and Mabou Mines, McGrath argues that 'the dominant cultural fantasies of surveillance – the protecting eye or controlling Big Brother – equate in many ways with the fetishized figure of the twentieth-century theatre director, controlling events from which he or she is absent through the creation of a structure that necessitates and depends upon continued obedience' (McGrath 2004: 3).

In addition to the power dynamics between directors and actors, theatre audiences spend economic capital to gain cultural edification and status, watching as actors, sets and props create representations of 'reality'. Theatrical representations of reality have long been influenced and even determined by the social, economic and political stature of the watcher. Marilyn Frye, in *The Politics of Reality*, links the etymology of the word 're-ality' to the political power of legitimating a range of representations from law, proper-ty and citizenship to the theatrical arts: 'Real in Spanish means *royal*. Real property is that which is proper to the king. Reality is that which pertains to the one in power, is that over which he has power, is his domain, his estate, is proper to him. [...] To be real is to be visible to the king' (Frye 1983: 155). Indeed, throughout history, theatre artists have often had to gain the right to perform by the permission of a royal governing body.[8] Moreover, the 'best' seat in the house has, in theatre practices that cross centuries and cultures, been reserved for either gods or members of the royal family. These practices of heirarchized viewing came to be embedded and normalized within theatre architec-ture and naturalized in theatre-going behaviour, as persons of political, economic and religious power were graced with the most advantageous view of the stage and actors.[9] While this kind of royal treatment is by no means transhistorical, similar traditions continue today as regional theatres, Broadway houses and West End theatres feature great disparities in ticket prices based on the best view of and proximity to the stage.

In theatre practices, the matrix of visibility and invisibility is somewhat different than in surveillance, but just as powerful and ingrained. Certain bodies and objects within a theatre space are presented as hyper-visible (actors, props, set), while others (audience members, backstage area, stage machinations) are carefully produced as in-visible or *given to be overlooked*.[10] The actors, sets and props are made intentionally visible in the theatre; they tend to be centrally located, elevated and well lit. In contrast, audi-ence members of twentieth- and twenty-first-century realist theatre productions have been conditioned to sit attentively and quietly in the dark in order to avoid disturbing the hyper-visible part of theatre – the actors and stage space – with their own visual or aural presence. Although cell phones and pagers have come to be among the expected personal effects of theatregoers in the last decade, our attempts as practitioners and au-dience members to silence these technologies (in order to avoid the potential disrup-tions they could stage) indicate that contemporary theatre audiences continue to co-operate according to habits of seeming invisibility.

In addition to functioning as visible markers of the theatrical world and narrative, hyper-visible elements of theatrical representation such as actors' bodies, props and set pieces reference certain external events, gestures and conditions of the 'real world' outside the theatre. These 'real world' referents are symbolically present but materially absent, inferred only by the actors' bodies and gestures, the set and the props. The 'real world' referents, themselves 'signs' of cultural processes and values, are visible through the representation of theatrical 'signs', making theatrical representation a layered system of in/visible signification (Fischer-Lichte 1995: 85).

In effect, whereas contemporary subjects are conditioned to 'not see' certain aspects of surveillance in public space, audience members are disciplined to see double. In the theatre, spectators watch actors and stage objects that perform both *as* and *in excess of* themselves. As performance theorist Peggy Phelan puts it:

> In moving from the grammar of words to the grammar of the body, one moves from the realm of metaphor to the realm of metonymy [...] Metaphor works to secure a vertical hierarchy of value and is reproductive; it works by erasing dissimilarity and negating difference; it turns two into one. Metonymy is additive and associative; it works to secure a horizontal axis of contiguity and displacement [...] In performance, the body is metonymic of self, of character, of voice, of 'presence'. (1993: 150-151)

For theatre audiences, the actors and props function simultaneously as theatrical sign, real world referent and material reality on stage. And yet, within the metonymical processes of theatrical representation and reception, the stage object or body of the performer is eclipsed by the referent that it can simultaneously never fully become.

Importantly, this uniquely theatrical relationship between 'reality' and 'representation' is 'unverifiable' in a similar way to the construction of the panoptic principle. Hyper-visible markers of theatre (actors, set, props) remain, to some degree, unverifiable, as their status as representational objects constantly oscillates between sign, referent and material reality on stage. Just as the panoptic prisoner internalizes the disciplinary gaze from the guard tower to the extent that s/he polices him- or herself, the theatregoer participates in a willing 'suspension of disbelief' through which s/he invests in objects, bodies and events that are simultaneously real and representational, material and abstract, actual and fictitious. Theatrical representations of real or imagined human experiences are different from other forms of media in that they come to being in the present, again and again, never as entirely fixed meanings or contained narratives but rather as performances that admit to 'the impossibility of securing the Real' (ibid. 192).

In contrast, 'securing the real' is, ostensibly, the central purpose of dominant surveillance systems: to provide stable evidence and seal the past into a cauterized story from a particular point of view. As Foucault – and more recently Lyon, Gandy, Haggerty and Erikson – have argued, surveillance systems are built and used to produce a 'secure' and 'reliable' version of an event or situation. And yet, if we take a moment to reflect constructions of theatricality back onto surveillant media, we can see that surveillance systems are fundamentally theatrical. The panoptic guard tower or CCTV camera functions as a symbol of visual surveillance, producing a form of disciplinary power that is based less on the material 'reality' of being watched and more on the interplay between the sign of visual surveillance and its implied disciplinary threat. That is to say, surveillance technologies in everyday settings, as in theatre, function metonymically as both real and representational technologies.

These parallels between historical practices and perceptions of theatre and surveillance are foundational to understanding processes of remediation and intermedial critique available through surveillance theatre productions. Such productions continue to create invaluable spaces in which cultural and individual interactions with new surveillance media and processes can be rehearsed, negotiated and critically reflected upon. In particular, surveillance theatre productions represent surveillance as a 'live' process that holds opportunities for interactivity and agency on the part of subjects and practitioners of surveillance. This is to say that live, co-present, theatrical practices, especially those that feature some aspect of interactivity on the part of audience members, can represent surveillance technologies in such a way as to offer audiences a valuable opportunity to critically consider their relationships to and interactions with everyday disciplinary interfaces in theatrical and surveillant contexts.

Having mapped some inroads within and between historic surveillance systems and theatrical practices, as well as between notions of active usership and passive spectatorship, I now return to *Contains Violence*. In this production, surveillance technologies serve as especially effective tools – weapons, we might say – to challenge habits of theatrical spectatorship and reconsider popular conceptions of surveillance. By giving audience members binoculars and earphones to spy off a rooftop in London, Rosenberg harnessed the potential of surveillance technologies to act as agents of theatrical violence, defamiliarizing the audience's sense of spectatorial identity and disorienting their perceptual senses. In creating these conditions, Rosenberg shifted the site of theatrical violence off of the actors and into the audience. The cartoonish 'on-stage' murder was, in the end, a dummy, a red herring: the theatrical production did indeed 'contain violence', just not of the kind or in the place the audience expected.

## Doing Violence to the Theatrical Container

*Contains Violence* gave audiences the rare chance to play at a cultural fantasy of rooftop spying, while simultaneously providing them with a new dramatic perspective. While the dramatic narrative of *Contains Violence* received mixed reviews, as critics were unenthused with the rather mundane murder plot, audience members and critics-at-large blogged enthusiastically about Rosenberg's bold integration of surveillance technologies into their theatre-going experience. Heralded with popular culture references such as 'The Office meets Rear Window' (Clapp 2008), every online response and review that I have read reflected indisputable fascination with the innovative formal elements of the show:

There's something gratifyingly unusual about being marshalled out on to a London roof terrace by surly, burly men with walkie-talkies, collecting binoculars and headphones [...] on the way and settling down to watch a play unfold in the windows of an office block across the road. How bizarre! How artfully creepy! (Jones 2008)

Susannah Clapp, in her online *Guardian* review, noted the rare and valuable opportunity the piece provided, writing, 'the inside-outsideness sets you up to look quite differently at your surroundings – which is not something *The Importance of Being Earnest* will usually help you do' (Clapp 2008).

Giving audiences this rare opportunity was, in fact, part of Rosenberg's fundamental goal. Rosenberg created *Contains Violence* as part of a two-year fellowship he had been awarded 'to research techniques that "facilitate participation and methods of empowering the audience"' (Hutera 2008). In this piece, he fostered audience participation by giving theatregoers the chance to play at classic, old-fashioned surveillance – a model of surveillance that satisfyingly echoed popular representations of surveillance in films, TV shows and news events but that everyday social subjects rarely have the opportunity to embody. As one audience member shared on a blog, the show's concept was immediate inspiration to attend: 'I went along as I like anything Hitchcocky and it also seemed a good way to indulge my creepy habit of looking out of the window and spying on passers-by on a more sophisticated level' (Dar 2008). Robin McKie of the *Observer* online could not help but compare the experience to 'Hitchcock's film *Rear Window*, in which a helpless James Stewart glimpses odd bits of action in the next apartment block and eventually concludes murder has been committed,' concluding happily, '[*Contains Violence*] is a perfect mix of paranoia and voyeurism' (2008).

While the opportunity to 'play' Jimmy Stewart attracted and thrilled audiences of *Contains Violence*, the surveillance theatre piece functioned as far more than a pleasurable indulgence of cultural fantasies. Rosenberg's creation led his audiences to the limits of the game of paranoia and voyeurism that he had invited them to play, and in doing so coaxed them out of the comfortable position of traditional spectatorship. McKie's statement (above) makes clear that, in spite of his active involvement as a spy, he also felt helpless as an audience member, just as James Stewart with his broken leg did. Voyeurism – the practice, some would say compulsion, of taking visual pleasure in a scene from a careful distance[11] – clearly adds to the mechanics of suspense, as the voyeuristic spectator cannot or does not intervene in the scene itself. At the same time, the helplessness of the voyeur, and the paranoia that can accompany such helplessness, lays bare a fundamental problem of spectatorship that, when reframed as surveillance, can offer a serious challenge to the 'peace of mind' of theatregoers.

The tension that emerged from balancing their new role as active surveillance agents and their habitual role of passive audience members struck some of the theatregoers as not only exciting but somewhat disturbing: 'Gradually, it becomes apparent that what you are watching is a thriller during which a woman will batter her victim to death, every sickening thud relayed through our ears, *while we do nothing, as if the events unfolding in front of our eyes are nothing more than a play'* (Gardner 2008, emphasis added). On one level, of course, the events *were* 'nothing more than a play'. Audience members had purchased tickets, the actors would be paid, the event had a set start and finish time, and no one was *actually* harmed in the staged violence. Further, 'doing nothing' seemed to be the only option, given the habitually passive behaviour of theatrical audiences and the large distance between the spectators and the unfolding action. And yet, audience members were torn, because they held in their hands surveillance equipment that symbolized the active duty to stop crime, enforce laws and bring offences to justice. As the audience was given the chance to 'play at watching' within the medium of surveillance, the seemingly simple question of what it means to 'watch a play' became suddenly troubling, new, unfamiliar.

The comment 'as if these events were nothing more than a play' serves as an especially telling clue as to the target of the actual violence that the production contained. Critics wrote reviews such as: 'the hard-to-follow plot, which has a vague Hitchcockian theme of voyeurism, culminates in an apparent murder, with a bit of blood smeared down glass, but for most of the time it staggers along from incident to incident with no sense of development' (Clapp 2008). In addition to being overly attached to Aristotelian forms of drama, these critiques missed the deeper impact of *Contains Violence*. The production masqueraded as 'nothing more than a play', and the surveillance equipment as 'nothing more than props' in order to perform a more subtle kind of violence. The tawdry stage violence and overwrought, under-written plot of the play that prompted complaints from critics were merely blanks fired to get attention in order to enact a dislocation of identity and perspective produced by blurred boundaries between the theatrical and the everyday, the symbolic and the material.

Returning to Rosenberg's use of remediation, in which he strategically layered two traditions of spectatorship upon one another, the architecture of his violent container becomes clear. Rosenberg rearranged the formal elements of traditional theatre, making small but impactful changes in traditional theatre practices with the help of some familiar symbols and practices of surveillance. He placed audience members and actors adjacent to, rather than inside, a traditional theatre space, separating them by a gulf that they could see but not 'act' across. He outfitted his audience with individually issued tools of surveillance that not only allowed them to see and hear the distant action but that also served as emblems of their limited roles within the dramatic action. And finally, once his audience sat on the rooftop of the theatre, clutching the 'props' they were given to enact their roles, Rosenberg relied upon the surveillance equipment to disorient and reframe their sensory encounters within the theatre performance.

These three main aspects of remediation at work in *Contains Violence* merit closer examination. First of all, the spatial arrangement of *Contains Violence* placed audience members, quite literally, on the edge of a traditional theatre space, peering over the rail of the Lyric's rooftop terrace. By spacing the audience and actors across the gulf of a real-life busy street, Rosenberg pitted the fictional frame of theatre against the 'real' world of the everyday and created a visible space that simultaneously demanded and limited the participation of the audience. The fiction of the murder that the audience watched for entertainment was powerfully framed and encroached upon by the bustling reality of the busy Hammersmith commercial district. As Susannah Clapp of the online *Guardian* observed, 'Beneath the imaginary acts of violence, as in a dreamlike backdrop, buses pass by silently, pedestrians bustle, and ambulances speed to real emergencies' (2008). The blurring of the two registers produced a unique and interwoven theatre of surveillance, as the 'staged violence' slipped between and around 'real emergencies'. From their rooftop vantage point, audience members could freely move between 'real' and 'staged' events, a perspective that some audience members were not quick to leave. As an audience member noted, 'the audience stayed in their seats, scanning the area with their binoculars for several minutes after the play was over' (Arendt 2008). In effect, the spatial frames between reality and fiction were made permeable, injecting the borders of theatrical spectatorship with productive doubt.

Secondly, the surveillance technologies that were placed in the hands of audience members functioned as *theatrical props*, casting spectators in 'empowered' roles as rooftop spies while simultaneously challenging embodied habits and perceptions of theatre spectatorship. Andrew Sofer, who writes extensively about the complex relationships between stage objects and audience members, suggests that theatrical props can indeed serve as particularly radical tools with which to challenge theatrical convention. As Sofer argues in *The Stage Life of Props*, 'the prop [can] become a concrete vehicle for confronting dramatic convention and revitalizing theatrical practice' (2003: vii). Sofer ascribes this to an important dual capacity of stage props, arguing that props function as 'visual emblems' or 'symbolic agents', as well as 'vital participants in the stage action' (ibid. vi). In other words, theatrical props function as symbols that reference cultural systems of meaning outside the frame of the play while simultaneously facilitating particular, material interactions within the play world itself. Sofer suggests that props contain:

> two temporal processes that move in opposite directions simultaneously within a given performance. On the one hand, props are unidirectional: they are propelled through stage space and real time before historically specific audiences at a given performance event. At the same time, props are retrospective: [...] they are 'ghosted' by their previous incarnations, and hence by a theatrical past they both embody and critique. (ibid. viii)

The surveillance technologies staged in *Contains Violence* can likewise be read according to these dual temporalities: in the first and more immediate temporality, they function materially within the frame of the play as tools that actively mediate processes of watching and being watched. Audience members had to interface with the surveillant media (binoculars and earphones) in order to access and follow the dramatic action of the play. In the second, retrospective temporality articulated by Sofer, the surveillance technologies invoke the 'ghosts' of their sociopolitical roles and contemporary cultural representations of reality TV and crime dramas. For the audiences of Contains Violence – historically specific in their familiarity with the technologies and gestures associated with rooftop surveillance – these 'ghosts' are familiar spectres of police on a sting operation, or Jimmy Stewart playing at vigilante sleuthing. These recognizable 'ghosts' attracted audience members to the theatre production in the first place, and implicitly instructed them to behave in certain ways once there. Rosenberg thus effectively drew on the radical potential of the stage prop; he counted on his contemporary audience's willingness to play along with familiar tools of surveillance, to treat them lightly, like props in a play, in order to open up their senses – and their senses of themselves as spectators – to the disorienting effects that the binoculars and earpieces had on familiar modes of watching and listening to a live performance.

Thirdly, Rosenberg furthered his sly attack on the habits of theatre spectatorship through a sensorially disorienting contrast between physical distance and mediated proximity. The significant distance between the audience and the performers – across a large, busy street in Hammersmith's commercial district – contrasted with the visual close-ups and aural amplification provided by the binoculars and earpieces. While the audience was several hundred yards from the actors, a distance much greater than most contemporary theatre spaces allow, the surveillance equipment permitted them to see and hear the action up close. Visually empowered by the binoculars, audience members could get up close and personal with the characters in a way that the medium of theatre does not typically allow. 'You make up your own long-shots and close-ups, using their binoculars to zoom in and out at will,' described one observer (Clapp 2008), as another extrapolated, 'the experience of being free to follow and zoom in on what interests you can give you a feeling of being closer to the action' (Dar 2008).

In contrast, the aural experiences of many audience members were unfamiliar and disorienting: 'You are, weirdly, much further away from the actors than usual but aurally much closer up,' wrote one observer (Clapp 2008), while another added, 'the sound is extraordinarily disconcerting, as if someone else has taken up residence inside your head' (Gardner 2008). According to one interviewer, Rosenberg hoped that the use of headphones would do just that: 'transport the audience into the rooms and into the heads of the protagonists,' as the audience hears not only what is audible to the characters, but also 'what is happening in their bodies: [such as] an accelerated heartbeat' (Hutera 2008). In another interview, Rosenberg shared that he was inspired to use this aggressive form of audio recording by a traumatic experience from his childhood in which his father, a neurologist, had him listen to a binaural recording of savage dogs howling (McKie 2008). The childhood memory seems to have inspired Rosenberg to create his uniquely violent theatrical container, as the intrusion of the soundscape into the very skulls of the audience was, by several accounts, the most physically palpable mode of sensorial violence.

Through these strategies Rosenberg attempted to counter traditions of realist theatre in which audiences are given a passive role, positioned both literally and figurative-ly outside the frame of the play. In contrast, Rosenberg forcibly cast his audience 'against type', outfitting them with props that cast them as active agents within the frame of the play. While Rosenberg's use of theatre conventions to represent the vio-lence in his murder mystery may have been nothing particularly new, his use of conven-tional surveillance technologies performed a far more radical act of violence to theatri-cal conventions of reception.

However, as I have continued to puzzle over the layers of actual and conceptual violence contained within the theatre piece, I cannot help thinking that Rosenberg could have used the surveillance technologies to enact an even more radical form of remediation. By positioning his audience within a frame of theatrical performance while simultane-ously placing them precariously at its edge, Rosenberg constructed the production to overstep its own boundaries, and yet, in the end, he fell short of what could have been a more extreme inversion of Althusserian interpellation, and a more cutting lesson in the stakes of voyeurism. Rosenberg's set-up never fully forced the audience of *Contains Vio-lence* out of their position of disciplined social subjects, or challenged them to see every-day surveillance in a new or critical way. Although the surveillance technologies they held seemed to interpellate them into the position of policeman, surveillance guard or vigilante neighbourhood watcher, audience members continued to behave according to traditions of obedient social citizenship.

This shortcoming of the production is shown most clearly in an interview with an audience member from the world of professional surveillance. As fortune and good press would have it, a private investigator by the name of Michael Colacicco attended *Contains Violence* during its run at the Lyric. In an online interview with the *Guardian*, Co-lacicco offered his perspective on the accuracy and effects of the representation, recep-tion and embodied experience of surveillance in the *Contains Violence* set-up, as well as some interesting ideas for future remediating dialogues between practitioners of sur-veillance and theatre. While some theatre critics of the show were bored by the compli-cated, somewhat slow-moving murder mystery plot, Private Investigator Colacicco had quite a different response: 'I wish my current surveillance jobs were half as much fun as this play. More happened in 70 minutes than I would normally see in weeks [...] In the 15 years I spent working for the police's anti-terrorism branch, I saw perhaps three or four acts of violence' (in Arendt 2008).

In other words, Rosenberg could have pushed his emulation of surveillance prac-tices much further and challenged theatregoers at a deeper level. He could have staged something more mundane than a murder, or even staged 'nothing' at all, and, in doing so, he could have used the play to put another set of habits under scrutiny. Recalling Rancière's critique of police-dominated vision in everyday life discussed above, *Con-tains Violence* could have interrogated the cultural limits and conditions placed upon what a 'good citizen', like a 'good audience member', *should* see. In fact, several of the audience comments shared above show that there was an active desire to test the borders between the theatrical and the everyday that the production made visible. Some participants noted that the binoculars gave them freedom to watch things that interested them, regardless of whether those things were inside the frame of the theatrical narrative or not, while others stayed in their seats after the conclusion of the 'play', scanning the street and other buildings for everyday dramas. What would have been the effect upon the audience's spectatorial identities and positions as voyeurs if the production had urged its audiences to watch the everyday in the same way that they watch a piece of theatre? How much more or less – or how differently – would they have watched? Would they have felt more or less responsible for what they were witnessing?

A particularly class-focused comment from one critic sticks out as a fruitful place to apply this line of questioning. Describing the interplay of 'real' and 'theatrical' action, Susannah Clapp of the *Guardian* wrote, 'Occasionally, a non-actor – a cleaner or late worker – gets snarled up accidentally in the action' (2008). Her dismissive tone clearly indicates that these figures are not 'worth' watching, and perhaps for reasons that go beyond their 'non-actor' status. As such, Rosenberg might have done well to use the permeable borders of *Contains Violence* to ask his audience members to examine the contours of their own *subjective* vision, the snap judgements and cultural assumptions they were making as they viewed the play and the busy Hammersmith district below.

Another observation from Colacicco suggests that a more pointed use of the show's overlapping frames of surveillance and theatre could have challenged unexamined subjective responses such as that of Clapp. The private investigator reflected, 'the show invites you to get inside the minds of the characters, something my training forces me to resist. A well-trained surveillance officer never allows himself to become involved. You don't make judgments, you never pre-empt. Everything has to be viewed objectively' (in Arendt 2008). This observation moved Colacicco to suggest that viewing shows like *Contains Violence* could be a 'useful training exercise' for inexperienced agents, as the challenge of watching the play without getting attached 'would teach them to be more objective' (ibid.). His observation also contains a prescient critique of the limits and possibilities of surveillance theatre. Colacicco points out contrasting levels of identification, judgement and objectivity encouraged by theatre and by surveillance. Even while *Contains Violence* invited audience members to 'play detective', Rosenberg did not use the production to challenge his audience's objectivity as viewers. In contrast, he encouraged his audience members to 'get inside the heads' of his characters, connecting actors and audience members through a recorded heartbeat.

Consider instead if Rosenberg had taken Colacicco's advice to surveillance professionals – 'everything has to be viewed objectively' – and applied it to his surveillance theatre audience. If Rosenberg had presented his audience with characters and scenes that blended more easily with the everyday world, then he would have more profoundly remediated the way his audience looked at the 'scenes' and 'characters' constructed before them. Looking for possible clues and seeking to understand the motives in the people and actions they watched, his audience would have examined the everyday world and its range of inhabitants with a new, investigative-spectatorial gaze. Either way, Rosenberg could have gained more by doing less. By employing a theatrical frame to interrupt – and in interrupting, hold up for inspection – his audiences' habitual judgments and blind spots, Rosenberg could have enacted a deeper-reaching form of violence aimed at habitual patterns of *over-looking* in the everyday world of sociopolitical surveillance.

## Concluding the Investigation

This article has explored unique and important strategies of remediation involved in surveillance theatre that productively revitalize and reframe contemporary understandings and experiences of surveillance systems and of theatrical practices. The medium of theatre can emulate, facilitate and challenge popular understandings of sociopolitical surveillance; at the same time, familiar practices of watching and being watched through surveillance technologies can effectively defamiliarize habits of representation and reception in theatre. David Rosenberg's *Contains Violence* remediated habits of spectatorship in theatre through the strategic use of surveillance techniques of technologies in three main ways: the production's spatial arrangement placed audience members on the limen between the theatrical and the everyday; the surveillance equipment had distinctly distorting effects on the visual and aural senses of the audience; and the surveillance technologies symbolically pulled audience members between passive voyeurism and active witnessing.

However, as discussed above, Rosenberg could have gone further with his remediation of surveillance through the medium of theatre. Had he more explicitly raised the question of what paying audience members are conditioned to see within competing and overlapping frames of the theatrical and the everyday, then *Contains Violence* could have become a sharper critique of the politics of vision in public space. In this way, Rosenberg could have further and more deeply challenged his audiences to critically consider the power structures and figures of authority that condition the parameters of their visible worlds, both in the theatre and in the everyday.

**Elise Morrison** recently received her PhD in Theatre and Performance Studies from Brown University. Her book project, *Discipline and Desire: Surveillance, Feminism, Performance*, looks at artists who strategically employ technologies of surveillance to create performances and installations that pose new and different ways of interacting with and understanding apparatuses of surveillance. She is a Lecturer on Dramatic Arts and Associate Director for Speaking Instruction at Harvard University.

## NOTES

1 The increased popularity and visibility of surveillance art is also evidenced by groups such as the Surveillance Camera Players, Yes Men, Institute for Applied Autonomy and artists as Sophie Calle, Jill Magid, Gilles Walker, Manu Luksch and Steve Mann, who use surveillance technologies to stage provocative interventions in performance art and installation pieces around the world. This trend is also reflected in the growing number of visual art installations curated around the theme of surveillance techniques and technologies, such as 'ctrl[space]' (ZKM, 2001), 'Anxious Omniscience: Surveillance and Contemporary Cultural Practice' (Princeton University Art Museum, 2002), 'Open_Source_Art_Hack' (New Museum of Contemporary Art, 2002) and 'Balance and Power: Performance and Surveillance in Video Art' (Urbana-Champaign's Krannert Art Museum, 2005).

2 I am using the concept of 'defamiliarization' as first coined in 1917 by Viktor Shklovsky in his essay 'Art as Technique' to describe a literary strategy by which artful or poetic language can be made to appear strange and unfamiliar to the reader, thereby breaking habits, expectations and 'over-automatization' in the reception of literature. Theatre practitioners and theorists such as Erwin Piscator and Bertolt Brecht applied this theory to theatre-making, using formalist, materialist strategies to 'alienate' familiar gestures, scenes and narratives for given audiences.

3 Diderot was most influential in the theatre world for his advice to the actor to imagine the fourth wall and behave as if he or she was not 'performing'. In 1758, he wrote: 'When you write or act, think no more of the audience than if it had never existed. Imagine a huge wall across the front of the stage, separating you from the audience, and behave exactly as if the curtain had never risen' (1981: 206).

4 Samuel Taylor Coleridge first coined the phrase 'suspension of disbelief' in his 1817 theoretical treatise *Biographia Literaria* to describe the process of willingly investing in a plausible fiction in the context of writing and reading poetry. Film theorist Jonathan Crary subsequently employed the phrase in his analysis of the observer and cinematic realism, as did formalist art theorist Michael Fried in his critiques of theatricality and artifice in visual and performance art.

5 See also Auslander (1999), Case (1996) and Schneider (1997).

6 Sonstegard uses the term 'coach' to describe the way in which 'Boucicault and the theatrical players had to coach audiences in 1859 to accept photography's role in resolving the conflict of this play' (2006: 376).

7 Terms such as Gandy's 'panoptic sort', Lyon's 'digital divide' and Murakami Wood's 'differential mobility' each refer to the creation and maintenance of techno-social borders and boundaries that 'threaten to divide contemporary societies more decisively into high-speed, high-mobility and connected and low-speed, low-mobility and disconnected, classes' (Murakami Wood & Graham 2006: 177-8). In *The Panoptic Sort*, Gandy asserts that these invisible and dispersed processes of sorting and dividing social subjects are the product of non-transparent engineering and programming of surveillance-software systems (1993: 18-20).

8  See Brockett and Hildy (2003) for censoring bodies and government regulations at various points in theatre history: for example, the Master of Revels (Brockett & Hildy 2003: 117-188) and other licensing acts (ibid. 214-215) regulated what could and could not be shown in theatres in Renaissance England. Regulations of this kind continue to be enacted through government funding organizations such as the National Endowment for the Arts (NEA). In a controversial decision that showed the conservative politics and cultural power of the NEA in 1990, chairman John Frohnmayer vetoed the grants of four performance artists (Karen Finley, Tim Miller, John Fleck and Holly Hughes, known as the 'NEA Four'), even after they had successfully passed through a peer review process.

9  See Camp (2007: 615-633). Camp points out that common architectural layouts in eighteenth- and nineteenth-century theatres (in France and elsewhere in Europe) were constructed according to the representation of space that dominated the natural philosophy of the Enlightenment. This is to say that the Enlightenment models of knowledge and power (which arguably continue today) conditioned the spectatorial and spatial relationship of theatre audiences to the stage.

10  It is also significant that the matrix of in/visibility of theatre has been used, linguistically and materially, to describe that which should or should not be given to be seen, both onstage and in the everyday world. Historically, the term 'obscene' derived its meaning from bodies or acts that, due to graphic, immoral or violent characteristics, were deemed improper to be shown on stage (in a scene).

11  See Freud (1955) and Burgin (2002).

## REFERENCES

Althusser, L., 'Ideology and Ideological State Apparatuses'. In: L. Althusser, *Lenin and Philosophy and Other Essays*. New York, 1971.

Arendt, P., 'Another View: Private Investigator Michael Colacicco on *Contains Violence*'. In: *The Guardian*, 8 April 2008. Web. <http://www.guardian.co.uk/artanddesign/2008/apr/08/art.dance>

Auslander, P., *Liveness. Performance in a Mediatized Culture*. London, 1999.

Bolter, J. D. and R. Grusin, 'Remediation'. In: *Configurations*, 4, 3, p. 311-358. Baltimore, 1996.

–. *Remediation*. Cambridge, 1999.

Brockett, O. G. and F. J. Hildy, *History of the Theatre*. Ninth Edition. New York, 2003.

Builders Association, 'Súper Vision'. s.l., s.d. Web. <http://www.superv.org/>

Burgin, V., 'Jenni's Room. Exhibitionism and Solitude'. In: T. Levin, U. Frohne and P. Weibel (eds.), *ctrl[space]. Rhetorics of Surveillance from Bentham to Big Brother*. Leipzig, 2002.

Camp, P., 'Theatre Optics. Enlightenment Theatre Architecture in France and the Architectonics of Husserl's Phenomenology'. In: *Theatre Journal*, 59, 4, p. 615-633. Baltimore, 2007.

Case, S. E., Domain Matrix. *Performing Lesbian at the End of Print Culture*. Bloomington, 1996.

Chun, W., *Control and Freedom: Power and Paranoia in the Age of Fiber Optics*. Cambridge, 2006.

Clapp, S., 'The Good, the Bad, and the Photocopier'. In: *The Guardian*, 6 April 2008. Web. <http://www.guardian.co.uk/stage/2008/apr/06/theatre2>

Crary, J., *Techniques of the Observer: On Vision and Modernity in the Nineteenth Century*. Cambridge, 1990.

Dar, A., 'Peeping Toms'. In: *Smudgeyink*, 5 May 2008. Web. <http://smudgeyink.blogspot.com/>

Deleuze, G., 'Postscriptum sur les sociétés de contrôle'. In: *L'autre journal*, 1, p. 3-7. Paris, 1990.

Diderot, D., 'On Dramatic Poetry'. In: O. L. Brownstein and D. B. Chaim (eds.), *Analytic Sourcebook of Concepts in Dramatic Theory*. Santa Barbara, 1981.

Dixon, S., *Digital Performance*. Cambridge, 2007.

Fischer-Lichte, E., 'Theatricality. A Key Concept in Theatre and Cultural Studies'. In: *Theatre Research International*, 20, 2, p. 85-90. Cambridge, 1995.

Foucault, M., *Discipline and Punish. The Birth of the Prison*. Trans. Alan Sheridan. New York, 1995.

Freud, S., *Three Essays on the Theory of Sexuality*. Trans. James Strachey. London, 1955.

Fried, M., 'Art and Objecthood'. In: M. Fried, *Art and Objecthood. Essays and Reviews*. Chicago, 1998.

Frye, M., *The Politics of Reality: Essays in Feminist Theory*. Freedom, CA, 1983.

Gandy, O. H., *The Panoptic Sort. A Political Economy of Personal Information*. Boulder, 1993.

Gardner, L., 'Contains Violence'. In: *The Guardian*, 5 April 2008. Web. <http://www.guardian.co.uk/stage/2008/apr/05/theatre2>

Geisekam, G., *Staging the Screen. The Use of Film and Video in Theatre*. London, 2007.

Haggerty, K. and R. Ericson, *The New Politics of Surveillance and Visibility*. Toronto, 2006.

Hopkins, D. J. and S. Orr, '*Measure for Measure*, directed by Simon McBurney'. Review. In: *Theatre Journal*, 57, p. 97-100. Baltimore, 2005.

Hutera, D., '*Contains Violence* at the Lyric, Hammersmith'. In: *The Times Online*, 4 April 2008. Web. <http://entertainment.timesonline.co.uk/tol/arts_and_entertainment/stage/theatre/article3672054.ece>

Jones, A., '*Contains Violence*, Lyric Hammersmith Roof Top Terrace'. In: *The Independent*, 9 April 2008. Web. <http://www.independent.co.uk/arts-entertainment/theatre-dance/reviews/contains-violence-lyric-hammersmith-roof-terrace-london-80627 3.html>

Lyon, D., *Surveillance Society. Monitoring in Everyday Life*. Philadelphia, 2001.

McGrath, J., *Loving Big Brother. Performance, Privacy, and Surveillance Space*. London, 2004.

McKie, R., 'What the Punters saw...'. In: *The Observer*, 16 March 2008. Web. <http://www.guardian.co.uk/stage/2008/mar/16/theatre1>

Murakami Wood, D. and S. Graham, 'Permeable Boundaries in Soft-ware Sorted Society. Surveillance and Differentiations of Mobility'. In: M. Sheller and J. Urry (eds.), *Mobile Technologies of the City*. London, 2006.

Phelan, P., *Unmarked. The Politics of Performance*. London, 1993.

Rancière, J., 'Ten Theses on Politics'. In: *Theory & Event*, 5, 3, p. 1-9. Baltimore, 2001.

Schneider, R., *The Explicit Body in Performance*. London, 1997.

Shklovsky, V., 'Art as Technique'. In: *Russian Formalist Criticism. Four Essays*. Trans., intro. L. T. Lemon and M. J. Reis. Lincoln, 1965.

Sofer, A., *The Stage Life of Props*. Ann Arbor, 2003.

Sonstegard, A., 'Performing Remediation. Minstrelsy, Photography, and the *Octoroon*'. In: *Criticism*, 48, 3, p. 375–395. Detroit, 2006.

# The Work of Art in the Age of Its Intermedial Reproduction

## Rimini Protokoll's *Mnemopark*

Katia Arfara

Based upon an actual railway model – on a scale of 1:87 – Rimini Protokoll's Mnemopark stages reality through an installation of mini-cameras manipulated by four modelists, retirees who are passionate model railway buffs. Max Kurrus was seven when he got his first small-scale locomotive and has since bought 12 engines and 35 cars. His railway landscapes are inspired by the Swiss Graubünden canton. Hermann Löhle received his first locomotive 50 years ago and has since acquired 53 locomotives and 290 cars. His landscapes reproduce Baden-Württemberg. René Mühlethaler bought his first locomotive with his first salary. With 40 locomotives and 150 cars, he has reconstructed America. His landscapes recreate the Swiss Berner Oberland and Wallis canton. The fourth railroad hobbyist is Heidy Ludewig. She made her first cars out of chocolate. Her landscapes are inspired by literature, more specifically by Erich Kästner's stories. In addition to the railroad hobbyists, there is an actress, Rahel Hubacher, who studied art and who grew up in the small village of Bannwil. The farmhouse she grew up in has been reconstructed in every detail by Kurrus: the wooden terrace, her room with a view of the chicken coop, the cows, even her family friend Jules who helped out on the farm for 63 years. Besides her personal biography, Hubacher also gives us some statistics about the forests and the grassland in Switzerland, the number of chickens consumed annually, the number of inhabitants, the size of the country, the number of railroad track miles and the important annual subsidies that the farmers have received from the federal government since World War Two so that the country can feed itself. She also introduces an Indian chicken called Import, which will be the guest of the show, and gives information about the total distance that the miniature electric train will have travelled by the end of the show. At the same time, she assumes her position as the 'control centre' of the stage game, controlling the mini-cameras attached to the locomotives in order to enlarge the details of the landscape onto a large screen in the centre of the stage.

Mnemopark emerges from patterns of Swiss geography that are treated without any nostalgia, sentimentality or romanticism. Director Stefan Kaegi highlights the landscape's capacity to serve as a symbol for national identity, although his depiction is based on intentional neutrality. Forestalling nostalgia prevents an escape into the past

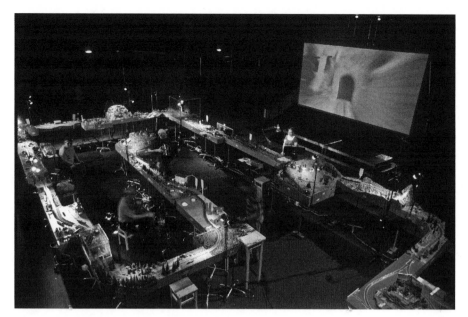

Fig. 1    Rimini Protokoll, *Mnemopark* © Sebastian Hoppe.

while allowing a wide range of 'meanings' to emerge, including those of cultural and social criticism. In order to introduce the spectator into the very specificity of rural populations, he juxtaposes the experts *real* memories of Swiss landscapes with their reduced reproduction. Biography and statistics, fictional and historical information come out twisted and blurred: Stefan Kaegi elaborates a counter-portrait of Switzerland as an alternative to the official history of his country. More specifically, he takes on the evocative power of the alpine landscape as it has been perceived inside and outside the Swiss borders. Rather than establishing a broad panorama, he questions the way in which the pictorial landscape tradition in Switzerland contributed to the shaping of its national identity and, consequently, its fossilization into geopolitical stereotypes.

The aim of this contribution is to explore the way in which the interaction between painting, video art and theatre introduces a hybrid theatricality while calling into question the very place of the spectator, thereby questioning the very notion of perception from an intermedial perspective. The reproduction of Swiss landscapes by new media technologies such as micro-cameras allows Stefan Kaegi to examine the so-called documentary theatre through the pictorial landscape tradition. While 'control centre' Hubacher observes that 'until the seventeenth century, in Europe, landscape was used only as background' and that it was only 'in the Romantic period [that] landscape was used as a main subject in paintings', the performance activates and, at the same time, alters the landscape heritage in order to reconsider some of the major questions revealed from the crisis of representation in the postmodern era, such as originality, authorship and authenticity. Following Fredric Jameson, the traditional fine arts are 'mediatized' because they 'come to consciousness of themselves as various media within a mediatic system.' It is a process of 'spatialization', which

> draws its effects from a place not above the media but within their system of rela-
> tionships: something it seems better to characterize as a kind of reflexivity rather
> than the more conventional notion of 'mixed media', which normally implies the
> emergence of a kind of super-product or transcendental project – the Gesamt-
> kunstwerk – from this synthesis or combination. (Jameson 2003: 162)

In *Mnemopark*, it is exactly this kind of reflexivity between the different media (theatre, film, painting) that calls into question the status of each medium in a given situation. More specifically, Stefan Kaegi deconstructs not only the inherent idealism of landscape painting as a vehicle for national ideologies but also, at the same time, the very nature of dramatic representation. Projected on the screen, the landscape's mechanical reproduction questions the authenticity both of the experts and of any image chosen to officially represent the country abroad. In particular, the use of the projected images in combination with the personal testimonies reverses the utopian vision of the 'alpinized' landscape that populates the Romantic imagery and proposes an alternative geographical history that dissolves micro-identities and regionalism in order to attain a distanced and thus critical perspective on the world. Stefan Kaegi appropriates the pictorial landscape tradition as a critical category from which new ways of spectatorship can emerge. Landscape, just like theatre, is always a way of seeing, a highly subjective composition of an 'eye' which is culturally and socially defined. In her conception of the play as a landscape, the American avant-garde writer Gertrude Stein points out that:

> The only thing that is different from one time to another is what is seen and what
> is seen depends upon how everybody is doing everything. This makes the thing
> we are looking at very different and this makes what those who describe it make of
> it, it makes a composition, it confuses, it shows, it is, it looks, it likes it as it is, and
> this makes what is seen as it is seen. Nothing changes from generation to genera-
> tion except the thing seen and that makes a composition. (1998: 125)

As Stein states, it is not the landscape that changes from generation to generation but our way of looking at it and our way of using it. In *Mnemopark*, the artificial landscape echoes with the artificiality of the stage condition. If theatre is not to serve as a mirror to the world, that does not mean that it should flee it either, but rather that it should reconstruct versions of it.

In Rimini Protokoll's performance, the stage composition becomes more complicated as it plays with our expectations concerning the dualistic relationship between the original and the copy, the true and the false. Because of the live video, the experts as well as the spectators are allowed a bird's-eye cinematographic perspective that virtually takes the form of a landscape painting seen from above. The three-dimensional miniature model installation coexists with the pre-recorded footage that is projected onto the screen, either from the experts' own houses and families or from Swiss farmers giving an interview on the use of bull sperm.

Additionally, the presence of an actress as the master of the game increases the impression that all memories are 'false', as they are media-based and therefore always subject to alteration and manipulation. Once again, Stefan Kaegi shifts the attention from the impossibility of the 'real' on stage to the (mediatized) perception of the world, as the performance demonstrates 'inauthenticity' as its main condition. In this way, Mnemopark deconstructs both the documentary tradition as a direct, unmediated experience of real-life issues and the heritage of Romantic contemplation of a landscape that still haunts the Western collective imaginary. In an industrially manufactured world, the documentary strategies of authentification cannot be involved. By erasing the distance between the modelists and their memories and, at the same time, distancing the modelists themselves from these memories through the use of media technology, the performance launches a feeling of insecurity about the solidity of values and of dominant aesthetics. Destabilizing the usual perception of reality could be an exercise in what Brecht calls 'complex seeing', which imposes a new acting style, the 'epic' style. More specifically, the experts' stage presence echoes Brecht's reflections on the 'street scene': this 'primitive type of epic theatre' does not need actors but demonstrators who will be able to repeat what they have witnessed on the street without being interested in creating pure emotions (Brecht 1964: 122). By juxtaposing personal biographies and geopolitical data, Kaegi prevents the reconstruction from becoming self-referential. Mnemopark is not auto-reflective but relevant to the 'here and now' condition operating in the larger field of a broader social, political and economical reality.

## Reconstructing Memory

Since its very beginnings, the Berlin-based collective Rimini Protokoll has been working on an expanded field of intermedial practices articulated around the concept of appropriation, i.e. copying, quoting or recycling aspects of popular culture. Resulting from the crisis of authorship and representation in the 1970s, appropriation was at first conceived as a critical position towards the modernist claim for an auto-referential, pure and 'auratic' art. Strategies such as the appropriation of photography masters by postmodern artists disintegrate the boundaries between art and non-art, rejecting any claim to conventional notions of artistic creativity.[1] Radicalizing its rejection of high art, appropriation art shifts the focus from the representation of action to the action of representation, aiming at an energetic spectatorship.[2]

Each Rimini production is based on the appropriation of different types of documents such as films, video recordings, diaries, audio archives and photos, as well as of different cultural traditions and popular stereotypes. Nevertheless, the primary source always remains the singular biographies of the experts. It is through the individual and the specific that they question social rituals, belief systems or political situations. Rather than reproducing their own interpretation of these situations on stage, they prefer to exhibit them in a sophisticated system of viewing instructions, focusing on the personal experience of their 'experts of the everyday'. Hence, *Mnemopark*'s theatrical installation stages a new way of looking at landscapes, while taking into consideration the very relation of modern man with his environment. The Romantic pictorial tradition looked at the landscape as a human being. Its shape supposedly reflected a specific physiognomy, while the human figure, whenever it appears, is depicted without characteristics. He is more in a state of passive contemplation which manifests his inner identification with nature (cf. Brion 2003: 31). The experience of the intact vastness that has been reflected within this sublime landscape acts as an allegory for the unrepresentable Cosmic Unity between God, Man and Nature (ibid. 24-25). Stefan Kaegi's theatrical landscape alters the way individuals are traditionally depicted in Romantic landscapes. His 'world of miniature trains' reflects the personal biographies of the four train masters and the actress. Their memories emerge from their familiar landscapes. In other words, they are based on landscapes as experienced by each one of them. Even if the stage game is articulated around separate lives and different backgrounds, each component of the staged landscape is finally related, in a more or less obvious way, to the other – they are all part of the same rural community; in other words, they participate in the same economic, social and political system, but they never form a homogeneous whole. On the contrary, their memories of the 'same' landscape focus on different aspects and bring to the surface different ways of seeing.

As such, these portraits do not become an allegory for either the human alienation in urban centres or the disintegration of rural society. Every single expert remains anchored in a concrete space-time, preserving his individual qualities as much as possible, far away from any effect of dramatization or idealization. What Stefan Kaegi wants to reveal by introducing these mechanical media on stage is a typology of a reality that cannot be perceived by the 'naked eye' without any mediation. He de-sublimates the Romantic memory and in one and the same move the persisting myth of the artist and his 'mission' to extrapolate, by his genius, the inner face of the world. In *Mnemopark*, it is the experts who become, literally, the landscape. With the micro-camera making close-ups of her face, Heidy Ludewig makes the following hypothesis: 'If I were a landscape, I'd be a landscape made of experiences. Valleys, mountains, plains, forests, sculpted rocks...where water has been flowing for ages. Craters... The storm devastated the fields.'

What Stefan Kaegi reactivates by this comparison of a face with nature is the old analogy of microcosm and macrocosm as inherited from Neo-Platonism. In *Mnemopark*, the macroscopic view of the landscape is altered with the microscopic views of experts' faces which allow us to look at their every pore in a nearly biological way. Accuracy being one of the main virtues of the mechanical eye, Kaegi privileges close-ups that restore the geography of the face compared to natural structures. As

Walter Benjamin remarks in his seminal essay 'The Work of Art in the Age of Mechanical Reproduction':

> With the close-up, space expands... By close-ups of the things around us, by focusing on hidden details of familiar objects, by exploring commonplace milieus under the ingenious guidance of the camera, the film, on the one hand, extends our comprehension of the necessities which rule our lives; on the other hand, it manages to assure us of an immense and unexpected field of action. (1986: 42)

According to Benjamin, this different reality that opens consciously to the camera, and not that which opens unconsciously to the naked eye, is one of the major dissimilarities between the artistic performance of the stage actor and that of the screen actor. The way Stefan Kaegi uses live video on stage, however, dissolves Benjamin's distinction between theatre and cinema. Contrary to Benjamin's analysis of the camera's power to introduce spectators to what he calls 'unconscious optics', Kaegi brings together filmic and theatrical devices in order to imply an energetic spectatorship. At the same time, he redefines the terms of use of the live camera: cameras do not so much document what is happening on stage as guide what we imagine is happening on stage. Assuming the power of his imagination, the spectator makes the final montage of the different stage elements, becoming thus a cameraperson him/herself: the experts' physical presence fuses with the miniature landscape not only inside but also outside the camera frame on screen.

More specifically, the spectator abandons his position outside the theatrical world and becomes part of the fabric of the theatrical composition, its 'making of'. By doing so, Kaegi suggests a double operation: not only does he dismantle the theatrical as well as the filmic illusionism, he also expands the limits of perception. In Mnemopark's paradoxical world, there are no established boundaries between traditional media nor between documentation and narrative, fictional storytelling; everything is relative and therefore ambiguous. Within that post-documentary context, the mutation of media could be perceived as interrogating the very notion of experience operating on a phenomenological rather than a metaphysical level.

At the same time, Mnemopark expands not only the perception of space but also of time. Just like in the landscape plays of Gertrude Stein, it is the compositional principles of landscape painting that enable Stefan Kaegi to resist the linear narratives and the conventional use of time. For Stein as for Kaegi, spatial principles such as simultaneity, juxtaposition and multiple perspectives resist the continuity that characterizes a conventional theatrical event while allowing us to witness different time levels at the same time.[3] More specifically, Stefan Kaegi shapes his theatrical landscape around distinct temporalities: the experts' actual situation as described with the help of video material and photographs, and the experts' past as re-enacted through flashbacks. During the first flashback of the evening, Heidy sees herself with a small bag at the Leipzig railway station, escaping East Germany, entering Essen's mining zone and getting a job as a bread packer. Some minutes later, Hermann 'wins' the second flashback which allows him to revisit 1961 – the year he got married, got his diploma as chief builder and his two sons were born.

It is exactly this game structure that interrupts the continuum of time and space, that enables the experts to re-experience their own past *in the present*. As Max Kurrus states, the rules of the flashback are simple:

> During the flashback, you'll see everything at a 1:1 scale. You must always look straight ahead. The simulation works only if you can remember. The time-jump happens when we reach 20cm per second. You have exactly 87 seconds. If you stay longer, your memory cells will melt away... and you'll become a plastic figurine.

It seems that there is no other way: remembering is an act that occurs in the present tense. We cannot re-enact memory unless we reconstruct it. Usually, recreated situations are 'live' and thus relevant to the here and now (Arns 2007: 41). *Mnemopark* is not about creating an isolated experience with an immersive effect but rather about providing a critical, reflective distance from the past by questioning what constitutes the so-called 'collective memory' in the present time.

## Mutating Media, Mutating Cultures

In *Mnemopark*, the Swiss director seems to materialize, in an artificial yet playful way, a Bergsonian perception of time as a continuum in which we live, move and change. According to the French philosopher's theory of simultaneity, there is only a single duration in which everything participates, including our consciousnesses, living beings and the entire material world (cf. Deleuze 2004: 78). What we experience here is the inner face of Time, in other words we are *inside* Time. To quote Gilles Deleuze:

> the past coexists with the present that it has been; the past is preserved in itself, as past in general (non-chronological); at each moment, time splits itself into present and past, present that passes and past which is preserved. (2005: 80)

For even if we take into account a succession of different temporalities, it is necessary that each of these temporalities remain when we pass to the next one. What we are witnessing in *Mnemopark* are different time levels, or, according to Bergson, 'a multiplicity of Time' – Time considered as the fourth dimension of space. By elaborating on this anti-naturalistic manipulation of Time, *Mnemopark* becomes a performance based on a memory system, a highly structured space that expands while activating the memory of those who have experienced the landscapes: after having an accident during his flashback, Max Kurrus 'time-travels' from the familiar past to the unknown future. On the screen we follow him 'landing' on a completely white, unbuilt model. He sighs: 'How can we build something that doesn't yet exist? We always build according to reality.

Models always depict the past.' Without any model for the future, the modelists imagine a white world with genetically modified fruits and aluminium UFOs. But without a 'real-world' referent, this white model becomes a simulacrum – i.e. according to Gilles Deleuze, 'an infinitely degraded icon' (2002: 297), which still produces an *effect* of resemblance. Once we can no longer define the simulacrum in relation to a model, no knowledge or opinion can be based on it.

Once Kaegi moves our attention to the potential disparity of the real, Swiss stereotyped prosperity becomes a kind of archetype for any falsified image that the Western world exports to the East, in this case Asia. In this context, Rahel Hubacher gives some striking facts about the actual situation in the mountains of Kashmir:

> For 30 years, conflict has been raging between India and Pakistan... in the mountains of Kashmir, India's most idyllic mountain range. That's why for 30 years Indian directors have been coming to Switzerland... to shoot the rhythm and dance sequences for their film without war. For the Indian film myths, they need: flowers, cows and luscious fields, in front of the snowy Alps. The Alps are for the Indian audience what turbans and camels... were for the Western audience in the 60s: a fairytale land.

By the intrusion of Bollywood films on the screen, Stefan Kaegi shows, in a non-emphatic yet highly critical way, how the simulacrum of a 'paradise land' serves to subvert the collective imagery of an entire country. The 'exotic' is now domesticated in the Western world, calling into consideration old stereotypes about the relations between 'home' and colonial land, centre and periphery.[4] In today's globalized world, the orientalized vistas of the Romantic scenography have been replaced by the normative imagery of Indian film industry. According to Deleuze, the simulacrum 'implies huge dimensions, depths, and distances that the observer cannot master' (2002: 298). Escaping any possible control, this timeless topography of the Bollywood industry turns into a hybrid geographic imagery that reflects the vast landscape as an allegory for an untouched cosmos. It is a kind of supra-naturalism that introduces another degree of 'authenticity' within *Mnemopark*'s Western theatrical landscape. The intrusion of film fragments taints the credibility of the miniature world mapped by the modelists – the mutation of media reveals the mutation of cultures. Rimini Protokoll's performance thus becomes a highly sophisticated system of viewer integration, in which alternative sites for personal experience and new understandings of the world could emerge.

*Mnemopark* proposes an alternative auratic experience through a technologically mediated liveness. In 'the age of mechanical reproduction', Rimini Protokoll juxtaposes on stage the unique, physical identity of the experts and their 're-enacted' memories in an expanded field of intermedial practices that excludes dogmatism and authoritarian schemas. Once memories integrate the 'here and now' condition of the stage, Benjamin's concept of authenticity can no longer be determined by its unreproducibility.

What Rimini Protokoll suggests by altering the conditions of the theatrical transmission of the 'real' is a new theory of perception.

**Katia Arfara** is researcher, doctor in art history and curator in the field of the performing arts. Her essays at the crossroads of theatre, dance and visual arts have appeared in various journals and publications. Her current interests focus on documentary theatre, new media practices and installations. She has lectured extensively in France and Greece. She is the author of the book *Théâtralités contemporaines. Entre les arts plastiques et les arts de la scène* (Peter Lang 2011).

## NOTES

1  On appropriation as the main activity of postmodernism, see Crimp (1995: 129).
2  See Inke Arns and Gabriele Horn's introduction in Arns and Horn (eds. 2007: 9).
3  On Stein's 'lang-scapes' and their sources in painting, see Bowers (2002: 132-144).
4  On theatrical orientalism and the modern geographic imagination, see Ziter (2002).

## REFERENCES

Arns, I., 'History Will Repeat Itself. Strategies of Re-Enactment in Contemporary (Media) Art and Performance'. In: I. Arns and G. Horn (eds.), *History Will Repeat Itself. Strategies of Re-Enactment in Contemporary (Media) Art and Performance*. Berlin, 2007.

Arns, I. and G. Horn (eds.), *History Will Repeat Itself. Strategies of Re-Enactment in Contemporary (Media) Art and Performance*. Berlin, 2007.

Benjamin, W., 'The Work of Art in the Age of Mechanical Reproduction'. In: J. G. Hauhardt (ed.), *Video Culture. A critical investigation*. New York, 1986.

Brecht, B., 'The Street Scene. A Basic Model for an Epic Theatre'. In: J. Willett (ed., trans.), *Brecht on Theatre. The Development of an Aesthetic*. New York, 1964.

Brion, M., Introduction. In: C. G. Carus and C. D. Friedrich, *De la peinture de paysage dans l'Allemagne romantique*. Paris, 2003.

Bowers, J. P., 'The Composition that All the World Can See: Gertrude Stein's Theater Landscapes'. In: Fuchs and Chaudhuri (eds.), *Land/Scape/Theater*. Ann Arbor, 2002.

Crimp, D., *On the Museum's Ruins*, Cambridge, 1995.

Deleuze, G., *Le bergsonisme*. Paris, 2004.

–. *Cinema 2. The Time Image*. London, 2005.

–. *Logique du sens*. Paris, 2002.

Jameson, F., *Postmodernism, or, The Cultural Logic of Late Capitalism*. Durham, 2003.

Stein, G., *Writings, 1903-1932*. New York, 1998.

Ziter, E., 'Staging the Geographic Imagination. Imperial Melodrama and the Domestication of the Exotic'. In: Fuchs and Chaudhuri (eds.), *Land/Scape/Theater*. Ann Arbor, 2002.

# Rimini Protokoll's Theatricalization of Reality

Frederik Le Roy

In 2000, Daniel Wetzel, Helgard Haug and Stefan Kaegi collaborated for the first time under the label Rimini Protokoll. *Kreuzworträtsel Boxenstopp* ('Crossword Pit Stop'), a stage production on old age and Formula 1 racing, initiated a string of acclaimed stage productions that have made Rimini Protokoll one of Europe's most prominent theatre groups. Rimini Protokoll is no tight-knit collective. For the founding members, the production of differences is more important than speaking with a unified voice. This model of productive dissent, of questioning and discussion, is also reflected in their work: their collaborations (often in different constellations or with 'outsiders') are project-based and pragmatic, often site-specific and focused on the exchange of particular ideas and experiences. Yet, despite their very diverse nature, their projects are mostly clearly recognizable as Rimini Protokoll productions. Over the ten years they have been working together, the group has been experimenting with a distinctive theatre poetics that is often designated as 'a kind of documentary theatre'.

According to Carol Martin, technological media play a vital role in contemporary documentary theatre as video, film or tape recorders are used to supplement the performed text and the performing bodies on the stage. Technological media are 'a primary factor in the transmission of knowledge' of documentary theatre because 'means of replication and simulation are used to capture and reproduce "what really happened" for presentation in the live space of the theatre' (Martin 2006: 9). In that sense, technological media in documentary theatre gesture beyond the presence of the performance toward a factual, historical or archival realm.

On 3 December 2010, in the context of this book on mutating media, I had a conversation with Helgard Haug to explore some of the intricacies of the use of different media in the work of Rimini Protokoll and the way in which technology was used to relate to what lies beyond the stage. As will hopefully become clear from the rendition of this conversation below, replication or simulation of reality is only part of the story of Rimini Protokoll's use of media. Rather than replicating reality to the theatre, one could say that they replicate theatre to reality, effectively pushing the boundaries of documentary theatre.

## Transporting Media

Logging onto Skype for my interview with Helgard Haug, one of three theatre makers working under the Rimini Protokoll label, I am reminded of *Call Cutta in a Box*, a project the group made in 2008. For *Call Cutta in a Box*, the spectator had to enter alone into an anonymous office space that turned out to be an interactive theatre installation. Like in most offices, the centrepiece of the room was a desk with a telephone and a computer. While I was exploring the room the telephone rang and I was connected to a call centre operator 10,000 km away, somewhere in India. During the conversation that followed, that 'somewhere' became gradually more concrete: pictures of the office building in Calcutta where the operator was located appeared on the screen, as did a photo of the call centre agent himself and his colleagues. He asked me to picture the sounds and smells in the street in front of the building. He gave me details about his life and as the dialogue progressed I did the same.

Rimini Protokoll rarely work with trained actors but with people they call 'experts of the everyday'. Their expertise is not in acting but in the specific topic of the performance (Rimini Protokoll have already worked with truckers, secret service agents, model train enthusiasts, ex-Sabena personnel, policemen, urban scavengers, etc.). The experiences they convey on the stage or in performance installations are theirs and theirs alone and so are the stories they tell, the clothes they wear, the accents in their voices and the specific qualities of their movements. For this 'intercontinental phone play' Rimini Protokoll had hired a group of students to work as call centre agents, this time not to sell credits cards (like they usually do) but as 'experts of the everyday' in order to create a performance piece that reflects on the increasing interconnectivity between people, businesses and cultures in a globalized world.

Like the famed 'global village' or like the Skype interview with Haug, the piece would have been impossible without the help of media and technology. As Haug explained, to make present what is elsewhere is the role that media mostly play in the work of Rimini Protokoll, even in the stage projects:

> Media are used first of all and very basically to transport life outside of theatre onto the stage. Photography, film and audio recordings defy the limits set by the stage: locations mentioned can be evoked through video or photographic representations. Material that was gathered during the research process, especially quotes from interviews with people who could not join the experts on stage, can be integrated in the performance.

As a consequence of their use of archival documents and of real-life 'experts', the work of Rimini Protokoll is often labelled 'documentary theatre'. However, the label is appropriate only to a certain extent to catalogue Rimini Protokoll's practice. Haug remarks that 'documentary theatre' has been a handy tool to distinguish their projects from more traditional forms of theatre with fictional or fictionalized characters. But the term 'documentary' can also be misleading, as it might suggest that reality is presented as it really is or was; as if the theatre can become a transparent window on reality. Rimini Protokoll, however, are more interested in the way reality is mediated and transformed, not only through the personal memories of the experts on stage but also through the very fact that it is shown in the frame of theatre. Haug emphasizes: 'The struggle between theatre and reality is an essential part of the work.'

## Constructing Authenticity

Already during the documentation phase of a project, this media awareness plays a crucial role. As they look for and meet people who will become the living, breathing and acting archives of the everyday on stage, the members of Rimini Protokoll first take written notes. Haug: 'Recording something or somebody influences the situation. Rather than recording the original statement, we ask somebody to repeat it and make a video statement.'[1] From the outset, the 'real person' is doubled as his or her original expression is immediately refashioned into a recorded one: the person copies him- or herself for the registration device. Once the experts become part of the performance, they retain something of this first moment of self-representation on tape. However, whereas the video or voice recording can be reproduced in the absence of the person, on the stage the person is present again. The expert is both himself and a stage performer. If the experts on the stage appear authentic, this authenticity is a dramaturgical construct or, as Florian Malzacher rightly remarked, the stage projects of Rimini Protokoll always present a 'scripted reality' (2008: 39-42).

Not only are the experts' lines and dialogues not spontaneous but rehearsed and repeated every night with each new performance, their stage presence is also mediated by the theatrical frame. This gap between the person in 'normal life' and the person on stage, between the self and the self performing him- or herself, is a crucial feature of Rimini Protokoll's theatre aesthetics. It will even be accentuated by the interjection of self-referential statements in the performance or by the use of theatrical devices akin to Brecht's alienation techniques.[2]

When I ask Haug how Rimini Protokoll projects relate to oral history, journalism, documentary or storytelling (disciplines their work is often compared to), she answers that 'we always link back to theatre, even if we work in or on different media. For us, the reference to theatre and to its artificial frame and traditional setting is always crucial.' It follows that when Rimini Protokoll initiate a project, they do so not only out of an interest in the subject matter or in the experts on stage, but always also to explore the codes of theatre. With Wallenstein (2005), for example, they started specific research on the relationship between text and performance. The research on dramatic texts and Schiller's dramaturgy in Wallenstein was continued with Karl Marx: Das Kapital, erster Band (2006) in which they challenged dramatic codes with the idea of 'staging' a major classical text that everybody claims to know, namely Marx's famous treatise on the economy. Breaking News (2008) closed this trilogy on the relationship between original text and performance: instead of an existing text, daily newscasts from different major news channels broadcast live on the stage on several television sets became the score of the performance. 'It turned out like a media critique,' Haug says, 'but it didn't start like that, since our first question was about the functioning of text in theatre.'

## Becoming the Camera

Still, a Rimini Protokoll project is never an autonomous, self-standing work that deals only with the medium of theatre. Their performances are permeable events: not only does the reality of the everyday fill the theatre space, theatricality also leaks into reality. For their project *Hauptversammlung* ('Annual Stockholders Meeting', 2009), Rimini Protokoll invited the audience of HAU (Hebbel am Ufer, Berlin) to buy shares from the car manufacturing company Daimler AG or become a proxy of an existing shareholder. The shares they bought subsequently served as theatre tickets: as shareholders of Daimler they gained the privilege to participate and vote in the company's yearly stockholders meeting. About 200 spectators attended the meeting together with 8,000 other small and big shareholders at Berlin's main conference centre. The point of departure of this project was simple: Rimini Protokoll declared that the shareholder meeting was theatre and found a (legal) way for people to attend it as a theatre performance. During the actual meeting they didn't intervene (even though they had the formal right to sign up to ask questions) but just observed and organized side meetings with experts of this theatre. The mechanism of their intervention was not unlike that of the ready-made: the shareholders meeting became a 'found performance', a real event that was framed as theatre.

Helgard Haug says about this project: 'we went and simply watched what normally cannot be watched. The spectator becomes the camera.' 'Simply watching' entailed a transformation of both the watcher and the watched. The watcher was encouraged by Rimini Protokoll to develop a gaze that documents this event as if he or she was a 'camera or microphone'. They gained an unmediated, first-hand experience of an event that is normally only accessible to the layman when it is mediated by reports in newspapers or newscasts. In addition, they also get the opportunity to observe those parts of the meeting that normally are not open to journalists, like the question round or the vote to (re)affirm the board of directors.

'Making the audience conscious of the effect of their observation and the different ways they can look at it' is an aim in many of Rimini Protokoll's projects. The presence of an audience among the 'normal' shareholders also changed the nature of the event. Rimini Protokoll's declaration that the event was theatre becomes a speech-act or performative utterance: the huge dais bearing the Daimler logo became a stage, the management became protagonists in a drama about a car company in trying economic times, the shareholders became actors in a participatory mass spectacle and the length of the event (no less than ten hours) made it into a genuine 'durational performance'. The presence of a theatre audience inevitably added a meta-reflective layer to the stockholders meeting, something the organizers of the *Hauptversammlung* disliked. One of the directors of Daimler, aware of Rimini Protokoll's presence, acknowledged this from the get-go when he opened the meeting with the words 'this is not a spectacle nor a theatre play.' But just like the drunkard's repeated denial of being drunk only serves to demonstrate his inebriation, the director's denial that this serious meeting had anything to do with theatre only boosted the audience's awareness of the theatrical codes at work.

Significantly, the project drew a lot of media attention: different media interviewed Haug, Kaegi and Wetzel; clips of activists disrupting the meeting were shown as if they were part of the performance (which they were not); the director's dismissal of the project was televised.[3] 'This discussion on the public forum was for us entirely part of the performance,' Haug says, for:

> While only 200 people were 'audience members' at the meeting, their presence contaminated the way others looked at this event. We planted the seed of something bigger that lies beyond the performance itself and that can start a reflection on modes of looking and perceiving these events as theatre.

To use the concept of this book: the news media were mutated into an annex of the theatre project.

This contamination of the news media has been an important facet of other projects of Rimini Protokoll as well. In 2002 they made *Deutschland 2*. For this project a parliamentary debate taking place in the Bundestag in Berlin was transmitted (on an audio/telephone-line) live to a theatre in Bonn where 237 audience members (all citizens of Bonn) each played one of the 237 members of parliament. When their double in Berlin took the floor, an audience member in Bonn would repeat their every word. Wolfgang Thierse, then president of the Bundestag, had prohibited the use of the former Bundestag building in Bonn where Rimini Protokoll had first planned to make the live recreation of the parliamentary debate for fear this 'live copy of a parliamentary debate' would debase the parliament. Reminiscent of Daimler's director, he stated that the parliament was not a place for theatre. Rimini Protokoll diverted to Bonn's Bonn-Beuel Theater but the seed was planted. Not only were the audience members incited to negotiate between their own personal opinions and those of the parliamentarian whose every word they were mimicking. The media debate that preceded *Deutschland 2*'s 're-presentation of representation' (Matzke 2008: 110) also incited non-audience members to reflect on some of the crucial questions of democracy. Where is the parliament? What is the space of politics? What constitutes political representation and how am I as a citizen represented? What are the codes at work in the theatre of politics?[4] The media contamination made it possible to expand Rimini Protokoll's proposition to the spectator to look at a segment of reality (in this case the space and performance of democracy) through the speculum of theatre.

## The Intimate Collectivity of Radio

One of the most striking ways Rimini Protokoll does this is by using a medium and a genre that now seems outdated: the radio play. There are some similarities between theatre and radio play: like theatre, a radio play happens at a specific moment in time. Unless you record the broadcast, you have to tune in at the right moment. Unlike in theatre, however, the listener does not share the same space with the rest of the audience. Haug explains: 'The paradox of radio plays is that on the one hand the amount of people you reach outnumbers the audience in a theatre, while on the other hand it is a very personal medium because it allows for very direct address.' The radio plays of Rimini Protokoll can be divided into two groups. The first type are original works that bear no relation to their theatre projects.[5] The second group does have a relation with plays but are not, however, 'bonus tracks to the performance, but independent works.'

As such, the radio play is used to revisit the experts that were in a performance, to underline different aspects from a topic addressed on the stage or to retell the story from a different angle. For the radio play *Welcome to you!* (2009), Rimini Protokoll explored the story of a South Korean girl doing an online DNA analysis to find out who her parents are, a theme briefly touched upon in the performance *Black Tie* (2008). For the *Karl Marx* radio play, the listener is taken to the coulisses of the performance but also to the kitchen of a Rimini Protokoll member to listen in on a discussion between the experts of the play. *Deutschland 2* sheds light on the workings of the German parliament through dialogues with voters, candidates for parliament and functionaries of the Bundestag (e.g. an usher and an interpreter).

Radio also presupposes a greater control over the material. Haug points out that it is one of the most flexible media, because voices and sounds are so easily cut up or re-arranged in post-production.

> Using 'mediated' documents is a totally different way of making use of the material we have. The situation of authorship changes: there is more freedom. We make more extreme decisions and play with the material people have given us. That is one of the main differences between working on stage with people versus working on radio plays (often with the same people). Theatre and radio are in that sense two extremes in our work.

Even though these are the two extremes, she adds that 'in a lot of projects we mix both approaches.' What this means is that Rimini Protokoll's stage plays often have a montage structure: monologues and dialogues are alternated with musical numbers, projects, or short choreographies. Radio, on the other hand, is 'theatricalized', which means that Rimini Protokoll highlight the machinery of the medium they use, as they do in their stage plays: 'when we work in radio we refer back to the rules of the radio play.'

## Growing and Shrinking

'One of the strengths of theatre is that it is not bound to one specific medium or restricted to one form,' Haug says. For Rimini Protokoll, theatre in a way is the medium *par excellence* because it can move beyond the designated theatre space to infuse reality with theatricality. Their aim is to invite spectators to look at the world from a theatrical perspective – a theatrical gaze that is sensitive to the dramaturgies of social and political events and of the personal lives that are involved in those events. Ultimately, the experts of the everyday that are the protagonists of almost every Rimini Protokoll performance are everywhere. Rimini Protokoll only amplify their presence. As Haug notes:

> People on stage are really growing or shrinking. Somebody 'small' or 'insignificant' can grow to become small again at the moment of applause. They leave the theatre like anybody else and step outside without the spotlights and without the amplified voices. It makes you realize that there are many, many of these people that you can give the right frame and make them grow.

**Frederik Le Roy** is a PhD researcher funded by the Flemish Research Foundation (PhD fellowship, FWO-Vlaanderen) and is affiliated with the research group Studies in Performing Arts & Media at Ghent University. He is co-editor of a special issue of *Arcadia, Performing Cultural Trauma in Theatre and Film* (2010) and of the books *No Beauty for Me There Where Human Life is Rare. On Jan Lauwers' Theatre Work with Needcompany* (Academia Press and IT&FB, 2007) and *Tickle Your Catastrophe. Imagining Catastrophe in Art, Architecture and Philosophy* (Academia Press, 2011).

#### NOTES

1   This working method during the documentation phase is fairly recent, as they used to record every conversation. Now, however, some form of scripting is initiated already at the first meeting with an expert.

2   In *Das Kapital*, for example, dialogues are interjected with self-referential pointers like 'Kucinsky says'. These theatrical techniques have a double effect: on the one hand, they point to the rehearsed nature of the dialogues, showing that the words are not spontaneous or natural expressions of the experts, actually undoing the authenticity of the words. On the other hand, this alienation paradoxically also underscores the authenticity of the person speaking these lines. The theatrical device not only shows that the expert is *playing theatre* and hence is ultimately an actor even if he or she is playing him- or herself, it also highlights the person behind the role. Alienation shows at least two poles of a character: the construct and the constructor.

3   Some of the newscasts dealing with *Hauptsammlung* can be consulted on Rimini Protokoll's website (http://www.rimini-protokoll.de).

4 To accentuate this even further, Rimini Protokoll made a spin-off of this project in HAU: an interactive installation called *Deutschland 2 Trainer*. In this installation you can practice mimicking the different parliamentarians on your own, or with friends or strangers.

5 For example: *Apparat Herz. Sondersendung zu Passierscheinfragen* ('Heart Machine. Special Broadcast: Permit Questions Phone-in', 2001), *Undo* (2002), *Alles muss raus!* ('Everything must go!', 2004), *Zeugen! Ein Verhör* ('Witnesses! An Interrogation', 2004).

**REFERENCES**

Malzacher, F., 'Dramaturgies of Care and Insecurity. The Story of Rimini Protokoll'. In: M. Dreysse and F. Malzacher (eds.), *Experts of the Everyday. The Theatre of Rimini Protokoll*. Berlin, 2008.

Martin, C., 'Bodies of Evidence'. In: TDR, 50, 3, p 8-15. Cambridge, 2006.

Matzke, A., 'Rimini's Spaces. A Virtual Tour.' In: M. Dreysse and F. Malzacher (eds.), *Experts of the Everyday. The Theatre of Rimini Protokoll*. Berlin, 2008.

# Digital Landscapes

## The Meta-Picturesque Qualities of Kurt d'Haeseleer's Audiovisual Sceneries

Nele Wynants

## Digital Landscapes

Theatre that incorporates other media into its performance space is as old as Greek tragedy. The integration of word, music, image and gesture in one frame presupposes theatre as the intermedial art practice par excellence. That is at least the basic argument of the Theatre and Intermediality Research Working Group, substantiated in their first publication (Chapple & Kattenbelt 2006).[1] Theatre, in Kattenbelt's formulation, has a distinctive capacity to be a 'hypermedium' that is able to 'stage' other mediums (ibid. 37). As the 'stage of intermediality', theatre mutates media into mixed forms that both thematize and question the role of media in our contemporary mediatized culture (ibid. 38). However, the mutating paradigm of the present issue of *Theater Topics* works in two directions and can be understood as the mutual interference and contamination of different media into 'new' or hybrid forms that are hard to categorize. In a text on hybrid art, Elke Van Campenhout, a Belgium-based freelance dramaturge and researcher, distinguishes 'mutants' and 'monsters' as two variations of a contemporary artistic practice operating in the grey zone between performance and visual arts, between science and the gallery. 'Mutants' are types of work that abandon their disciplinary frames, but at the same time (and by doing this) they inquire, question and reinforce the existing disciplines. The second category she characterizes as 'monsters': artworks as a hotchpotch of elements that by no means refer to a particular discipline or identity (Van Campenhout 2008).

The versatile artistic practice of Kurt d'Haeseleer (1974) exemplifies the difficulty, even the impossibility, of cataloguing this kind of hybrid work into one particular discipline, resulting in both mutants and monsters. With a background as a video artist, d'Haeseleer designs visual machineries by combining elements of painting, video clips, cinema, performance and installation art. After his studies at Sint-Lukas (Brussels), he was invited by Peter Missotten to join the collective De Filmfabriek. Recently this collective mutated into DE WERKTANK, a factory for new and old media art, which is coordinated by d'Haeseleer and Ief Spincemaille. The early collaboration with Missotten resulted in several monumental video installations for intermedial theatre, opera and dance projects, such as *The Woman Who Walked into Doors* (2001) and *Haroen en de Zee van Verhalen* (2001), both directed by Guy Cassiers for Ro theater. D'Haeseleer further designed the videography of other international productions, of which his collaborations with Georges Aperghis and Ictus (*Paysage sous Surveillance*, 2002 and *Avis de Tempête*, 2004) and choreographer Isabelle Soupaert (*Kiss of Death*, 2007) have been the most noticed. Many of these video designs are already canonical in their profound reshaping of the use of (new) media in live performances. They exemplify how theatre functions as a hypermedium in 'staging' other media.

Next to these 'videographies', d'Haeseleer developed self-proclaimed visual machineries such as *S*CKMYP* (2004) and *Scripted Emotions* (2006). Together with his participation to Joji Inc's relay performance *ERASE-E(X)* (2006), these 'mutants' will be the focus of this chapter, as I consider them as paradigmatic for his multifaceted practice. Notwithstanding the interdisciplinary nature of this work, however, there is a distinctive feature that characterizes the majority of d'Haeseleer's oeuvre. Whether it concerns an experimental short film, the VJ or live cinema of a music performance, an interactive installation or the videography of a performance, all of these works appear as digital landscapes as a result of their outspoken pictorial cinematography. Based on state-of-the-art digital montage and production technologies, d'Haeseleer builds video sceneries that far exceed the specificity of the cinematographic medium, expanding the image into a sculpted story world. It is no coincidence, then, that the singularity of d'Haeseleer's varied practice is often described in graphic terms, emphasizing the picturesque quality of his cinematic universe. As a digital painter he is said 'to give life to the bare pixel material of seemingly everyday shots in wonderful, organic and associative images' (World Wide Video Festival). The landscape might thus function as the appropriate figure to gain insight into the mutating mechanisms operating this growing oeuvre.

In this light, I will demonstrate how Kurt d'Haeseleer constructs digital landscapes that furthermore can be considered as a specific kind of meta-picture. In the line of Gertrude Stein's *Landscape Play*, this pictorial motif functions as a theoretical concept, which enables us to relate d'Haeseleer's video designs to the aesthetic tradition of the landscape. In addition, it hints at the spatial and immersive dimension of his cinematographic environments causing a shift from a mere understanding to an embodied experience as the spectator is called upon his/her active presence. Eventually, by putting parallel cinematographic environments *en abyme*, the digital landscapes of d'Haeseleer appear to be 'meta-pictures' in which aspects of time and space are juxtaposed. This concept introduced by W. J. T. Mitchell can be described as 'pictures that show themselves in order to know themselves: they stage the "self-knowledge" of pictures' (Mitchell 1994: 48). In short, meta-pictures are pictures that refer to themselves or to other pictures and as such they provide their own meta-language; they consist of a levelled structure that offers a reflection on its own status as image and, by extension, an involved observer.[2]

It is our argument that d'Haeseleer's landscapes stage the act of looking by drawing in the active presence of a spectator. Moreover, the formal use of *mise en abyme* appears to comprise the central motif in d'Haeseleer's post-apocalyptic imagery. As we will demonstrate, these nested landscapes visualize the hybrid and networked space we live in. Working from the premise that this interdisciplinary practice can be qualified as 'meta-pictures', it is considered a 'theoretical object' (Mieke Bal 2002: 61). Instead of mere illustrations to theory, it 'pictures theory' (Mitchell 1994: 49). Put differently, the notion of the landscape functions both as a metaphor and as a theoretical concept to investigate and picture what this particular practice can add to the understanding of intermedial or hybrid forms of performance art.

## Abysmal Landscapes

As a specific kind of meta-picture, the notion '*mise en abyme*' points to a particular representational structure (or strategy) that places related parallel worlds behind – or within – each other. Mostly known as a narrative figure denoting 'a play within a play' or 'a story within a story', *mise en abyme* in fact originates from a pictorial tradition, referring to an image that infinitely doubles oneself as a reflective split off from the stem world.[3] The mechanism is harder to define than to indicate as some illustrious examples have become canonical. In Shakespeare's *Hamlet*, for instance, a troupe of actors stages a play in which key actions of the main plot are dramatized. In a pictorial tradition, Vélazquez' *Las Meninas* is the classic example of a picture-within-a-picture. Even more popular as a clarifying exemplar is the 'Quaker Oats principle'. The expression refers to the packages that include in their design a smaller picture of the package itself, duplicating its framing image (also called the Droste effect). This spatial figure breaks open the depicted narrative landscape and hints at underlying parallel worlds by means of an embedding strategy: a frame opens a window to another world beyond that frame, which opens again a new window, etcetera.

Given its cheerful play with mirrors and reflection and its feasibility to picture infinity, the *mise en abyme* became an attractive visual device for surrealist painters. René Magritte, for instance, frequently made use of mirrors and windows to frame a parallel surrealistic universe beyond that frame. But probably the best known for his labyrinthine use of the infinity motif is the Dutch graphic artist M. C. Escher. His complex landscapes turn out as never-ending loops. Combining mirror images of cones, spheres, cubes, rings and spirals with a perfect knowledge of perspective, these scenes mislead the senses and cause an effect of breathtaking infinity. Exactly this structure of infinity is one of the characterizing features of the *mise en abyme*, which at the same time constitutes its paradoxical double nature. The never-ending motif has the compelling power to immerse the beholder in a tunnel of infinite multiplications, while its ability to disorient and disrupt the representational totality in which it appears draws attention to its own artificial status.[4] This self-reflective nature counts for the disposition of the *mise en abyme* as a meta-picture: its layered structure incites a reflection on its own status as image and, by extension, an involved observer.

Fig. 1    S*CKMYP © Peter Missotten.

## Embedding the Landscape

S*CKMYP, a production based on a text by Peter Verhelst, was d'Haeseleer's first full-length experimental film produced by De Filmfabriek. In the installation of the same name, which premiered at the 2004 World Wide Video Festival in Amsterdam, the moving pictures (chapters) were split up over four projection screens, while the hypnotic voice of Peter Verhelst and the soundscape by Köhn, a project of Belgian composer Jurgen Deblonde, drove the visitors along an endless succession of never-ending stories. By means of parabolic speakers, the sound was organized to enclose the visitor in an aural area before the screen, banishing the surrounding sounds to background buzzing. Following an individual track along the different tableaux, the visitor could discover several parallel unfolding narratives. In other words, the set-up allowed for an individual trajectory along the different sceneries reminiscent of the cut-up structure of the pageant plays of the Middle Ages.[5] This arrangement resulted in an endless variation of story chains, personally threaded by the wandering visitor. Consequently, the cinematographic experience became extremely individualized, as the multilinear story lines incite a multitude of interpretations and experiences. Much as in reading Verhelst's prose, which is always highly individual and full of ambiguities, it is up to the 'reader'/viewer to weave the modular story fragments into a coherent and meaningful experience.

By making use of visual fragmentation and narrative modularity, Kurt d'Haeseleer builds further on the so-called 'expanded cinema' projects of the 1960s in which video

164

artists experimented with the limitations of the conventional frame in order 'to free film from its flat and frontal orientation and to present it with an ambience of total space' (Youngblood 1970: 361). Opening up the image-space and offering a multitude of narrative perspectives to the visitor of the diegetic environment provoked a significant disruption of traditional linear forms of narration.

A similar shift occurred in theatre practice, where 'classic' linear dramatic forms of plot development were replaced with more spatially oriented dramatic forms in which narrative elements were juxtaposed. Inspired by the aesthetics of landscape painting and nineteenth-century panoramas, Gertrude Stein, for instance, introduced the notion of the Landscape Play to characterize her own drama texts. Although Stein's dramas are neither scenic landscapes nor the verbal depiction or evocation of a landscape, she considered her texts as landscapes (Stein 1998b). According to Stein expert Jane Bowers, the analogy is based on a specific use of language. That is why Bowers suggests the term 'lang-scapes' as a more accurate neologism for such plays, as they are more involved with spatial configurations of language itself that, like landscapes, frame and freeze visual moments and alter perception (1991: 26). Stein considered the theatre stage as a platform on which landscapes of words could be arranged and put in motion. Although initially a rather conceptual notion – Stein's plays were hardly performed on stage – the notion of the landscape play was picked up by Hans-Thies Lehmann to conceptualize what he called 'postdramatic theatre': plays that move the focus from the text to the overall scenic atmosphere without a causal logic steering the course of the narrative. 'Just as in her texts the representation of reality recedes in favour of the play of words, in a "Stein theatre" there will be no drama, not even a story; it will not be possible to differentiate protagonists and even roles and identifiable characters will be missing' (Lehmann 2006: 63).

This approach of narrative as a landscape, with a structure open to discover, is in accordance with a contemporary notion of narrative in cognitive science. Proceeding from cognitive psychology and perception theory, these paradigms no longer regard narrative as a literary discourse but as a way to organize human experience. In the spirit of a Gombrichian thesis of the beholder's share, cognitivist art theory attributes an important role to the reader/viewer in the construction of narrative content and experiences.[6] Stories are 'mental constructs that we form as a response to certain texts, artworks, discourse acts and, more generally, as a response to life itself' (Ryan 2006: 647).[7] Narratives are the semiotic realization of these mental constructs: their inscriptions as texts, images and sounds are the material output of this desire. To reconstruct a story, the reader will do what Wolfgang Iser has called 'filling in the gaps' to construct a plot – i.e. imagine untold episodes that glue lexica together to a meaningful and coherent story world (Iser 1972: 285).[8] In the case of S*CKMYP, for instance, the 'multilineal verbosity' (Rieser 2002: 148) of Verhelst's prose and the open structure of the corresponding sound and imagery leaves a certain freedom to the visitor to wander through the narrative and 'fill in the gaps' according to one's own discretion. (S)he can do so by framing expectations about upcoming events, fit actions into larger frameworks and apply schemas derived from personal knowledge and experience and literary and cinematic tradition (Bordwell 1985). In this view, narration can be broadened to the human capacity to understand abstract data as meaningful structures by means of interpretation patterns.

The narrative world of S*CKMYP is indeed a fragmented landscape, with the cut-up structure of a dream. The spectator is dropped into a kaleidoscopic labyrinth, driven through the landscape of screens by the mesmerizing voice of the author as a narrative guide:

> Maybe you have the feeling you've stepped into a dream
> In which someone dreams it's the real world.
> Maybe, someone whispers, we live in a parallel world
> That in the end is no different from our own.
> (D'Haeseleer & Verhelst 2004; transcription)

Although Verhelst's address is very intimate and direct – 'you remember her smell, her warmth' – one is never certain whether the voice reports on a vague memory, an interior monologue or a daydream. Rather than illustrating the spoken words, the successive tableaux on the four screens depict a threatening and alienated atmosphere of people, bodies wandering through a postmodern industrial landscape. The camera pans along nocturnal sceneries of suburban (Flemish) districts and new housing estates. The people inhabiting these scenes resemble slowly moving sculptures; contrary to the speed of the camera, they stray through the landscape in slow motion. These tableaux visualize 'a collection of the stolen dreams, fears and thoughts of its unsuspecting inhabitants' that is melted into an impressive audiovisual universe (D'Haeseleer & Verhelst 2004).

Following two people, a man and a woman, the beholder is only partly able to see what these characters are doing as they gradually become overgrown by a web of visual layers, encapsulating them in their own world. At the same time, one seems to observe the scenery from a distant, capsular position, as a lot of film shooting is done from within (or on top of) a driving car (or moving vehicle) scanning a generic urban landscape. This clearly detached, voyeuristic viewing position – often manifestly that of a surveillance camera – contrasts sharply with the direct address of the narrating voice. The specific personal address in sentences such as 'maybe you have the feeling you've stepped into a dream' repeats irrevocably the tone of the hypnotist who carries the dreamer away in the labyrinth of one's memories. From the apparent distanced position, the visitors of S*CKMYP discover how successive worlds roll out as a *mise en abyme*, submerging them in a rabbit hole of continually underlying stories. The manifold structure is in fact evoked in the text read aloud, unfolding its different narrative levels:

You sink into the bottom of a sleep. There is really nothing to worry about. [...] You sink into the bottom of a new sleep. [...] You sink through a bottom whereupon you sink again through a bottom. Etcetera. Maybe all this is just a joke. Maybe you are the privileged witness of your own death. It's the end of an ordinary day. Maybe you are finally part of a story, whose coherence hadn't yet been grasped. (D'Haeseleer & Verhelst 2004; transcription)

Verhelst thus makes this form of never-ending stories explicit, providing the key to unlocking the meta-levels of the narrative experience. 'Maybe you are part of a story,' the voice suggests, referring to a type of frame-within-a-frame story in which the act of mirroring both integrates the beholder/reader and at the same time makes him/her aware of the fictional nature of the event. This play of mirrors and reflection is exactly one of the characteristic features of the *mise en abyme*: in the act of construction and deconstruction, meaning turns out to be unstable and the story becomes aware of its own ontological status, 'a story whose coherence hadn't yet been grasped'.

As mentioned, d'Haeseleer does not visualize the narrative content of Verhelst's poetry on a literal level. Nevertheless, he does mimic the structure of the narrative, which is a succession of parallel cut-up worlds, spread out along the multiple screens, which relate to each other as fragments of a dreamlike tale. But also on a visual plane the pixel dramas of d'Haeseleer reflect the 'multiverse' of parallel worlds by repeating it on a micro-level: zooming in on seemingly unimportant details of the images, enlarging them to the granular character of their pixel structure, the apparent imperceptible material character of the vibrating electronic networks become visible, almost tangible, opening up and referring to the existence of networked spaces. The dialectics at work between text and image (and sound, although not the focus of this analysis) creates in this way another meta-picture – installing another frame around the previous frames – that brings the hybrid ontology of reality in a digital age to the surface, reflecting a multiverse composed of parallel possible worlds.[9]

## Metapicturing the Landscape

The promise and despair of the postmodern urban condition are recurring topics in d'Haeseleer's digital landscapes. *Fossilization* (2005), for instance, an experimental video commissioned by the International Film Festival of Rotterdam that received a prize at the COURTisane Festival in Ghent (2005), was also perceived and described in an apocalyptic idiom as a hermetic meditation about the cheerful downfall of Western society (COURTisane, 2005). In a self-proclaimed 'filthy cocktail of pixels', d'Haeseleer tackles contemporary issues such as oil dependence, social segregation, mass tourism and mass media. Through a process of morphing which has become his artistic method and signature, seemingly everyday images are rendered as if they are stretched out, crumpled and folded open again. This computer procedure in which one image is smoothly transformed into another, or combined using digital tweening, gen-

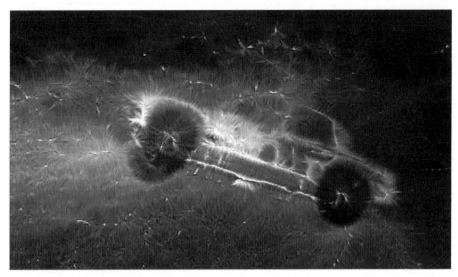

Fig. 2    *Fossilization* © Kurt d'Haeseleer

erates an unpredictable special effect. Although this rendering is a digital procedure, the resulting granular and contaminated imagery is surprisingly reminiscent of former analogue processes of image making. 'At first sight,' a critic describes, '*Fossilization* looks as if the magnetic video tape escaped from the cassette, was badly wrinkled, then stretched out again and fiddled back onto the reel' (Vinken & van Kampen, s.d.). Both appealing and alienating, the outcome of this 'poetics of ambiguity' is once again a digital landscape inhabited by people carrying heavy loads whilst struggling against the wind, and somersaulting cars that seem to float. Offering once more a reflection on the influence of digital technology on our contemporary living condition, d'Haeseleer elaborates on issues he already explored in early films such as *File* (2000). This short film has been characterized as a crossbreed between a video clip, an essay, an action movie, a documentary and a commercial about a relationship between two people losing each other in a world of digital overdrive.

In *Scripted Emotions* (2006), his subsequent interactive cinematographic installation which was awarded with special honours at Transmediale in Berlin, this 'poetics of ambiguity' must be conceived somewhat differently. Two tourist binoculars generate a *trompe l'oeil*, a panoramic landscape that seems to be a visual translation of a world wherein every detail is predicted. However, the landscape changes as soon as the beholder looks in another direction. The movable tourist binoculars of *Scripted Emotions* look out on both sides of a cinematographic panorama. The first pair provides a view over a gloomy car park in the shadow of a desolate cinema complex. The second, placed diametrically opposed to the first, opens up to a shiny tableau of cheerful fountains in a park. Whenever one changes viewing direction by panning through the landscapes, the haunted characters of this environment disappear and reappear once more. Lonely figures roam through the landscape and turn out to have disappeared once you look back. Someone is taking his dog out. A couple is loading a car. Another character is crawling on hands and knees out of a bush. A dark woman yells at you from a distance. All of a sudden you face a man who stares back at you. But when you look away and back he seems to have vanished.

Yet again d'Haeseleer generates a story world without a fixed path or ending. Built on the foundations of the software from an old first-person shooter game, the installation engenders a surround environment that corresponds to the subdivided composition of early modern viewing apparatuses such as panoramas and dioramas. The surround imagery is split up in strips that function as separate frames. Within these invisibly demarcated frames, an image or object can transform independently from its adjacent frames. As a result, the rhythm, direction and succession of events are dependent on the movements of the spectator, who steers the narrative by panning around with the binoculars. In this regard, d'Haeseleer explores the possibilities of an interactive montage or editing that instead of following a sequential causal logic, once again opens up a countless range of possibilities.

With the aspect of interactivity in art, we enter a fuzzy zone. The term 'interactivity' refers mainly to the relationship between a person and a machine, notably in modern technological media calling for the viewer's participation. This participative aspect, however, seems to be the main reason for its generic and ambiguous use, as it recalls different types of activities. Interacting with a work of art is at once to look at it, touch it, sense it, enter it, manipulate it, comment on it, criticize it and so on (Kreplak 2008: 6). Although one or more of these criteria can be ascribed to a wide range of artworks, the prominence of action as a dimension of the work seems to be the determining feature here. Its attractiveness probably marks a paradigm shift from a distanced contemplation of art in favour of an active, participative relation privileged in contemporary art practices and cognitive theory, following again Gombrich's thesis of the beholder's share.

Although we support this general interactive approach of the aesthetic relation to art and media, we believe that calling every piece of art 'interactive', however, would miss the point. Interactive practices do indeed have a common and at the same time distinctive feature: the wish to develop less autarchic forms of art, in which the co-presence of work and visitor is an essential aspect of the mutual effects of the art practice. Significant in this context is the act of placing the beholder at the centre of the artwork, which amounts to his or her inclusion in the work not only as a subject looking at the art but also as a participating agent. The visitors thus find themselves reflected or implicated in the work, engaged in the action, becoming in the words of Boal a 'spectactor', which irrevocably determines one's relation to the work. Placing the viewer on 'the inside' of the image is, nonetheless, more than a shift from perception to engagement. As it radically changes one's position and perspective towards the depicted events, it demands a fundamental reconsideration of our relation to artworks.

In this light, we can consider the apparatus of *Scripted Emotions* as a digital re-enactment of the diorama crossed with the set-up of an early modern peepshow. As 'a kind of theatre without actors and storylines, partly optical and partly mechanical', the diorama was a moving variant of the panorama, originally conceived by Louis Jacques Mandé Daguerre and the artist Charles Marie Bouton (Huhtamo 2010: 249). In this modern viewing machine, the audience was placed central in a sloping amphitheatre that mechanically rotated around its axis. The appeal was based on the trick of atmospheric transformations and animated view by means of a play on light and transparency painting, mechanical motion and elaborate sound effects. After several minutes, a bell rang which indicated a *changement de décor* by means of a crank-operated mechanism that rotated the auditorium.[10]

These early mechanical viewing devices are generally considered as important predecessors of moving pictures. But even more important in this context is that these apparatuses caused a crucial shift in modern viewing conditions, in particular with regard to the way of seeing the landscape in the twentieth century. Since the Renaissance, artists had used linear perspective to structure space and landscape. According to Una Chaudhuri, the spectator of perspectival landscapes is formally an outsider, and this position is 'considerably alleviated by the concomitant projection of passivity on the world represented' (Fuchs & Chaudhuri 2002: 19). The thrilling effects achieved by perspective depended, according to this same author, upon the distance and fixed position of the onlooker and, further, upon denying both of these. This fixed and detached relation between the viewer and the image became the dominant disposition of theatre and film. Moreover, perspective turned out to be the theatre's fundamental spatial disposition. Framed by the manteau of the theatrical stage, the staged scene is always directed/oriented towards a central 'perfect' – and thus fixed – viewing position.

Modern culture, however, established with its nineteenth-century viewing devices other, more fragmented ways of viewing and experiencing visual attractions. The panorama and diorama are good examples here, as they seem to be the direct inspiration for both Stein's conception of the landscape play and d'Haeseleer's installations. The panorama was a circular landscape painting displayed on the inside walls of a rotunda. Spectators could wander around on a central platform to contemplate the spectacular surrounding environment. Different from central-perspective painting, the source of perception in panoramas was not the single-eyed fixed gaze but the entire body that projected the perceiver into the landscape. From that position, the imagination of the viewer was free to construct the image world from multiple perspectives.

What inspired Gertrude Stein, however, was not only the panorama's imaginative power and free embodied perception but also its potential to encourage a new way of looking at landscapes as well as a new relationship of the embodied self to the environment (Stein 1998a). After all, the panorama was, among other contemporary spectacles, a performative landscape that emphasized the mechanics by which the illusion was created. As a viewer of the panorama, one becomes aware of the process of illusion, which is an aspect of attraction that constitutes the thrill of the experience.

*Scripted Emotions* can also be understood in the frame of this modern dialectic between fascination (illusion) and deconstruction, distance and proximity, inside and outside, first- and second-order representation.[11] Moreover, this double logic is reminiscent of meta-pictures' dialectical disposition. Positioned behind the binoculars, the spectator again becomes a voyeur, 'scripted' as a Peeping Tom. This voyeuristic role of the viewer is also made explicit in the set-up of the binoculars, becoming a tableau itself worth looking at. Queuing visitors in turn observe the peering spectator. The act of looking is thus once more reframed on a meta-level: the image of people looking at people looking at people evokes an 'interactive' dialogue between the observer and the nested image in this self-referential picture. As a matter of fact, this 'dialogue' or the relation between the observer and the observed is the actual subject of this work, turning the entirety of this installation into a meta-picture. Consequently, the self-referential character of *Scripted Emotions* serves a double function. It not only offers a reflection on vision itself, it also generates a self-awareness on the side of the beholder who needs to negotiate a new relationship to the depicted environment. The reflective character of a so-called 'multistable' meta-picture, then, has as much to do with the observer as with the meta-picture itself. It is for this reason that Mitchell calls the multistable image 'a device for educing self-knowledge, a kind of mirror for the beholder' (1994: 48).

Fig. 3    *Scripted Emotions* © Kristof Persoons - www.perreonline.be.

## Remembering the Landscape

The interactive video environment of *Scripted Emotions* was later implemented in ERASE-E(X), a relay-performance of Joji Inc, selected for the Festival d'Avignon 2008. For this chain performance, Johanne Saunier invited several choreographers and artists, including Kurt d'Haeseleer, to erase and (re)create the dance phrase of the previous. Inspired by *Erased De Kooning Drawing* (1953), a painting of Robert Rauschenberg in which the American pop artist erased a drawing of Willem De Kooning, a similar method developed the choreography. In ERASE-E(X), the act of erasing is not so much a negation but rather a rewriting in which each artist is challenged to set up a dialogue with the universe of his/her predecessor. This seemingly destructive act is of course a conceptual one, which highlights the main issues of postmodern art by questioning the position of art and the artist, the problem of authorship, inter-referentiality and legibility. Translated to the domain of dance and performance art, these issues are even more precarious because of its ephemeral ontological status and the absence of a universal notation system. The performance thus builds on an existing discourse on poststructural semantics, based on the ability of the observer to understand the complexity of narrative layers and references as a coherent and consistent event.

In his detailed analyses of the first three instalments of this choreography, Johan Callens neatly unravels the multiple references underlying ERASE-E(X). First in line, the Wooster Group was asked to rework a dance phrase of Anne Teresa de Keersmaeker. This interpretation, performed by Saunier, returned to de Keersmaeker only to be re-erased again. In a third phase, Isabelle Soupaert directed Saunier, this time in a duet with the male dancer Charles François. Callens extensively discusses Jean-Luc Godard's canonical *Le Mépris* (1963) as a central motif in the first three instalments of the performance. This theme was established by the Wooster Group, who recycled the soundtrack and gestural vocabulary of the opening scene of this film. Featuring the Austrian director Fritz Lang in the role of a movie director, this making-of movie already functions as a meta-image, picturing the act of filmmaking in reference to the existing cultural canon.[12] Taking the soundtrack of the first scene as a starting point of the performance, ERASE-E(X) irrevocably takes along the gender issues of that particular scene in which a naked Brigitte Bardot invites her partner to admire her body. In his article, Callens points out how 'the relevance of *Le Mépris* for ERASE-E(X) extends to the movie's autobiographical subtext, which turns both works into private commemorations, as well as gender explorations and self-conscious historicizations of their medium, all the way up to the present' (2007: 95-97). The performance is thus not only a self-conscious reflection on 'the permanence and belatedness of art', it also echoes on a narrative level the classic topos of relational issues through the creative re-enactment or citation of the cultural canon (ibid. 99).

D'Haeseleer was the fourth in a row to erase and (re)create the performance. Parallel to Godard's soundtrack in the first instalment, d'Haeseleer started his part with the soundtrack of David Lynch's *Mulholland Drive* (2001), a film bearing innumerable references to Le Mépris and other movies. Godard's film ends with a car crash and the death of Emilia played by Brigitte Bardot. D'Haeseleer staged Saunier as a Bardot after the crash, mirroring the beginning of Mulholland Drive. The dancer slowly crawled along the scene. Her fractured movements were registered by a surveillance camera scanning the theatrical space and projected on a screen above her. When she entered a specific zone before the camera, she apparently seemed to activate the 'mental images' of the performance. In reaction to her movements, fragments of dance phrases from the previous instalments were projected as flashbacks behind her. D'Haeseleer reframed these fragments in one video environment – the same software environment he had used for Scripted Emotions. The landscape was thus used as a frame to take together and reposition all the different instalments into one single cinematographic space. This projected landscape was steered live by a technician, as if he scanned the panorama with a pair of binoculars. Containing multiple images of a dancing Saunier at different moments in the performance, the landscape reflects the mental pictures of the performer wandering through that scenery. Moreover, it appeared as if she was able to interact with these images of 'her' lost memory. In the act of remembering her past identity, she mirrors at the same time the amnesia of Rita, the protagonist in Mulholland Drive.

Summarizing, we can state that d'Haeseleer's episode of ERASE-E(X) contains all the discussed characteristics of his work in a performative context. By introducing his own cinematographic medium on the theatrical scene, he inevitably installs the existence of a parallel world, through an embedment of a cinematographic environment en abyme. The screen opens up to a landscape containing all the performative repetitions of the 'same' but erased dance phrase. On a first level of this mise en abyme, the screen functions as a mirror or window that reflects the infinite repetitions of the performance's memory. On a second, meta-level, it pictures the impossibility of a comprehensive remembrance and, by extension, a 'perfect' re-enactment. The interaction of the actress with her projected 'mental images' reflects at the same time the remembering/reconfiguring act of the witnessing audience. The use of the related soundtrack, for instance, immediately triggers the audience's 'cultural memory' and invites the viewers to construct meaning and 'fill in the gaps' between a multitude of references and (personal) recollections. In this respect the construction of meaning parallels both on a textual and visual level postmodernist thought, which itself can be considered a mise en abyme or an endless web of cross-references. In deconstructive literary criticism, mise en abyme is used as a term to denote the intertextual nature of language and its incapacity to refer to reality. Signification in this postmodern paradigm is understood as a mise en abyme of signifiers, where authorship and spectatorship are merely rhetorical/ grammatical constructs – every signified is nothing but another signifier, literality is but another trope, depth a play of surfaces. Poststructuralist Jean Baudrillard coined the term 'simulacrum' to postulate this postmodern problem of the original. In our contemporary society saturated with images, the status of that image (representation) in relation to an external reality has become blurred. To characterize this hybrid ontology of reality, Baudrillard polemically stated that reality seems to have disappeared behind the multitude of copies, simulations: images, or models without origin or reality; a hyper-reality (Baudrillard 1981).

However, to reduce the work of d'Haeseleer to the paradigm of 'hyperreality' would be wide of the mark. Although his post-apocalyptic universe definitely relates to postmodern aesthetic theory, his digital landscapes are too material (too human) in nature to be characterized as simulacra. The depicted spaces are not empty and infinite, as the signs of Baudrillard are, but on the contrary are layered and complex. In that sense they can be considered as hybrid – a denominator that entirely connects to the register of mutating media. To characterize d'Haeseleer's surroundings as 'hybrid' is an effective way to overcome the unproductive distinction between physical space and the intangible flows of informational space.[13] Instead, d'Haeseleer's digital landscapes seem to visualize, almost materialize, the layered character of postmodern space, in which parallel worlds are embedded and interwoven within each other. The human body appears to be the go-between then, hovering around in parallel worlds spanned by electronic networks. This complex play between material 'spaces of place' and immaterial 'spaces of flow' (Castells 2000: 409) is exactly the scope of his most recent performance (at the time of writing), which exemplifies our concluding remarks. In Je Connais Des Gens Qui Sont Morts (2009), d'Haeseleer and Bérengère Bodin again perform a landscape, this time populated by inflatable objects and puppets that successively swell up and deflate again. Based on Zygmunt Bauman's La Vie Liquide, the theme of a society that is entirely driven by flexibility and change recurs. The manipulated objects and floating video images form the background for a strange, alienating courtship dance. D'Haeseleer's visual poetics of morphing adds again to the material, almost organic, quality of these sceneries, turning his digital landscapes into pictorial hybrid surroundings. Slowly deforming figures emerge as dancers. The empty membranes are wrenched in anatomically impossible positions. In the end, two corporeal bodies of the performers are determined to endure in the swiftly transforming digital landscape.

**Nele Wynants** is a junior researcher at the University of Antwerp (film and theatre studies). She studied Art History (performance and media arts) at the University of Ghent and the Université Paris X, and scenography at the Royal Academy of Fine Arts in Antwerp.
Since October 2008, she has been a fellow of the Research Foundation – Flanders (FWO), conducting her PhD on visual narratives in immersive performance and installation art.

NOTES

1   The book is the result of a collective effort by the members of the Theatre and Intermediality Research Working Group within the International Federation for Theatre Research (www.iftr-firt.org). Recently the group published a second volume, Map-

ping *Intermediality in Performance* (Bay-Cheng et al, 2010), in which they focus on digital culture and the implications for theatre of what has been called the 'intermedial turn'.

2  For an extensive overview of all kind of meta-pictures, we refer to the catalogue of the exhibition *Une image peut en cacher une autre: Arcimboldo, Dali, Raetz* organized by and in the Galeries nationales of the Grand Palais in Paris, seen in July 2009. More information on the exhibition and catalogue can be found at: http://www.rmn.fr/ une-image-peut-en-cacher-une-autre.

3  The term stems from the domain of heraldry describing a coat of arms that appears as a smaller shield in the centre of a larger one – thus, 'placed into infinity' or, literally, 'placed into the abyss'.

4  Lucien Dällenbach was among the first to elaborate an extensive theoretical ground for the *mise en abyme* as a figure. He methodically divided these two categories (which he called paradoxical reflection and simple reflection) into subtypes, and posited a third category of infinite reflection in which the parallelism between the part and the whole is multiplied by repetition and embedding. In 'Mise en abyme et iconicité', Mieke Bal proposes some critical amendments to Dällenbach's theory (Bal 1978). Since both Bal and Dällenbach mainly focus on the literary tradition of the figure, we leave these approaches out of the picture of this essay.

5  Pageant or mystery plays played simultaneously on different platforms spread out over the city or an open square.

6  In reference to E. H. Gombrich's 'beholder's share', I will give preference to the term 'beholder' instead of 'spectator'. It was the key concept of Gombrich's canonical *Art and Illusion* in which he claims that perceiving images is always influenced by our knowledge of the world and of other images. With 'the beholder's share', he denotes our interpretative activity in reading and accepting notations. 'All art originates in the human mind, in our reactions to the world rather than in the visible world itself, and it is precisely because all art is "conceptual" that all representations are recognizable by their style' (Gombrich 1984: 71).

7  Cognitivist thought considers our response to art 'primarily [...] as a rationally motivated and informed attempt to make sense of the work at each of the levels it presents: sensory stimulus in light and sound, narrative, and object charged with higher order meanings and expression' (Currie 2004: 155).

8  Marie-Laure Ryan points to the limits of this 'filling in the blanks', as it is simply not possible to construct a coherent story out of every permutation of a set of textual fragments, because fragments are implicitly ordered by relations such as logical presupposition, material causality and temporal sequence. Ryan's aim is to deconstruct this 'Myth of the Aleph' – or the utopian idea of hypertext narratives with its unrestricted possibilities and meanings – as a theoretical model with limited practical value. Instead, she proposes the jigsaw puzzle as a more accurate model that describes the reader's activity as the arrangement of textual segments into a global pattern that slowly takes shape in the mind. Although her definition of narrative is very

broad, her detailed dissection of digital textuality is very much in favour of unambiguous stories, leaving more experimental poetics of narration aside (minimizing these forms to an arcane academic genre). See Ryan (2002).

9 The narratological application of the notion of possible worlds is an adaptation of a model developed in modal logic by philosophers of the analytic school. Marie-Laure Ryan (2006) explores how narrative fiction deals with the notion of a multiverse composed of parallel worlds, drawing on the concept of parallel worlds in philosophy, logic and technology and in literature and the visual arts. The foundation of the possible worlds theory is the idea that reality is a universe composed of a plurality of distinct worlds (analogous to the many-worlds cosmology, a theory in physics). This universe is structured like a solar system: at the centre lies a world commonly known as 'the actual world', and this centre is surrounded by worlds that are possible but not actual. Umberto Eco describes the narrative text as a 'machine for producing possible worlds' (1984: 246).

10 For an extensive study and overview of how the diorama evolved, see Huhtamo (2010).

11 Film and media scholars such as Jonathan Crary and Tom Gunning have, following Walter Benjamin, extensively elaborated on this specific dialectical principle of the modern viewing experience.

12 With references to other films like *Voyage in Italy* (1953, Roberto Rossellini), Alberto Moravia's *Il disprezzo* (1953) as well as literature such as Homer's *Odyssey*.

13 We borrow this approach from Eric Kluitenberg, who introduces the concept of 'hybrid space' to characterize the stratified nature of our contemporary physical space and the electronic communication networks it contains. Speaking with Kluitenberg, our contemporary public space 'is reconfigured by a multitude of media and communication networks interwoven into the social and political functions of space to form a "hybrid" space' (Kluitenberg 2006: 8).

**REFERENCES**

Bal, M., *Traveling Concepts in the Humanities. A Rough Guide.* London, 2002.

–. 'Mise en abyme et iconicité' In: *Littérature*, 29, p. 116-28, Palaiseau, 1978.

Baudrillard, J., *Simulacres et simulation.* Paris, 1981.

Bay-Cheng, S., C. Kattenbelt, A. Lavender and R. Nelson (eds.), *Mapping Intermediality in Performance.* Amsterdam, 2010.

Bordwell, D., *Narration in the Fiction Film.* London, 1985.

Bowers, J. P., *'They Watch Me as They Watch This.' Gertrude Stein's Metadrama.* Philadelphia, 1991.

Callens, J., 'Erase-E(X): Embodying History in Postmodern Dance'. In: L. van Heteren, C. Kattenbelt, C. Stalpaert and R. van der Zalm (eds.), *Theater Topics. Ornamenten van het vergeten.* Amsterdam, 2007.

Castells, M., *The Rise of the Network Society.* Oxford, 1996.

Chapple, F. and C. Kattenbelt (eds.), *Intermediality in Theatre and Performance*. Amsterdam, 2006.

COURTisane festival, 'Winnaars Belgische competitie kortfilm/video'. Press release, 16 May 2005. In: *Courtisane Editie 4*. Gent, 2005. Web. <http://old.courtisane.be/editie_4/pers/winnaars.doc>

Currie, G., *Arts and Minds*. Oxford, 2004.

D'Haeseleer, K. and P. Verhelst, *S*CKMYP*. Ghent, 2004. DVD and booklet.

Eco, U., *The Role of the Reader. Explorations in the Semiotics of Texts*. Bloomington, 1984.

Fuchs, E. and U. Chaudhuri (eds.), *Land/Scape/Theater*. Ann Arbor, 2002.

Gombrich, E. H., *Art and Illusion. A Study in the Psychology of Pictorial Representation. The A. W. Mellon Lectures in the Fine Arts 1956*. New York, 1984.

Huhtamo, E., 'The Diorama Revisited'. In: A. Altena (ed.), *Sonic Acts XIII. The Poetics of Space*. Amsterdam, 2010.

Iser, W., 'The Reading Process. A Phenomenological Approach'. In: *New Literary History*, 3, 2, p. 279-299. Baltimore, 1972.

Kluitenberg, E., 'Netwerk van golven. Leven en handelen in een hybride ruimte'. In: *Open*, 11. Hybride Ruimte. p. 6-16. Rotterdam, 2006.

Kreplak, Y., 'Quelles interactions en art contemporain?'. In: *Esse*, 63. Actions réciproques/Mutual Actions. p. 5-8 Montréal, 2008.

Lehmann, H.-T., *Postdramatic Theatre*. London/New York, 2006.

Mitchell, W. J. T., *Picture Theory*. Chicago/London, 1994.

Rieser, M., 'The Poetics of Interactivity. The Uncertainty Principle'. In: A. Zapp and M. Rieser (eds.), *New Screen Media. Screen/Art/Narrative*. London, 2002.

Ryan, M.-L., 'Beyond Myth and Metaphor. Narrative in Digital Media'. In: *Poetics Today*, 23, 4. p. 581-609. Durham, 2006.

–. 'From Parallel Universes to Possible Worlds. Ontological Pluralism in Physics, Narratology, and Narrative'. In: *Poetics Today*, 27, 4. p. 633-674. Durham, 2002.

Stein, G., 'Pictures'. In: G. Stein, *Writings 1932-1946*. New York, 1998a.

Stein, G., 'Plays'. In: G. Stein, *Writings 1932-1946*. New York, 1998b.

Van Campenhout, E., 'Hybride kunsten. Over monsters en mutanten'. In: *Courant*, 84. p. 10-13. Hybridisering. Brussel, 2008.

Vinken, J. and M. van Kampen, 'Fossilization'. In: *Netherlands Media Art Institute – Catalogue*. s.l., s.d. Web. < http://catalogue.nimk.nl/>

World Wide Video Festival, 'Solo: Kurt d'Haeseleer'. In: *Festival 2004*. Amsterdam, 2004. Web. <http://www.wwvf.nl/2004/ohaeseleer.htm>

Youngblood, G., *Expanded Cinema*. London, 1970.

# The Productivity of the Prototype

## On Julien Maire's 'Cinema of Contraptions'

Edwin Carels

In his artworks and performances, Julien Maire (b. 1969, France) systematically re-invents the technology of visual media.[1] His research is a manifest hybrid between media-archaeology and the production of new media constellations. His output consists of prototypes that perform exactly what their etymology promises (from '*protos*', 'first' and '*typos*', 'impression' or 'model'): proposing unique technological configurations that produce a new, specific image quality. As industrial prototypes, these original creations – no matter how technically clever and refined – are rather useless: they are too complex, too delicate and too clunky to ever be considered for mass production. As artistic statements, the main function of these full-scale constructions is to provoke an effect of wonder, alerting the viewer to the ambivalent status of moving images produced by a machine.

In a contemporary context of mutating media, Maire's works are at once innovative and archaic, seemingly simple yet unique in their radicality, both at the conceptual and the aesthetic level. This radicality is one that incites fundamental questions about the characteristics of the image and the position of their viewer. Working on the interstices between installation, performance and media art, Maire's creations are decidedly original, as he never combines art forms merely for a provocative or innovative effect. His manipulations are always motivated by a questioning of prevailing categories and visual strategies in the digital era.

Deconstructing time-based media such as video, film, slide projections and performances, Julien Maire underlines in the first place their durational aspect, making us aware of our own experience of an image in time. His prototypical contraptions confront immobility with movement, reality with illusion, and interrogate the notion of time and memory in the moving image. With his work, Julien Maire clearly enters into dialogue with the history of media, paradoxically through the design of new technological *dispositifs*. Working against the rhetoric of technology as progress and promise, Maire instead recalibrates technology and its effect on mediation. He modifies obsolete cinematic techniques to develop alternative interfaces that produce moving images.

Overcoming a simplistic opposition between analogue and digital media, Maire's work readily invites both a strategic reconsideration of indexicality and of apparatus theory. As this highly reflexive oeuvre has thus far triggered very little theoretical writing, the first step is to map out the terrain, introducing the work and at the same time establishing the discursive vantage points that are implicated in the work. A multidirectional approach imposes itself, motivated by the problematizing of any linear tradition that forms a subtle yet systematic concern throughout Maire's work.

Julien Maire operates at the intersection of two complementary approaches to the history and genealogy of media. 'The contents of one medium are always other media,' Marshall McLuhan already proclaimed in the opening chapter of his *Understanding Media* (1994: 18). But conversely, the past is also important to go back to and rediscover what we forgot to see in earlier media configurations. Siegfried Zielinski's self-proclaimed 'anarchaeological' approach to media-archaeology promotes the motto: 'do not seek the old in the new, but find something new in the old' (2006: 3).

The media that Julien Maire wants to remind us of are less distant in time from us than the pioneers reintroduced by Zielinski (e.g. Empedocles, Giovan Battista Della Porta, Athanasius Kircher). They are actually quite recent, yet their unique characteristics are constantly being contaminated by ever newer media. While slideshows are replaced by PowerPoint presentations and other data projections, Maire revives the legacy of the magic lantern that fed into the traditional presentation with a slide projector. His most popular work to date, the performance *Demi-Pas* (*Half Step*, 2002), is a high-tech update of the mechanical slide principle, allowing the limited animation of transparent flat or three-dimensional objects during projection. With its duration of approximately half an hour, Maire's only narrative piece to date evokes through consecutive series of animated slides a wordless tale with an extremely simple storyline: the daily routine of a factory worker walking, working, eating and sleeping. This deconstructive mini-movie elegantly demonstrates a critique on Taylorization, the automation of human labour, the industrialization process that concurred with the advent of cinema (Banta 1993). This monotony is constantly reinterpreted by the process of projection, which problematizes the cinematographic image, the fluidity of time, the consistency of reality.

Figs. 1-2    *Demi-Pas / Half-Step* © Julien Maire, 2002.

The live production of small, often looped movements within the projected image (e.g. smoke coming out of a chimney) gives the presentation a paradoxical sense of immediacy and hypermediacy at once, the two complementary characteristics that come together in what Bolter and Grusin have described as the effect of remediation (2000). Updating McLuhan's ideas, they use the term 'remediation' to refer to the representation of one medium in another and turn it into a defining characteristic of new digital media. Immediacy in their terms denotes a 'style of visual representation whose goal is to make the viewer forget the presence of the medium (canvas, photographic film, cinema, and so on) and believe that he is in the presence of the objects of representation' (ibid. 272). Hypermediacy, on the other hand, is a 'style of visual representation whose goal is to remind the viewer of the medium' (ibid.), making us hyperconscious of our act of seeing (or gazing).

With Demi-Pas, however, Julien Maire performs an act of reverse remediation: instead of smuggling old content into new technology, he reactivates and updates old technology and invests it with new imagery. The impact on the viewer is an unsettling combination of analytical observation and pure fascination. A computer-assisted slide projector is able to produce a 'film' consisting entirely of three-dimensionally projected objects, a collection of diapositives or 'projection modules'. 'By layering image and performed interventions into the projected scenes, the images and operations differentiate themselves spatially with perceived realities weaving in and out of perceptibility' (Druckrey 2003: 447). Demi-Pas is a performative piece that cannot exist without the manipulation by Maire himself. It plays on the interaction between machine and image to provoke an intricate reconsideration of what Timothy Druckrey has described as 'the cinemaginary interface' (ibid.).

The technicality of the performance is in itself as much part of the spectacle as what appears on the screen. His mechanical slides could only be made with laser cuttings and micro-electronic aids; the interfaces applied are both pre- and post-cinematographic. Instead of reconfirming the dualism between analogue and digital paradigms, between the industrial and the post-industrial, the photographic and the post-photographic (Mitchell 1992), Maire infuses the convergence of media with a strong sense of materiality. Against the illusive ephemerality of new media culture, Maire posits a materialist approach. Through his reverse engineering practices, he analyses the new imaging technologies by linking them up to older, still familiar formats of optical media.

## Cinema Extracts

Julien Maire describes his references to the cinema as 'extracts' in the culinary sense: as juices or a kind of paste that contains a distillation of what is essential in cinema.[2] For instance, in several of his works he revisits one of the most typical effects of cinema, or 'the cinemaginary interface' – slow motion. In the performance Ordonner/Tidying Up (2000), he demonstrates an improbable slowing down of cardboard boxes being

Fig. 3    *Model for the Apocalypse* © Julien Maire, 2008.

passed on from one person to another during a house move. In *Double Face/ Two-Faced* (1999-2000), the cinematographic slow motion predominates the theatricality of the staging as the viewers witness (the illusion of) a gradual slowing down of the movements of a coin during several heads or tails, until the coin stops completely in mid-air. In *Model for the Apocalypse* (2008), a man shapes amorphous little heaps with 'slow-motion material' made from micro steel balls with a special glue. This time there isn't any manipulation of the viewer, the mass actually appears to disintegrate in slow motion. A camera records the 'action' in detail and this live transmission is projected onto a screen next to the performer, thus conflating real-time perception with mediated vision. Resembling a bizarre form of minimalist tabletop animation with caviar-like matter, the performance is preferably stretched out for many hours, adding another layer to the already conflated perception of time by the slow movement of 'sculpture' and the mediated slow motion on the screen.

Maire thus questions to what extent our vision is conditioned by tropes from diverse media. How does our eye distinguish the features of three-dimensional silvery grains on the table from the recording of the grains, translated into a frame filled with fuzzy pixels? What connotations does this automatic reading trigger? Whether in the form of installations, performances or two-dimensional objects, the work of Maire is making obvious the slippage from analogue to digital media. From his earliest pieces onwards, the artist has been addressing the process of mediation rather than the epistemological, the content of the media.

With *High Voltage/Tension Photographs* ('Photographies à Haute Tension', 1995), he demonstrates the organizational principle of photography: putting things in perspective from a singular point, fixating the image as captured by a *camera obscura*. As each image – a geometric constellation of points that suggest a three-dimensional drawing not unlike Ucello's famous perspective study of a vase – is a multi-exposure consisting of nothing but minute dots, taking up to ten hours of exposure time per picture. Maire simultaneously alludes to the composite nature of electronic imagery. Not a 'single' moment is captured in these multi-exposures, and nothing really existed in front of the lens. They are virtual images, made up of electronic sparks produced in total blackout. And still these hollow images (almost holograms) are essentially photographic, literally 'written with light'. Only the 'warm' texture of the images and their imperfections distinguish them from synthetic imagery.

This investigation of the sensuous qualities of the images and their accompanying connotations inevitably raises the question of their aura. Already in 1931, Walter Benjamin (1979) wondered why the oldest photographic portraits possess an aura that seems evaporated from more recent ones. In *Das Kunstwerk im Zeitalter seiner technischen Reproduzierbarkeit* from 1936, he explains how the loss of 'aura' is a cultural process whereby the artwork as cult has gradually transformed into the artwork as exhibit (1955). The authenticity that comes with the aura is traded for an increasing scrutiny of reality through lens-based, automated technology.

But whereas Benjamin signalled the loss of aura accompanying the mechanization of the image, Maire makes a reverse observation about the delicate distinctions in picture quality when the same image or visual motif migrates from one medium to another. In his *High Voltage* pictures there is no room for any optical unconscious – in Benjamin's eyes a revelatory quality compensating for the loss of aura – as there is nothing to see, just an empty construction, no factual content. Maire analyses media less as a tool for a better, sharper, more detailed perception of the world but rather turns our attention towards a deeper awareness of the medium itself. With his installation *Les Instantanés* (2008), Maire imitates the distinct phases of a drop of water hitting a surface, in the style of Harold Edgerton's famous stroboscopic photo captures. Yet the frozen moment comes to life again through alternating slide projectors. On closer inspection, Maire's image-cycle appears to consist not of 2D images but of a series of framed miniature glass sculptures, a stunning *trompe l'oeil* that reminds us always to look twice.

'The photograph opens up a passageway to its subject, not as a signification, but as a world, multiple and complex,' claims film historian Tom Gunning (2004: 46). With his visualizations, Maire also invites a cultivated attention for delicate differences in image resolution and for the characteristics of the image, eluding a simple true-or-false opinion about the status of what we see. Debating the notion of the post-photographic and the presumed shift in paradigm from the analogue to the digital realm, Lev Manovich argues for a graphic essentialism, claiming that we should see the digital mode not as a post-photographic but simply a graphic mode, one of whose many possibilities is the photographic effect and, by extension, the live-action cinematic effect. Gunning prefers not to polarize:

Fig. 4    *Les Instantanés* © Julien Maire, 2008.

To refer to the digital as the 'post-photographic' seems not only polemic rather than descriptive, but most likely mystifying. The translation of photographic information into a number-based system certainly represents a revolutionary moment in photography, but one not unlike the replacement of the wet collodion process by the dry plate, or the conquering of exposure time with instantaneous photography, or the introduction of the hand camera. (2004: 47-48)

Although the transmission of information is not a central concern in Maire's work, indexicality nevertheless plays a role, questioning to what extent a lens-based image is a record, or rather a product, a construction. Are we really looking for truth, or for images that live up to certain conventions and expectations? Both photographic chemicals and the digital data must be subjected to elaborate procedures before a picture will result. Gunning: 'The indexicality of a traditional photograph inheres in the effect of light on chemicals, not in the picture it produces. The rows of numerical data produced by a digital camera and the image of traditional chemical photography are both indexically determined by objects outside the camera' (ibid. 40).

According to Thomas Elsaesser, digitization could be understood to have 'freed' us from a long-overdue superstition, namely that 'to see is to know':

So deeply ingrained and widely shared was the belief in script, imprint and trace as the foundation of our concepts of record and evidence, and the (peculiar kind of) 'truth' preserved in them, that even where this presumed truth of the image was denounced as illusion, as ideology and cultural constructions (as in the Althusser-Lacanian critiques of the cinematic apparatus), there remained the implicit assumption that a certain type of veracity could be ascribed to the products of mechanical vision, once its ideological operations had been understood. (1999: 33)

In this era of hyper- and hybrid mediatization, medium-specificity remains as complex as it is crucial. Understanding the characteristics of technology is essential for understanding its impact on our awareness of the world. Whereas consumer electronics become increasingly smaller and at the same time continue to expand their memory capacity, Julien Maire celebrates the sheer materiality of a deconstructivist display, foregrounding a whole configuration of machines necessary for the production of just a few images. Traditionally, photographic media are said to keep our memories alive. But how do we perceive the historicity of the image as such?

## Mnemotechnology

The attention to resolution and image definition is elaborated upon in a much more complex framework within *Memory Cone* (2009), a performative installation that again produces a perception of paradoxes, aiming to activate the memory of the participating viewer. It is a crucial work for Julien Maire, as it brings together all his concerns into one constellation, adding an important new dimension: the agency of the viewer. For his first large-scale solo exhibition *Mixed Memory* (M HKA, Antwerp, 2011), Maire confronted a collection of artefacts from the history of cinema with four variations on the principle of *Memory Cone*. With each of his 'mnemotechnical' works, Maire problematizes the status of a transparent slide that travels through different technological mediations to emerge as a single yet unstable image, endowing the visual outcome with a quiet sense of duration. These images feel like they have always been there, always incomplete, always in need of reanimation, waiting for the act of remembrance.

The set-up is each time an intricate combination of machines that conjure up an experiment in image production, whereby a slide-image is downscaled through projection rather than being enlarged. The still image is reduced by lenses and is concentrated on a 'digital mirror' or DMD (Digital Micro-Mirror Device), as currently used in video projectors for digital light processing or DLP. At the same time, a video camera records the hands of a person organizing strips of white paper on a table, literally recompositing an image of a bygone era. For this installation, Julien Maire uses family pictures, pedagogic images and miscellaneous slides bought on a flea market. (This again makes clear that although Maire is not entirely indifferent to the choice of images, his

Figs. 5-7
*Mixed Memory* at M HKA:
exhibition overview and
details © Alexandre Causin

interest lies not so much in the pro-filmic world as such but in the materiality of an image and the process of mediation.) The whiteness of the empty paper puzzle triggers the micro-mirrors that orient a section of the 'found' image on a screen and thus seem to open up 'photographic windows'. By moving the strips of paper, the visitor of the installation selects and gradually reconstructs an image from the past.

Fig. 8
*Memory Cone* projection view
© Julien Maire, 2009.

For any cinephile, witnessing this meditative process, two obvious references spring to mind: *Blow Up* (Michelangelo Antonioni, 1966) and *Blade Runner* (Ridley Scott, 1982). In *Blow Up*, a fashion photographer obsessively enlarges details from an outdoor shoot, penetrating the flat image with the desire to walk around the scene of the crime. In *Blade Runner*, a 'replicant' electronically zooms in and investigates a polaroid-like image, hunting for a detail that might help him understand his own identity. This close reading of the image is a reading against the logic of the grain, or of the pixel. Although the algorithms for image enhancement may have developed considerably, to endlessly enlarge an image step after step, without a radical loss of definition, remains an illusion. The same goes for spatial immersion in or penetration of the image – no matter what the 3D technology of our contemporary multiplex cinemas promises.

With his *Memory Cone*, Maire invites us first of all to explore the nature of the grain in the image and to question its apparent motionlessness. Ever since the Lumières first projected a photographic image and stunned their audience by putting it into motion,

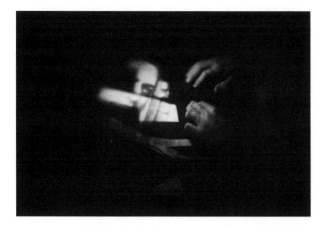

Fig. 9
*Memory Cone*
© Julien Maire, 2009.

the tension between the fixity of a recording and the 'live' effect of its animated presentation continues to fascinate due to the oscillation between document and illusion, stasis and motion, past and present. People were by then used to seeing large still projections of black and white photographic recordings, but in 1895 the reproduction of the intricate movement of trembling leaves in the background reputedly caused a big sensation.

The status of the image in *Memory Cone* can be described neither as a photograph nor as a slide, a video still or a film still. A video image without pixels? A quietly vibrating photograph? The projection on the white paper fragments seems neither purely digital nor analogue. To a simple opposition, Julien Maire prefers a conflation, or hybridization, a new prototype. In one of his variations on the project, *Memory Plane* (2009), he infects a static slide projection with the restlessness of a digital animation. What we see is again neither a video nor a still, but a kind of discretely disorientating electronic composite.

*Memory Cone* is a work that deals with memory and, for the first time, Maire also literally alludes to the past through the title of this interactive installation: the concept of *Memory Cone* is admittedly taken from Henri Bergson's *Matter and Memory* (1896). At the heart of his constellation of machines is Julien Maire's translation of Bergson's metaphor into an optical process: the inverted cone that hits the micro-mirror. As Bergson explains in his book, the base of the cone represents the entire collection of memories of our lived past – the *pure memory* that exists in the recesses of our mind and of which we are mostly unaware. The summit is our present condition, our recollection of the past at the time we interact with the world. Our perception is continuously injected with past experiences.

Bergson distinguished two types of memory: the automatic, strictly utilitarian one, inscribed in the body as a habit or automatic behaviour, and the pure (personal) memory, registering the past in the form of *image-remembrance*, and at times re-entering consciousness. Memory can thus be understood as a form of remediation of the past in a new context each time, either unconsciously or consciously, with immediacy or with hypermediacy, to reprise Bolton and Grusin's terminology.

But for Bergson, memory is in the first place duration: a prolongation of the past into the present. An image is immobile, while duration is 'pure mobility' (Bergson 2002: 165). Bergson was the first to devote an essay specifically to film ('L'illusion ciné-matographique', in his 1906 book *L'évolution créatrice*), but he later realized that cinema could only represent immobile images of movement, and hence no filmed image can actually represent duration. Thus, although Bergson was the first philosopher to turn to cinema as a metaphor for the mechanism of our thinking, he preferred the image of a cone or a telescope when describing true memory in action, to suggest a continuous spiralling movement downwards. For Maire, the cinema is also a major reference and yet, far from a self-evident *dispositif*, there is no stable visual regime anymore. Considering the dimension of time, an important distinction is to be made between an electronic image and the image captured on film, the latter always implying an 'after the fact' whereas the former allows for instant, live representation and manipulation. Playing with new technologies, Maire is concurrently testing our memory and experiences of 'old' media.

## Disciplining the *Dispositif*

With his reference to Bergson, Maire takes us back to the very beginning of film theory, when film was not yet entirely separated from other media and when the technology itself was an important component of the spectacle. At the end of the nineteenth century, the phonograph and the cinematograph were the new storage systems that finally allowed time to be recorded with other means than still text or images. The theorist Lev Manovich has looked at morphological similarities between early data storage devices and film projectors. He thus creates a connection between information storage machines and visual technologies that predate the electronic computer.

For Maire, it is not the volume of memory capacity of the machine that counts; his works are, on the contrary, rather minimalist in their use of imagery or data. What matters is the (re)animation of the image, the live moment when man and/or machine activate an image. This perceptual self-awareness is largely due to the restrained, yet theatrical way in which Maire presents his works, both performances and installations. 'Theatricality is a way of highlighting representational strategies that more or less openly acknowledge the beholder/spectator and, thus, in a sense, the alterity of representation,' Jan Olsson notes (2004: 3).

It is not just the image/representation nor the presentation of the machine producing it but the dynamics of the whole constellation that make up Maire's *dispositifs*. But whereas Michel Foucault, 'the last historian or the first archeologist' (Kittler 1999: 5), introduced the critical notion of *dispositif* (and archaeology) as a theoretical approach to look into social formation and the disciplining powers at work behind it, Maire is more focused on the technology as such, freeing familiar *dispositifs* from their conventional use by reconfiguring them. As he does not want to entertain us with any conventional *dispositif* (the transparency of most narrative cinema, the television set as a technological fireplace, etc.), he deals with prototypes, or specific hybridizations. Instead of a movie theatre, where oblivion rules and everything is arranged so as to forget the fact that we are watching, Maire invites us to step into a distinctly theatrical configuration, a 'cinemaginary interface'. His installations are laboratories for self-reflexive research on our cultural and cognitive responses to an image. What do we know of cinema, still? What is the common sense of the contemporary use of the word 'film'?

Every kind of cinema (and film theory) presupposes an ideal spectator, and then imagines a certain relationship between the mind and body of that spectator and the screen. The apparatus theory of the 1970s maintained that cinema is by nature ideological because its mechanics of representation are ideological. So is the central position of the spectator within the perspective of the composition. Ideology is not a topic, it is structurally inherent in the construction of the *dispositif*. Structuralist (or materialist) film, on the other hand, militated against dominant narrative cinema. On many accounts, Maire's works tie in with the demystifying, non-illusionist strategies of structuralist film, always reminding us that 'viewing such a film is at once viewing a film and viewing the "coming into presence" of the film, i.e. the system of consciousness that produces the work, that is produced by and in it' (Gidal 1976: 2).

In his high-tech sequel to the structuralist (or materialist) cinema of the 1970s, some of Maire's recent works (*Horizon* and *Ligne Simple*, both 2008) even physically resemble the austere mountings of *Arnulf Rainer* (1960), the black-and-white filmstrips projected or pinned like an abstract mosaic against the wall by Peter Kubelka. Only Maire's mosaics are now infused with a sense of duration, and they are essentially electronic. *Low Resolution Cinema* (2005) is a projection installation based on a high reduction of the image resolution. The projection is produced with a special projector using two black-and-white Liquid Crystal Displays (LCD). Each LCD has been half destructed – literally cut in half – in order to display only the upper or lower half of the image.

In the decades that followed the heyday of apparatus theory, the technological *dispositifs* have become increasingly complex, the screen itself has become extremely versatile and ubiquitous (mobile phones, game consoles, GPS, hybrid portable objects, etc.), and now even mainstream filmmakers often switch between formats and media. The interface has replaced the *dispositif* as a theoretical model, and the agency of the user (formerly 'viewer') has been drastically increased, so the notion of the *dispositif* seems to have become less relevant. Yet it remains important to understand the agency of a medium in all its dimensions – including the setting and spatial implementations – as Maire indicates by his demonstrative configurations.

## The Operating Room

According to media-archaeologist Friedrich Kittler, 'aesthetic properties are always only dependent variables of technological feasibility' (2010: 3). Devoting such strong attention to optics and technology does not make Maire a formalist – on the contrary.

As Kittler distinguishes: 'Optics is a subfield of physics; vision is a subfield of physiology, psychology, and culture' (ibid.). Maire may spend a serious amount of work on elaborating unique optical pathways for the image, not taking any mediation for granted, but his real topic is vision, the orchestration of our contemporary viewing patterns.

The installation *Exploding Camera* (2007) offers his most direct allusion to the ideological power of the media. Maire conceived a seemingly chaotic installation that produces 'live' in the exhibition space an experimental historical film reinterpreting the events of the Afghanistan war. The premise of the installation is that the camera that exploded during the assault on Commander Massoud continued filming the events that followed his death. Two days before 9/11, Commander Massoud, the most senior war commander and the most credible opponent to the Taliban was murdered. Two al-Qaida suicide bombers posing as journalists killed him with a booby-trapped camera at his camp in Afghanistan's remote Panjshir Valley.

As if on an operating table, the piece is constructed with a TV monitor connected to the dissected body of a video camera lying on a table. The camera still works, but the lens has been taken out and is not used anymore. A transparent disc containing a few photographic positives is placed between the lights and the light sensor. By using simple external light in the room that the installation is in, as well as LEDs and lasers placed on the table, the video images are produced live by direct illumination of the camera's light sensor. Illuminating the picture from different angles makes the picture appear to move. The resulting imagery, projected in real time on the wall, evokes the grainy, saturated night vision and infrared aesthetics we have come to associate with war reports on television.

'It confronts us not with the camera eye as a Virilio-esque fatal projectile, but with the speculative perceptions of a machine eye that lingers in a state of near-death,' states Andreas Broeckmann (2007). Indeed, Maire's take on the exploding camera – at once a reconstruction and a deconstruction – does not cultivate speed as both essence and form of contemporary logistics of perception, instead he reverses the whole process, slowing us down to contemplate a surgically 'vivisected' camera still in operation. 'To understand cinema also implies breaking open the machine,' the artist confides.

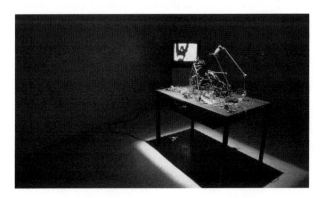

Fig. 10
*Exploding Camera* installation
view at Wood Street Galleries,
Pittsburgh
© Julien Maire, 2009.

'I work in a similar way to Leonardo Da Vinci's one, when, to draw in the best possible way the interior of a human body, he simply needed to look into it to understand what it was like. I have many ideas on how to work exactly when I understand the deep functioning of a machine' (quoted in D'Alonzo 2008).

Maire literally dissects and amputates cameras, and presents this as a contemporary version of the anatomy lesson. With his recent *Open Core* performances (2009), he revisits the public anatomical dissections from the sixteenth century. In the performance he opens up some machines of vision such as cameras and webcams while also feeding a VHS tape through a 16mm projector in operation. The anatomical theatre was indeed one of the original sites for the construction of modern spectatorship in its early stages. Matching the highly theatrical spirit of Renaissance science, painters such as Rembrandt and medical instructors like Fabricius of Aquapendente shared audiences devoted to the workings of the human body (Bleeker 2008). Yet Maire never suffices with a dismantling or paralysing analysis; he always implies a new synthesis, a re-animation, creating new forms of 'living' images without any negative, Frankensteinian bias. His approach is always constructive. 'Media are spaces of action for constructed attempts to connect what is separated,' Zielinski professes in his *Deep Time of the Media* (2006: 7).

## Cinema of Contraptions

'We knew nothing of our senses until media provided models and metaphors,' writes Kittler (2010: 34). Or, as McLuhan noted before him: media operate at the intersection of technology and the body. Throughout history, media has always offered us a training of our senses. And so does the work of Julien Maire. Almost ervery one of his pieces includes a performative component, converging the agency of the machine, the live artist and the viewer.

The performance *Digit* (2006), for instance, is located between a cinematographic process and the process of writing, only achieving its effect in the presence of a live audience. A writer sits at a table, writing what appears to be a script. Simply by sliding his index finger over a blank piece of paper, printed text magically appears under his finger. There is no visible hardware, no computer, no display, no noise, no projection. The spectators can come very close to the 'writer' and read the text following the movement of the finger or during the short pauses when the writer, thinking of what to write next, takes a walk around the space. The performance is simple but quite disturbing. The striking visual absence of any interface or extension problematizes our whole notion of the 'graph': in this very fluid and controlled demonstration of 'automatic writing', nothing seems to come between the thoughts and the printed words.

'*Digit* is a kind of "soft machine",' posits Maire, referring to William Burroughs. An invisible one at that. The attractiveness of the performance lies in its demonstration of a pertinent absence, the actual source of the printed text. It is a magician's act, relating Maire's working method back to Méliès' at the time when he was incorporating cinema into his live acts when working as an illusionist at the theatre Houdin. In the early days

Fig. 11    *Digit* © Julien Maire, 2006.

of cinema – best characterized by Tom Gunning and André Gaudréault with their influential term 'the cinema of attractions' (Strauven 2006) – the wondrous productivity of the machine was still an integral part of each séance, a projection felt like a performance and cinema's connotations of circus, magic and vaudeville were still very strong. Here again, we can draw an analogy with the principles of immediacy and hypermediacy: the alternation between a focused admiration for the machine and captivation for the magical effects it produces. From this often funfair-like setting of the earliest film projections, amidst a host of other visual attractions, film screenings started to develop their own distinct conventions with the success of the nickelodeon and its non-stop projection of short films.

Zielinski is currently expanding on his concept of variantology in the 'deep strata between art, science and technology' (2005). Beyond its obvious association with the variety theatre and with the musical praxis of the variation and difference in interpretation, variantology refers further back to the era 'before their categorical split from the performing and fine arts' (ibid. 10). Zielinski notes that since classical antiquity and even before – in Byzantine, Arabic and Chinese civilizations – there have been both artistic and scientific praxes of technical experimentation realized with and through media that form relevant case studies of contextualizing the hybrid origins and development of media applications. Before their categorical split from the performing and the fine arts, generations of philosophers, medical doctors, engineers, physiologists and mathematicians were using all sorts of audio-visual contraptions to develop and then manifest their insights.

Maire is not so much a historian who recuperates prototypes from the past but someone who conceives his own variations. The agenda of Zielinski is just as contemporary: 'Cultivating dramaturgies of difference is an effective remedy against the increasing ergonomization of the technical media worlds that is taking place under the banner of ostensible linear progress' (Zielinski 2006: 259). The investigation of ergonomization is intrinsically aimed at economic profit. Besides the illusion of a controlled speed of rotation in his performance *Double Face/Two-Faced* (1999-2000), several other works by Maire present coins. These *trompe l'oeil* studies in anamorphosis question perspective, trace, presence, seriality. For his *Pièces de monnaie* (1997), Maire has made a series of fifty twenty-centime coins, perfect copies of real coins, but in perspective. Laid out on five trays, they describe different stages of the rotation of a coin in space or at different distances. For example, one coin gradually shrinks to become tiny. Maire also makes rubbings of his coins on A4 paper, combining a forged perspective view with a sculptural consistency, thus causing puzzlement in the spectator by being both true and impossible.

Fig. 12

*Pièces de monnaie* rubbings

© Julien Maire, 1997.

From his earliest works onwards, Maire has kept on reminding us, as Pingree and Gitelman write, that all media were once 'new media':

> There is a moment, before the material means and the conceptual modes of new media have become fixed, when such media are not yet accepted as natural, when their own meanings are in flux. At such a moment, we might say that new media briefly acknowledge and question the mythic character and ritualised conventions of existing media, while they are themselves defined within a perceptual and semiotic economy that they then help to transform. (2003: xii)

When successful, each new medium helps to produce a distinct audience. As Jonathan Crary describes, each technology always brings along a set of rules to observe: 'Vision and its effects are always inseparable from the possibilities of an observing subject who is both the historical product *and* the site of certain practices, techniques, institutions, and procedures of subjectification' (1990: 5). In Crary's terms, an observer is more than a spectator, it is someone who unconsciously confirms his actions, complies with what he sees and observes certain rules. As an engineer of hybridity, conceiving impractical prototypes and contradictory contraptions, Julien Maire purposefully produces a set of paradoxes: between old and new media, between absolute control and total freedom of the viewer, between the machine and the image as the centre of our attention. He allows us to become conscious contributors, experiencing, exploring and completing mediated images with our own memory and subjectivity.

**Edwin Carels** (1964) is a researcher in the arts at the Faculty of Fine Arts of University College Ghent. Carels is also a programmer and curator for the International Film Festival of Rotterdam and for the Museum of Contemporary Art in Antwerp, where he has curated thematic shows such as *Animism, The Projection Project* and *Graphology*. He has developed solo exhibitions about and with Chris Marker, Zoe Beloff, Robert Breer, Quay Brothers and Julien Maire, among others.

**NOTES**

1  A selective overview of the work of Julien Maire can be found on his website, containing text and illustrations to all works cited in this paper: <http://julienmaire.ideenshop.net/>

2  From a conversation with the author.

**REFERENCES**

Banta, M., *Taylored Lives*. Chicago, 1993.

Benjamin, W., 'A Small History of Photography'. In: *One Way Street*. London, 1979.

Benjamin, W., 'Das Kunstwerk im Zeitalter seiner technischen Reproduzierbarkeit'. In: *Walter Benjamin. Schriften*. Band I, herausgegeben von Theodor W. Adorno. Frankfurt am Main, 1955.

Bergson, H., *The Creative Mind*. New York, 2002.

–. 'L'illusion cinématographique'. In: *Creative Evolution* [L'évolution créatrice, 1907]. Trans. A. Mitchell, ed. K. Ansell Pearson, M. Kolkman, and M. Vaughan. Basingstoke, 2007.

Bleeker, M., *Anatomy Live*. Amsterdam, 2008.

Broeckmann, A., 'Exploding Camera'. Exhibition text. Berlin, 2007.

Bolter, J. D. and R. Grusin, *Remediation*. Cambridge, 2000.

Crary, J., *Techniques of the Observer. On Vision and Modernity in the Nineteenth Century*. Cambridge, 1990.

D'Alonzo, C., 'Julien Maire, Leonardo and the Visual Anatomy'. In: *Digimag* 37. s.l., 2008. Web. <http://www.digicult.it/digimag/article.asp?id=1288>

Druckrey, T., 'Julien Maire's Imaginary Archeologies'. In: J. Shaw and P. Weibel (eds.), *Future Cinema*. Cambridge, 2003.

Elsaesser, T., 'Truth or Dare. Reality Checks on Indexicality, or the Future of Illusion'. In: A. Koivunnen and A. Soderbergh-Widding (eds.), *Cinema Studies into Visual Theory?* Turku, 1999.

Gidal, P., *Structural Film Anthology*. London, 1976.

Gitelman, L. and G. B. Pingree (eds.), *New Media 1740-1915*. Cambridge, 2003.

Gunning, T., 'What's the Point of an Index? Or, Faking Photographs'. In: U. Carlsson (ed.), *The 16th Nordic Conference on Media and Communication Research*. Special issue of *Nordicom Review*, 1-2, p. 39-49. Göteborg, 2004.

Kittler, F., *Optical Media*. Cambridge, 2010.

–. *Gramophone, Film, Typewriter*. Palo Alto, 1999.

McLuhan, M., *Understanding Media*. Cambridge, 1994.

Mitchell, W. J., *The Reconfigured Eye*. Cambridge, 1992.

Olsson, J. and J. Fullerton (eds.), *Allegories of Communication*. Eastleigh, 2004.

Strauven, W., *The Cinema of Attractions Reloaded*. Amsterdam, 2006.

Zielinski, S., *Deep Time of the Media*. Cambridge, 2006.

–. *Variantology 1*. Köln, 2005.

# The Theatre of Recorded Sound and Film

## Vacating Performance in Michael Curran's
## *Look What They Done To My Song*

Marco Pustianaz

## Theatre and the Installation of Media

Fig. 1    View of the installation © Matthew Tickle.

The ontology and location of theatre have undergone many strange mutations over time. Its cultural status has also waxed and waned. On the one hand, notions such as theatricality or spectacle, whether intended positively or negatively, have tended to expand theatre beyond the strict confines of the performing arts and have turned it into a globalizing medium, occupying the whole of the social scene. On the other hand, ever since the rise of cinema, television and now digital media, theatre has often been depicted as an increasingly residual form, under siege from newer technologies of representation, as though theatre were, in itself, inherently less technological because of its reliance on the raw materials of human bodies, time and space. As a result, whilst the-atricality has been increasingly influential as a notion in contemporary art practices ever since the 1960s – heralding among other things the performative turn of perfor-mance art, the spatializing turn of installations and the relational turn of participatory art – the traditional boundaries of theatre have appeared to be more permeable and un-stable. All along, theatre appears to have been perennially in crisis, its fragile ontology plunged into the middle of socio-technological revolutions that have deeply affected the definition of all its seemingly 'natural' properties.

In this chapter I address the fraught relationship between theatre and media through the lens of installation art and its performative relation to 'spectatorship'. The notion of extended theatricality is brought back to a particular site and temporal interval (instal-lations are generally ephemeral, like live performance), where the stage is set for other performative presences to act. Under certain circumstances, installations can fore-ground the relationship with media, shown, staged and experienced as a theatre – that is, in a particular mode whereby media are themselves subject to mediation and shown in the midst of mediation. Interpreting the relationship between media and theatre simply as a power struggle between hegemonic and residual forms contributes to a dis-course centred on a confrontation of distinct technologies whose outcome can only be either integration and assimilation, or resistance and refusal. Thus it becomes easy to assume that media inform the new cultural landscape while theatre represents an older paradigm, whose own mutation is induced by the dominant paradigm of mediatiza-tion. It is a narrative that ends up reinforcing the hierarchy between the two as well as their otherness: the mutating agency of media as an external cause and the consequent adaptation by the weaker or residual cultural form as its effect.

For my purposes here, I will take theatre as a mode or condition in which representa-tion itself becomes reflexively mediated for a subject and through a subject, according to what Samuel Weber has termed 'the irreducible opacity' of theatre as a medium (2004).[1] I wish to explore a modality of theatre where media (particularly media record-ings), instead of events, can 'come to pass' before a spectator. In this sense, I do not think the relationship between theatre and media can be treated as an external one, or that the question of the subject's mediation can be left out altogether. Seeking help to complicate our notions of theatre by the detour of mediation – the spectator being the last, or first, of these mediations – I shall revisit a recent installation by Michael Curran, Look What They Done To My Song (2007).[2] As a visitor to the installation, I would like to in-vestigate, three years after the event, its installation of recordings, their reverberations and effects on spectatorship, following their affective trails until now.

The installation process was described in the gallery press sheet as follows:

Three songs were performed and filmed in the exhibition space of Matt's Gallery, creating an open recording session and film set for three days. Through the sub-sequent editing process, the recorded material is subjected to radical temporal shifts through the use of overlays, speeding up, slowing down and repetition.

The installation is made up of two films (one of which is split-screen), a recorded soundscape and the remains of the recording studio, organized in two adjacent spaces separated by a curtain: a vestibule and an inner space. A CD with the final edit of the three songs provides yet another recorded item, a more permanent sound object offered as a gift to the visitor.

*Look What They Done To My Song* is a complex installation of representational media (sound and film recordings of a musical performance) that unsettles the equation of present and liveness by repeatedly staging their relationship, the final time as a palimpsest of traces before a live spectator. By reconnecting the times of the live event, of recording and of spectatorship, Michael Curran's installation constructs a theatre by using those technologies that apparently alienate live performance. Far from being somehow outside mediality, theatre is painstakingly conjured up by the artist out of the recordings and remediations (repeated mediations) of a vacated presence. Each of these creates a posterior effect (an affect) of presence. What defines the singular quality of this theatre of mediation, then, is the effect/affect of 'presentification', the repeated *making of the present* through a series of imagined relationships with past events. Curran represents our own mediated relationship with reality through a legacy of recordings that do not allow for a linear temporality, only for repeated returns. He places us in the middle of them, the 'viewer' being the ultimate medium in installation art (Bishop 2005) as well as its final 'revenant'.[3] Although some forms of mediation are taken to be more technological than others, Curran's theatre suggests that every chain of mediation must ultimately produce and include the mediation of a subject: the subject is installed through mediation while performing a mediated relationship with the real. Subjectivity is a product of mediation.

*Look What They Done To My Song* mirrors this mediated relationship by staging a vacated theatre, a left-over space overlaid by recorded sound, visuals, traces bearing witness to the technology of sound and film recording.[4] The visitor is invited into a theatre of ruins, where a group of musicians and a singer have previously rehearsed, played and recorded behind closed doors three songs chosen by the artist. Grown as a reflection on the power of music, on its transformation and memorialization through recording, the installation addresses temporal, spatial and psychic relations that are also central to any consideration of theatre as a testing ground for the performative constitution of subjectivity. At the same time, the layers of remnants on display (visual, aural, sculptural, technological, textual) allow the spectator/listener to enter a resonant vault that opens up liveness to its ghostly other. Theatre/installation calls into question the boundaries of time and place, and by doing so questions the very definition of performance as posited in a singular 'here and now'.

A subject has entered a theatre, whether or not a performance is actually going on or a living act(or) is presently acting.[5] Through a theatrical mise-en-scène, our relationship with recording technology can be denaturalized, i.e. detached from its claim to reduce everything to the present tense in order to preserve and prolong time. A subject in front of a recording already makes for a ghostly summoning. Mediality is haunted by spectrality. As theatregoers know, there may be no fuller presence than the recording of one, as Samuel Beckett found in *Krapp's Last Tape*.

## Losing Sight of Theatre

Fig. 2    View of the installation © Matthew Tickle.

In response to wide-ranging contemporary approaches that have sought to redefine theatre from the hybridized perspective of intermediality, virtuality and performativity, thus denaturalizing certain of its ontological anchors, my strategy seems to take a slight detour. By exploring the scene of Curran's installation, I am not suggesting ways to accommodate within an expanded definition of 'theatre' the growing artistic practices that actively blur the boundaries between media forms in the context of live performance. In other words, I am not referring to critical discourses that hinge on the post-dramatic turn (Lehmann 2006) or on the complex relationship with the new media increasingly incorporated in theatre practice and critically investigated by theatre and performance studies. Most approaches that have taken up theatre and redefined it in terms of media studies have done so in the belief that, unless it were wrenched away from its ontological opposition to mass-mediatization, it would be doomed to disappearance or to cultural marginality. In the introduction to *Intermediality in Theatre and Performance*, for instance, editors Freda Chapple and Chiel Kattenbelt state that their approach concerns 'the subject of intermediality from the perspective of theatre', taking as their starting point the acknowledgment that 'a significant feature of contemporary theatre is the incorporation of digital technology [...] and the presence of other media within theatre productions' (2006: 11). Whilst situating the notion of intermediality at the crossroads between convergent media practices and discourses, it seems to me that by claiming that 'theatre has become a *hypermedium* and home to all' (ibid. 24), theirs is a perspective that domesticates the space of theatre through a move that helps to revive an integrative concept of theatre as a total art form. The effect is the restitution of theatre to the centre stage of the contemporary media space, even going as far as identifying the two: theatre as 'the stage of intermediality' (ibid. 20).[6]

My detour here will opt for a less situated notion of theatre, a delocalization that issues from a radical non-habitability of 'theatre', either as a discipline, as a home/space (however inclusive and intermediatized) and, ultimately, as a perspective. Precisely by *not* starting from the perspective of theatre one can hope to encounter its othering possibilities, excavated from beyond its ontological edges.[7] We might embrace a more radical transdisciplinarity and question disciplinary spaces by inhabiting them *as if they* were other.

Opening up a term must always entail the risk of losing it, in the unbundling of a certain set of assumed constitutive elements which, through repetition, perform it as an object (if only an object of study). Are there other ways of opening up and losing one's own object? Is it imperative to reconfigure a space for theatre, under whatever new name, invested with whatever degree of amplitude, just to be sure that we know where it is and if we are in it? We might also ask: What is made to stand its ground in the midst of a definitional crisis, whilst some attributes of a term are allowed to fall away? For there is always some residue that is posited as the non-negotiable, without which both term and object would lose consistence, vanish offstage. In order to prevent this, many have posited as the non-negotiable limit of theatre its live element, defined as a relation between time, space and inter-subjectivity: present, presence, representation. According to this view, failing these, theatre would become invisible, unlocatable: it would disappear. Assessing the failure of theatre to become – or remain – theatre, is harder than it seems, though: it is never a single failure, involving as it does, in its disappearing act, each and every multiple and potential failure: of the present, of presence, of representation. Each of those terms is historically and culturally contested; in fact, the renewed and always different failures enacted within and between those terms prove that, far from marking the disappearance of theatre, they have paradoxically marked its reiterated survival. Since theatre can fail and will fail, in any number of ways, and since it can disappear and will repeatedly disappear no matter how we try to save it through remediations or hypermediations, it makes sense to unground it carefully and differently, to test its survival, or revival,[8] beyond the locations where it has stood its ground, even beyond the (un)founding terms of its conventional liveness. Because liveness is never a given, is always bio-political. Present, presence and representation, then, will no longer function as those terms whose conjunction makes theatre possible, but as those whose inherent instability allows for altogether different scenes to emerge.[9]

These issues particularly resonate with Curran's work, because its centre is a 'secret' live performance, occluded from our view, yet at the same time recorded as two *separate* memorial objects (a film and a CD). The 'loss' of the event is artificially sustained, even lovingly crafted. Whereas many installation works present 'leftovers from the aftermath of an opening event' (Bishop 2004: 55), the crucial difference is that the opening event here is not shared. It is a private music session staged by the artist and exposed to his own will to remember, and dismember, the affective core of the live event. Liveness is here preserved through a paradoxical use of the recording technology coupled with editing: a process of selection that mimics the work of the subconscious through condensation, dislocation, secondary revision. If theatre has been characterized by the co-presence of performer and audience, this installation experiments with a co-presence where the performers have not just abandoned the stage but recorded on the verge of appearance and disappearance. Unlike the more generalized theatricality of installation art, then, Curran's can be defined as theatrical in virtue of its affective and contagious sustainment of the event's temporary liveness through a panoply of recordings. It is not simply loss but our relationship with loss that furthers an endless series of recordings.

In the field of performance and media studies, the debate around liveness has often centred on the controversial role played by reproduction and representation in saving and memorializing the live event. Influenced by recorded sound theorists such as Steve Wurtzler, Auslander has contested the binary between the live and the recorded (Wurtzler 1992; Auslander 1999). Liveness is a concept that is historically contingent, and is furthermore dependent on experiences of the mediatized. As Auslander puts it:

> ...historically, the live is actually an effect of mediatization, not the other way around. It was the development of recording technologies that made it possible to perceive existing representations as 'live'. Prior to the advent of those technologies (e.g., sound recording and motion pictures), there was no such thing as 'live' performance, for that category has meaning only in relation to an opposing possibility. (1999: 56)

Look What They Done To My Song pursues a slightly different tack. It is not content to have done with the 'live' as a technological and ideological effect; it cultivates modes of relationship that cling to the 'live' by holding on to its peripheries, at the points of attachment with subjectivity. Recording technologies are shown as vehicles of transmission, even though the content of the recorded has already missed the point. This is what Auslander's quote does not acknowledge in its rather mechanical deconstructive reversal of priorities (the 'live' emerging after recording). If contemporary 'liveness' is indeed an effect of mediatization and the notion of presence is already fractured by the recording of presence, the resulting spectral present opens up a scene of mediated interpellation for the subject. This means we must be prepared to dislocate the visible staging of theatre, to desynchronize the multiple operations of its mediatizations: in short, we must conjure up theatre as a technology of disappearance and presentification, a technology less defined in terms of media than in terms of the subjective experience of mediation, a flickering scene where a subject is caught in the ever-so-slight delay of time and space that installs representation.

In this way it is possible to visit Michael Curran's installation *sub specie theatri*, a scene intentionally staged and rehearsed for its evacuation and subsequent re-installation. The mise-en-scène of the loss of the original performance (the live music session) is produced through the excess of recorded simulacra and a scenography of inscriptions, traces, material residues. Nostalgia is hinted at in the title's plaintive tone, *Look What They Done To My Song*, stringing together film and video ('look'), sound ('my song') and audiovisual recording technologies ('what they done'). On the other hand, nostalgia ceases to be a private, incommunicable affect once its impossible return is staged as a scene of transformation, trauma, mediation. It is, indeed, a theatre that has lost its 'original performers'.[10] The only one left to take over their exhausted roles, caught out in the split terrain of a vestibule and a gallery – a lobby and a theatre – is the belated spectator/listener, a witness *après coup*, left to wander in a theatre of media and representations whose temporality is literally *asynchronous*.

## A Drama of Representation: Sound

Fig. 3    The audio recording session © Matthew Tickle.

The previous notes on the delocalization of theatre call for a somewhat different attention and a certain disruption of the perceptual hierarchies that allow us to see theatre wherever it is given to be seen. As a specific 'distribution of the sensible', visuality hinders other visualizations.[11] If visuality is said to be of the present and in the present tense, paying attention to the auditory field contributes to a paradigm shift that also affects how we visualize space. As Steven Connor writes, 'the most important distinguishing feature of auditory experience' is 'its capacity to disintegrate and reconfigure space' (2004b: 56). A similar capacity would suggest the possibility that the auditory 'disintegration and reconfiguration of space' might serve to overlay another mode of perception, simultaneous yet dissonant with the space of the visual. It is a supplement that does not simply enhance perception.[12] Through the auditory experience of the soundscape, the visitor of Curran's installation may be able to see as sound what is proved absent by sight. Relocated in the vault of the soundscape, sight may see double – an *oversight* – and create a perception of presence that is 'visibly' not of the present.[13] Such presence(s) can only be cryptic, hidden within one another.

I want to give in to this double habitation of time. For this reason I start by listening to the soundscape, in the inner space of the gallery, even though this means that the account of my visit will be in reverse, retrospective like my writing. The soundscape provides an experience that resembles full presence, as if, by way of contrast with the visually evident evacuation of the gallery, it could neutralize its sense of loss with a fantasy of absorption, with a direct access to an experience I have been denied. What holds me a long time within the space of the installation is less the archaeological nature of the place, its ruinous visuality, than the lingering resonance of the soundscape, which feels aurally 'real'. Thanks to this auditory layer – added later, as a recollection – the vacated scene fakes a fullness that eerily contrasts with its evident visual referent. Through the later, un-original installation of the soundscape, Curran generates a further site within the womb of the former, an enfolded, spectral site where past performance is encountered as a fragmentary sound loop, right in the wasteland of its previous shell. The sound loop makes me walk round the gallery, in circles. I start writing in the disjunction between the auditory and the visual theatre – the one resounding, the other silent.

In the gallery I walk around recording equipment, a microphone stand on a stage, acoustic screens and foam pads, pinboards (with jottings, photographs, paper clippings, installation plans), as well as wall drawings, a Dansette record player and a pile of records in a corner. All visual vestiges are part of the enveloping scenography which Curran set up for the original session, with the additional framing provided by Louisa Minkin's wall drawings: classical figures referring back in time to tales of the ambivalent power of sound, to the myths of Orpheus, Pan, Marsyas, Scylla. The visual scenography, it is to be noted, *preceded* the music session and its recordings; during the course of the session it could be seen scattered all over, around the musicians and the technical crew, sometimes hidden in unpredictable corners. The drawings, together with the pinboard materials, were able to create an allusive immersive theatre for the musicians, setting up a web of references that entangled Curran's performers in a larger scenario and in a wider time span. This earlier installation served as a set, turning the performers into film actors, a live film being recorded in one take. The fictionalized setting and the liveness of the recording, typical of *cinéma vérité*, coincidentally collapse record and performance, recording as performance.[14] The same theatre, once more restaged, would host the later wandering visitors. The installation, therefore, has been installed twice, the first time for the rehearsal and recording session, a second time for us, with the session itself incorporated as recorded material within the initial installation.

The memorial space of the gallery is filled with a twelve-minute loop in Sensesurround, a dense auditory field, whose vocal and noise ambient sound has been put in place to haunt the original scene. Its density is not just a question of syncopation and temporal shifts. The soundscape has also attracted odd fragments of sound that bear no relation to the time of the recording session, for example Curran's murmuring thoughts on his work, or the sound of the staple gun hitting the surface of the acoustic screens during the building phase. These heterogeneous sources find their way into the sound mix even though their inclusion might be considered improper. Having read in the info sheet provided at the entrance that a performance has happened right in the gallery, the visitor is led to link the soundscape to the visual remains as though they belonged to each other, sharing one single origin. Together with the two film edits in the lobby, one could then be tempted to reassemble all the scattered evidence in order to reconstruct the imaginary fullness of an original event. Curran's installation would become the scene of a *documentation*, whose mediality, staged as the site of a coming together of every recording, might hail the imaginary return to the performing theatre. Yet, time and again, the installation prevents a return to the uniqueness of the performing event. The installation is not a puzzle: there is nothing to be saved in the end, only expenditure.

By focusing on the editing of recorded sound for the soundscape, I would like to show how Curran stages a confrontation between media technologies in order to provoke a 'crisis, or drama, of representation'.[15] One drama of representation is acted out from a distance by the soundscape and the CD, belonging to the two adjoining and separate spaces of the vestibule and the gallery. They are teasingly separated by a curtain, through which we have to step as we pass from the film/video parlour (the lobby) into the vacated theatre (the gallery). This particular display foregrounds three different notions of sound recording, which Steve Wurtzler has situated historically. There is recording conceived as: a) 'the documentation of a pre-existing event'; b) 'the construction of an event'; and c) 'the dismantling of any sense of an original event and the creation instead of a copy for which no original exists' (Wurtzler 1992: 93). Compared to the CD – a realist object (a) created out of a constructed event (b) – the nature of the soundscape seems to fit into the third type mentioned by Wurtzler. Coinciding with no single event-time, the audio edit is dramatically returned to the space of its actual recording, as an echo belonging and not belonging to it. We might call Curran's audio vault a 'mnemonic space', a composite of presence and absence that resonates with the wider crisis of temporality in postmodernity (Huyssen 1995).

Despite the claims that sound recording provides an immediate access to an original, its temporality is all but unified and complicates the binary opposition between live and recorded sound, when the latter is understood as original versus copy. Writing on the notion of the 'original sound event', James Lastra has argued that the latter is always dependent on iterability, similar to the Derridean notion of a sign as signature/event

(1992). Similarly, the original sound event is both present and absent in the installed soundscape. The loop I am listening to (a hybrid also because it is a compound of analogue and digital technology) is no longer a recording of any original. It produces a new site, a cryptic reverberation of the space in which it was recorded: a para-site. Site (the visual given) and para-site (the aural evocation) bounce off each other; their dissonant vibration engenders a spacing ready for the installation of a subject who is him/herself a parasite, a witness come too late upon the scene: for whom a scene is carved out in that disjunction, occasioned by his/her lateness, between a seeing and a listening that cannot be synchronized.

It is worth remarking that, instead of this hybrid para-site, another strategy might have been available. For instance, a selection of unedited sound sources might have been mimetically returned to the gallery as a kind of restored 'original'. However, the raw sound material was handed over by Curran to his sound recordist, Derek O'Sullivan, as a source for a new supplement, a new 'cover'. Unlike a faithful reproduction, recorded sound plays here as a further resonance, a phantom reverb compiled out of different times, not necessarily from the three-day recording session, as we have seen. It might be called a 'timeful sound' (Ihde 2007), exceeding the notion of single event.[16] This later sound brings about the dispersal of the original, held and lost at the same time.

Now that the installation has been dismantled – like the performance that was hosted in it – the visitor holding the CD owns a sound object whose meaning is likely to have changed dramatically because of its retrospective relationship with the various audio recordings he or she has met earlier on, including the audio of the film edits. This final translation into the reproducible medium of the CD can be seen as the concluding act of the installation, the last scene in the crisis of representation enacted by Curran's theatre. It is a listening scene that can only take place after leaving the installation, an off-scene. Coming after the liveness of the soundscape, it is ironical that the permanence of the CD is such an inadequate token to compensate a loss. On the other hand, it is this feeling that proves that I have performed an act of memorialization for a performance whose original I cannot possibly remember and whose prior 'originals' (the three songs that were covered) I had never heard before.[17] I have come to mourn a loss that is not mine.

On the CD, soprano singer and trained actress Sarah Redmond sings Melanie Safka's 'What Have They Done To My Song, Ma?' (1970):

look what they done to my song ma
look what they done to my song
well it's the only thing
that I could do half right
and it's turning out all wrong ma
look what they done to my brain ma
look what they done to my song ma
well they tied it up in a plastic bag

According to Curran, the lyric is 'a lament [...] against the requirements of representation, mediatization and commercialization',[18] an angry response to the recording demands made by the singer's record label. On listening to the complete song for the first time (the edited recordings of the installation had only afforded me snatches, loops, fragments of rehearsals), the lyrics belatedly cast an entirely different light on the installation. Instead of being a final resting place – the entombment of the event – the CD retrospectively compels yet another return to the scene. It is as if the soundscape of the gallery had now become *my* original. The CD can only sound as a poor representation of the sonorous envelope that held me captive. Even the distinction between representation and reproduction is shaken. As Rick Altman notes, every sound recording is more a *representation* than a *reproduction*, even though its purpose is to create an illusion of presence. Every sound recording is an iteration that cannot help adding its own dissonance, doubling with its own spatial and temporal signature as both representation and event: 'Recorded sound [...] always carries some record of the recording process' (Altman 1992: 26). Embedded in a chain of deferred representations, relayed through alternations of presence and absence, the heterogeneous sound I have been listening to does not cease to reverberate, back and forth. On the one hand, it is pointing towards my posthumous listening of the CD; on the other, it is filling the empty vaults of the once-again vacated theatre with the imaginary memory of an original time and place.

## A Drama of Representation: Sight

Fig. 4    View of the installation © Matthew Tickle.

In the inner vault filled by the soundscape, the subject – or rather, the subjects (the spectating[19] and the listening subject) – are at odds, given the absence of a predetermined perspective to guide us. The space is visually scattered, clustering in stations that I explore for clues, round and round. My experience of circularity is probably induced by the sonic articulation of the loop rather than by the spatial disposition that lets my gaze wander. Acoustical events are always inevitably spatializing (Kolesch & Krämer 2006: 7-15).[20] The auditory experience of absorption has often been called 'oceanic' because its pleasure enacts the fantasy of a crossing of thresholds, a retrospective representation of a primary experience – the murmuring house of the womb – inaccessible by definition (Schwartz 1997: 8). As a consequence, the reverberation of the loop seems to lend the auditory theatre a circular shape, a cave or a womb where the subject undergoes an immersive experience, partly losing him/herself. As a loop, though, it is also a shape of time, a fragment standing still, the shape of the past.[21] The immersive feeling of absorption, then, is repeated, i.e. interrupted. What happens to spectating under these circumstances? How can I inhabit the gap between what I hear and what I see? Even though the subject here may try to match listening and seeing, thus attempting to overcome the split, the fact that the loop temporally conspires to refute and withhold the present makes what he or she sees asynchronous, anachronistic. The vacated scene 'proves' that one is clearly seeing in the present (the present as what is left of the past); the vacated scene also 'proves' that one is clearly glimpsing into the past (the past as ruin). Therefore the very condition enabling us to inhabit this scene as a theatre is no less than the repeated installation of delays and fractures having to do with time, space and representation.

So far I have tried to show how listening and seeing are constructed in the fissured space of the inner theatre, which I have called 'auditory' mainly on account of the dominant fullness of its soundscape, even though the prevalent performance by the visitor will be that of an inconclusive *looking on*, i.e. of spectating. In order to apprehend the full effect of the installation, it is necessary for the subject to accept that immersion and integration belong to the imaginary scene he or she is performing rather than to the theatre which is hosting it. The theatre of recording, then, cryptically holds within itself what is in effect a theatre of the subject. Curran's theatre works resolutely against the spectacle. Spectacle commands the attention of the spectator by forging an imaginary seamless space of the image, capable of integrating the viewer into its own powerful and wondrous unity. This kind of spectatorship collapses the perception of a distance in space between spectacle and spectator, so that the latter's capture seems immediate (i.e. unmediated) and immediate (i.e. simultaneous).[22] In contrast with such a conflation of the intervals of time and space, the disposition of Curran's installation repeatedly marks and performs spatio-temporal intervals, so that spectacle never comes to fruition. In its place, subjectivity is endlessly mediated to itself: it sees itself not captured, but refracted (like a particle of sound, like a recording of a recording).

The spacing that hosts the appearance of the subject as mediated is also performed, or refracted, by the architecture. There is, to start with, the material division between vestibule and gallery enacted by a curtain. It entails a compulsory spatial itinerary, since the vestibule is the passage I have to cross before stepping through the curtain, a membrane of permeability. A series of tremblings transmit themselves through this membrane: an earlier trembling in the inner theatre – an effect of the emotional saturation of live recording given the demanding conditions imposed by the artist; a perceptual trembling experienced by the visitor confronted with a depletion of sight and a sonic dominance.[23]

The audiovisual disjunction of the inner theatre reverberates through the whole architecture of the installation, particularly in the differential between outer space and inner space. This is one reason why Curran's installation cannot be entirely consumed, nor does it allow the subject a resting place. With the curtain as a membranous separation, the whole theatre flutters inwards and outwards like a movable threshold, a *limen* repeatedly crossed by treading and passage.[24] Vestibular spaces like this one are always crossed doubly, *proteron-hysteron*. Like other vestibular spaces, this one, too, is likely to be neglected. The visitor will probably dismiss this space as a mere prologue to the installation, something that is *not yet* the installation proper. Whether as appendix, supplement or para-site, the vestibule and the disposition of its audiovisual materials crucially question notions of priority and context. As a preliminary to the installation, the vestibule naturally points *forward* to the theatre inside; the inner theatre, in turn, refers *back* to the vestibule as a promise of explication because of its own failure to unify a single place or time. Hence, the deferral of signification (instanced by the delay of the record) may be the most significant performative core of the installation: an excessively empty core.

In contrast with the auditory theatre inside, the vestibular space introduces itself as an essentially visual parlour. But where does one look? If I watch the film on the bigger screen, I cannot see the other one playing higher up on a monitor behind my back. This smaller monitor is playing a different edit, in split screen, generically referring to the same music session. The visual segregation produced by the two monitors is overruled by an auditory overspill: although I can only watch either one edit or the other, I cannot help hearing both. Each screen not only has its own soundtrack but is also punctured by the other at its back, same and different because of the shared references. The competing array of recordings creates a disjunctive perceptual field that is hard to name: no longer simply audiovisual, it is a ground where audio and visual are opened up within themselves, a terrain of multiple splittings brimming with redundancy and loss. I sympathize whit those who quickly pass through. This is a space of non-identity, where none of the audio/visual objects can hold us in place. The aural overlay from the two films doubtlessly deepens the space of the vestibule, but it does so by integrating and disintegrating.

Seen from the lobby, the voyage towards the centre of the installation is a regression that, starting from the vestiges of film recordings, moves back in time and space to the original vault of performance. However, the non-unified signs of the recorded performance are evidence that the space waiting for us on the other side must be empty by now: something had to disappear and pass away in order to reappear as a record.[25] If that is so, the space of the vestibule will have been the only space capable of propping the fiction of a performance: its necessary delayed supplement. Meanwhile, in the transitional space of the lobby, I am waiting for something that has already happened. The business of looking and hearing will have no end: the two films are loops.

## Splittings

Fig. 5    The filming session © Matthew Tickle.

The use of video and film in artists' cinema has often investigated the relationship between the 'in-frame' and the 'out-of-frame' and paid attention to the gallery space, which represents the outer frame within which the frame of the screen operates (Connolly 2009). Installations allow a particular reflexivity as to where cinema 'takes place', engaging any number of relationships with: a) the location of the visiting spectator (him/herself a passer-by); b) the centripetal or centrifugal movement of the images on screen; and c) the constellation of other sensory objects (including other screens and monitors) sharing the space. Film and video are thus relocated in settings that foreground the activity of spectatorship; at the same time they make us aware that there is no longer a single, 'natural' place for the screen or the monitor.

In this case, the doubling of monitors is the signal of a wider web of duplicities (of which audio/visuality is patently one), whose prevailing relation is never one of mechanical opposition or negation. On the one hand, the nearly symmetrical positioning of the two monitors produces a splitting of the visual field: two opposite aesthetical approaches face each other in the shape of a confrontation between a flat screen with a single image and a monitor with a divided screen. On the other hand, the two screens are placed like two mirrors 'looking' at each other. The splitting is actualized only when a spectator enters who, interjecting between the screens, will inevitably blot out either of them by performing the pivotal act of turning/not turning. With this insertion, the audio-visual medium of film is itself subjected to mediation, thereby making visible what would be left transparent: the middle space where the spectating subject is inserted. The median space is possible because two films have been installed instead of one, an excessive liberality that makes room for a theatre of film. Mediality is shown here as an ever-present virtuality, internalized through an act of mediation (the insertion of the spectator) that comes between a specular film. A theatre is opened up where there was none: an 'intra-mediality' (an internalized mediality) that suspends the automatic operation of the medium.

What is shown by one film will not remain the same once the film becomes two. Neither film is whole *without* the other, neither is whole *because of* the other. The more obvious decision would be to give precedence to the larger screen, as it is the one showing the 'primary'[26] film: firstly, because it is more prominently in view, secondly, because it shows itself as undivided, a visual equivalent of the immersive lure of the soundscape. Yet this 'natural' hierarchy is questionable because the split-screen structure of the 'ancillary' film is fully consistent with the performative strategy of *Look What They Done To My Song*. Moreover, its inconspicuous placement can be reversed into a commanding position; possibly referencing the pervasive, though often hidden, presence of surveillance cameras, the monitor's gaze – spying over us from the back – casts a kind of critical and controlling look over our spectatorship (as long as we are blind to it, of course).

The split-screen film consists of short fragments fading out into black frames. It shows the early preparatory stages of the recording space: early talks about the project; the artist investigating the empty space, marking it, testing it; the camera crew moving equipment; a red sign warning of a 'Recording in progress'; a spotlight on an empty chair, etc. The video highlights the apparatus of film production and reminds us that there is always another side, the backside, to the haunting. Behind our backs the installation exposes itself, busy at work around what is still largely a blank canvas. Through the choice of its source material, this film 'at the back' carries out an explicitly metafilmic approach; it also elicits a remarkable expansion in the timeframe of the performance thanks to the addition of outtakes from the whole three-month preparatory period. Whilst the film 'in front' is engaged in creating counterpoint and flow by closely investigating the affective dynamics of the rehearsal session, the split screen chooses to problematize the external boundaries of a performance, what precedes it, the time(s) of its inception.

Its split bar enacts difference by way of vibration, as rhythm; the two halves become permeable visual channels, playing on contrast, repetition, migration, association. Once again, like the curtain, the splitting turns into a space of passage, in this case a dynamics of visual signs. As Curran notes, 'a strange call and response seems to evolve between all the different modes of production taking place. [...] The use of the split screen allows ideas of progression, movement and momentum to be potentially undone or problematized by the action and sound beside it'.[27] This is evident when the splitting of this screen spreads to the establishing shot of the other[28], which shows the pianist Nicholas Bloomfield patiently waiting for the technicians to finish setting up their cables. The shot is framed so that his image is exactly mirrored by the reflecting surface of the shiny black lid of his baby grand. While the technical setup for the recording goes on in full view of the camera, the mirror reflection bisects the frame along the diagonal, so that the single-screen film itself begins with an inner splitting. Specularity is shown here as another instance of splitting.

Meanwhile, another significant split is at work between audio and video. In the flat screen film, audio and video are most of the time de-linked, de-synchronized. I see the pianist sitting still while the notes he has just played or is about to play are heard. What I see could be him listening to his own playing, either before or after he has done so.[29] His anachronistic listening might be called my own: the disjunction between seeing and hearing generates an in-between, where not only the pianist's listening and playing selves fail to coincide but my own listening and viewing selves part ways, too. The film plunges the viewer, and the listener, into anachronism, into the time of untimeliness. From the temporal dislocation introduced by the asynchronous editing, waiting moments have sprung up that were not there. Critically, and affectively, these are intervals where reflection can enter.[30]

Such disconnections and hesitations are plentiful in the film. The use of non-synchronization questions the spectator's realist expectations and experiments with other temporalities excavated within the frame of performance time.[31] Such temporalities are non-linear, imaginary, circular, slowed down, fashioned in the folds of linear time. Instead of documenting the recording session of the three songs, the single-screen edit deconstructs the sequential time of the rehearsal, freely moving backwards and forwards in time to construct the filmic equivalent of the experience of *being in performance*. As a result, the sequences documenting real-time snatches of jamming and rehearsal are remarkably rare; more often we find ourselves following the slow flow of circular shots lingering over expressions of concentration, ecstasy, release, languor, tenseness in the performers. Moments of actual playing are shown alongside moments of preparation and introspection: the eruption of music can only be sensed in the intervals of time, in the exploratory repetitions of rehearsal.

The hesitant temporality of the editing subverts the linearity of recording. Curran's montage brings about the suspended narrative of an event that is about to happen, despite the fact that we 'know' it has happened (only because it was recorded, that is). This un-happened, or virtual happening, is all that can be glimpsed in the energy surfacing in the musicians' bodies, who are shown as charged, moved, possessed, expectant, listening attentively. Slumped on the floor, with their eyes closed, twitching, smiling, the performers undergo a transformation, manifesting itself in certain body parts (hence the close-up details), a transcendence, which, in order to be filmed, must be theatricalized. This is why the recording session is staged like a ritual (a holy masquerade, a 'drag show'), fictionalizing its own construction as a theatre of performance. We are shown, for instance, the performers dressed up, a musician receiving his make-up (only to be strikingly unmasked), the band who played *How Does It Feel To Feel* posing for the final group portrait. Curran's film, like a musical trailer perversely withholding its song, defers the event allegedly to be recorded, choosing instead to focus on the rituals of foreplay, the 'peri-performative' (Sedgwick 2003), rather than the fully-fledged, spectacularized performance. Another boundary, the uncertain *limen* between performing and rehearsing performance, trembles and stutters, made visible by the calculated dis-appearance of the performance, edited out of sight.

## On Record

Fig. 6    The audio CD and the film reels © Matthew Tickle.

As we have seen, *Look What They Done To My Song* is a space that contains and displays memory traces of an event. These traces are not just the residues and remnants of a vacated performance (e.g. an abandoned set) but a spatial configuration or ordering that includes a variety of recordings, all of them edited and extensively reworked. None of these recordings, though, function here as a replacement for the lost event. The record (what has been recorded) is folded back into the vault that originated it, alongside the technical apparatus of its own production (a lone microphone, headsets left on the floor, a mixer placed on a long desk). The temporal experience of this installation, then, is dominated by the asynchronous simultaneity of different layers of recorded strata. The archaeology of this site does not differentiate between record as legacy and record as remnant. In other words, the logic of recording, projected towards a futurity, is stalled by a counter-movement that insists on a scene, again and again, in order to throw it back to the recordings that preceded it.

There is a compulsion to repeat, evidenced for instance by the sound loop and the film loops. The loop, of course, is nothing else than a recording that will not let go, that circles back to find itself again and again. The effect of presence that I experience is affectively produced by the insistence of this desire. Essentially, my own investment in this presence is radically forgetful of the performance that Curran purports to memorialize, whilst in effect refraining from reproducing it. Witness the inconclusiveness of the 'documentary' film, mythologizing rather than historicizing the music session. Recording is displayed in this installation as a medium, which, because it so insistently misses the object, cannot help but falling back on the subject, producing and reproducing it in that gap. By means of the recording performance, the record comes to pass in the guise of an impelling affect rather than as an achieved object of desire. As such, it can only be staged as a repetition in the space and time of longing. The disappearing act of performance is reframed, after the event, as the persisting effect of a recording apparatus which can take many shapes. This array of media, though, can only mediate, i.e. come between what is to be recorded; in so doing, mediality mirrors (re-performs) the separation that propelled the recording performance in the first place.

Installed in this theatre, recording (from the Latin *recordari*: to remember, to bring back to the heart as the seat of memory) is above all a performance of memory rather than a technology of reproduction. Through the record we come face to face with a mirror image of our desire to remember ourselves and the objects of our desire. In this respect, technology's intimation of futurity, which underpins the overwhelming impulse to record and archive ourselves *for the future*, may have nothing to do with a future. The sense of duration that we trust the record will affirm is a duration founded on retrospection. It is therefore retrospectral in that the duration of the live can only be proved through a specular encounter with its ghost. The record is one of those ghosts.

In Curran's case, we are brought into the midst of a theatre of recording to sense that all its instances of recording double back on a previous recording, and so on. The only tangible thing we get in return is a CD, which plays here the part of the surplus, the enigmatic token, the unwanted gift reminding us of what we failed to hear in our visit. The CD will make sure that we will keep on failing. As for our experience inside the installation, the theatre of recording must keep us recording, caught in a desiring catastrophe with no end ahead of itself.

Preserving recording as the insistent desire to hover, circling around one's own objects, or wandering around their vanishing point, we look in vain for our elusive object (each to his or her own, beyond the songs of the performance). This makes me return to the site, recording it in writing, in stolen photos, in passing (performing the installation as passage-work). I make my entrances and my exits, my perambulations, my lookings and my listenings. The recording theatre moves me, keeps me on the move, adding my own recording to the record.

*Past the pinboards on the side wall, I journey to the furthest end, to the corner which is blocked off by a curved wood panel. It allows for a slight gap inside which I peer. I glimpse mirrors and frames, an easel. The hidden mirrors seem to defeat their purpose: is the installation a display or a hiding place? Some mirrors have become screens, others are carefully folded away. Trying to sneak behind the panel I find that I can indeed pass through, hiding myself away, for a while. There I am, recording, recorded.*

Fig. 7
Visiting the hidden nooks of
*Look What They Done To My Song*
© Marco Pustianaz.

**Marco Pustianaz** is Associate Professor of English and Theatre at Università del Piemonte Orientale (Vercelli, Italy). He has published on queer theory, on theatre affects and on performative documentation. Together with Annalisa Sacchi and Giulia Palladini, he curated in 2010 the international conference 'Affective Archives', bringing together artists and performance studies scholars.

**NOTES**

1   Samuel Weber's emphasis on the mediality of theatre is important in arguing that as a medium, it precludes transparency: 'Theater marks the spot where the spot reveals itself to be an ineradicable macula, a stigma or stain that cannot be cleansed or otherwise rendered transparent, diaphanous' (Weber 2004: 7). In his remarkable book, Weber discusses theatricality and its scandal for self-identity through a wide-ranging array of philosophical texts from Plato to Aristotle, Heidegger, Benjamin and Adorno.

2   I am indebted to the artist Michael Curran, who has supported my writing and generously shared a wealth of background information on his artistic process for *Look What They Done To My Song* (Matt's Gallery, London, 19 September - 18 November 2007). I also wish to thank Robin Klassnik of Matt's Gallery for assisting my research on the installation. My article itself was born as a kind of writing installation, merging initial notes taken within the gallery with a later text I delivered as a paper

for the conference 'Theatre Noise. The Sound of Performance' (London, 22-24 April 2009). All these previous writings have been substantially reworked for this essay. On Curran's work, especially on video, see Curran et al. (2003); for a bio and a selection of videoclips, see the artist's page at http://www.luxonline.org.uk/artists/michael_curran/index.html.

3 Claire Bishop is not the only one to have argued that installation art is not medium-specific. The relational turn of installation art (and other contemporary performative and social art forms) necessitates a critical examination of the type of experience it structures for the visitor-performer. I would add that it also requires a spectatorial engagement in the archiving of such an experience. My essay is an attempt in that direction.

4 I have first encountered the term 'vacated performance' in connection with the English performer Rose Finn-Kelcey, who coined it to define some of her own works in the early 1980s.

5 'As regards installation art, the precondition for establishing [the] relationship between the viewer and the work is the theatrical arrangement of the work as an environment into which the viewer must enter' (Petersen 2009: 473). Petersen's alignment of installation with theatre is significant for my reading of Curran's work. For a discussion of the production of meaning in the engaged and bodily relationship between viewer and work, see chapter 6 on 'Installation Art between Image and Stage'. Petersen's book is in Danish, but a summary is provided in English at the end. Cf. also Petersen (2005). Bishop, too, comments on the 'theatrical mise-en-scène' of installations, specifically what she calls 'total installations' structured for an experience of contemplation (Bishop 2004). This is not the case with Curran's work.

6 Though Kattenbelt elsewhere remarks that he no longer speaks of theatre and media but only of media (Kattenbelt 2008: 21). In this later introduction to 'Intermediality in Theatre and Performance', he prefers to emphasize the co-relation of media within a media ecology in which it is harder to speak of the ontology of individual media.

7 I am indebted to Mark Wigley's commentary on Derrida's strategy of deconstructing space (Wigley 1993). Derrida's figural poetics of the crypt or vault as an aurally resonating space linked with the spectral duplicity of difference has inflected my own writing on Curran's installation. See Pustianaz (2009) for a starting exploration of some interstices glimpsed in the pauses of theatre and in spectatorial documentation. I have also been influenced by Rebecca Schneider's critique of the oculocentric regime of theatron (Schneider 2000). The field of performance studies has long dealt with the affective, temporal and site-specific dynamics of audience relationality. On installation art as a performative arrangement of 'sets', see Bishop (2005). The term 'relational art' has been proposed by curator and critic Nicolas Bourriaud (Bourriaud 2001). See also Doherty (2004).

8 In 'Teatro superstite' (Pustianaz 2009), I have tried to search for theatre before and

after for its event, as with the series of photographs Empty Stages by Hugo Glendinning and Tim Etchells, or the photographic documentation by Ivan Kralj of his own body after the one-to-one performance Secret Service (2002), by Felix Ruckert dance company. In addition, Doris Salcedo's installation Shibboleth (2007-2008) at the Tate Modern suggested the exploration of that relational installation (another resonant vault) where the visitors tentatively and playfully performed the huge space fissured by a seismic cut on the floor. In this case, what moved me to writing was the collective act of recording by a large number of spectators – a reflexive archive of the visitors' own performances in the installation.

9   The conference on 'Theatre Noise' in London (22-24 April 2009) has shown how the debates around sound practice, recording and representation, sound event and so on are now investing the field of theatre studies. On digital virtuality, theatre and performance see Giannachi (2004) and Dixon (2007).

10  There are no original performers. The original performers would be the artists whose songs are covered here. It is not coincidental that repetition is also a way to recover former traces. Recording is a technology of recovery.

11  I am freely borrowing Rancière's term 'partage du sensible' (Rancière 2004). The term 'distribution' (distribution of power, of resources, of means) has a spatial and architectural counterpart in any partition that excludes or any passage that allows flow. It can thus intercept forms of intelligibility, what can be said or recognized as existing. In The Future of the Image (2007), Rancière explicitly contests aesthetic disciplinarity: what is paramount is the aesthetico-political redistribution of the sensible, the change brought about in the representational regimes (here, of image and word).

12  On 'auditory distress' (where the use of sound contrasts or unbalances the experience of sight) as a strategy in contemporary music theatre, see Verstraete (2009).

13  On critical theories focusing on sound to counterbalance and destabilize the primacy of the visual, see Bull and Back (2003), Cox and Warner (2004), Erlmann (2004), Ihde (2007), LaBelle (2006), Schwartz (1997) and Voegelin (2010). Recording plays a central role in many reflections on modernity: cf. Milner (2009), Sterne (2003) and Altman (1992). For a Lacanian reading of recorded sound, 'fidelity' and the desire for coherence in the face of the recording's disruption of the real, see Malsky (2003).

14  On sound recording as sound event, see below. In this sense, recording is not the other of performance: it is another performance, even though it purports to be a simple parasite of the recorded performance.

15  Personal communication with the author.

16  Ihde's phenomenological investigation concentrates on the experience of listening as a temporal span: we do not hear sounds, we hear durations, punctuated by more or less structured rhythms. Because sounds converge and diverge from different sources, the auditory field is always full of temporalities, diverse yet shaping the perception of 'a dance of time'; cf. Ihde 2007: ch.7. Curran's editing, on the other hand, achieves a non-referential fullness of time through a soundscape that merges

different sound events occurring at different times. Its timefulness is a product of sound recording technology.

17 Since the performed songs were themselves covers, the recorded live performance has been made possible by a previous history of recording and commodification. It is the kidnapping of voice of which Melanie Safka sings in the song that gave the title to the installation.

18 Personal communication with the author.

19 Rachel Fensham has suggested speaking of 'watching theatre' in order to move away from notions of spectatorship that emphasize visuality at the expense of other senses and affects (2009). I use the awkward 'spectating' here because of its etymological sense of 'viewing repeatedly' (from the frequentative Latin verb 'spectare'). There is an added connotation of waiting, of expectancy, since there is nothing in the installation that compels watching. Curran's spectator, then, is deprived of any spectacle, if by spectacle is meant an integrative sensory experience. The connection with the spectator theorized by film studies is also relevant, since the spectator here is called upon to perform different acts of looking, including film. In fact, there is no single term that adequately sums up the variously interpellated subject of this installation. Petersen speaks of a 'viewer-performer' (2009: 479).

20 As Verstraete has remarked, sound can also disrupt the sense of place because of its essentially invisible and therefore 'a-topical' character: 'In the theatre, sound can equally intervene and disturb a visual experience in being essentially "invisible" and "a-topical" (placeless), while urging for correspondences to what is seen' (Verstraete 2009: 68).

21 A sound loop can also be seen as a sustained sound that, according to Brewster, becomes 'a spatial thing, a quasi-object/quasi-landscape' (1999: 103). On aural architecture, see Blesser and Salter (2007); for a theatre devoted exclusively to sound sculpture, see the Audium in San Francisco (http://www.audium.org/).

22 Commenting on Aristotle's Poetics, Weber notes that there are different notions of theatre's mediality. The medium of theatre takes place literally as a middle space, 'a spatial interval between two points'. One way of conceiving the medium is that of a bridge, joining through separation: 'The medium is what bridges the distance between the two, between origin and end [...] and thereby allows an indirect contact, a transmission or communication, to take place.' In Aristotle, such a scenic medium must fade into transparency if the plot of drama can emerge. Spectacle, likewise, needs to collapse the middle space of the medium, however slight the interval or spacing might be. In the concluding reflections to his essay 'Spectacle, Attention, Counter-Memory', Jonathan Crary (1989) wonders if the notion of spectacle is still relevant today, when the global system of flows and information is elusive and non-spectacular. On the other hand, the management and distribution of spectacle can also work diffusively, in a scattered web-like manner, which does not mean random.

23 On visual deprivation as enhancement for an acousmatic listening (a listening un-

coupled from sight), see Verstraete (2009: 64-68).

24 For a reading of installation art as passage-work and heterogeneous genre, situated 'between visual arts and something else', see Petersen (2009: 2).

25 Recording technology is no scandal to performance: it may embody the general passing away elsewhere of any theatrical happening. Weber writes: 'such happenings never take place once and for all but are ongoing. This in turn suggests that they can neither be contained within the place where they unfold nor entirely separated from it. They can be said, then, in a quite literal sense, to *come to pass*. They take place, which means in a particular place, and yet simultaneously also *pass away* – not simply to disappear but to happen somewhere *else*' (Weber 2004: 7).

26 The film (described as 'video work') was also shown at Arnolfini Gallery in Bristol (Dark Studio and Reading Room, 17 September 2007 - 6 January 2008).

27 Personal communication with the author.

28 Curran refers to viral metaphors when writing about possession by music and the transmission of a song refrain (2007: 17). In this theatre of recording, though, 'possession' becomes further mediated by a host of mediating objects: among them, recordings, or even their empty shells (the pile of empty vinyl covers on top of the Dansette which used to play them – to the artist, we imagine). Keywords such as possession, influence, infection all mark a contact without touch, or nearly intangible, and the passage of affect through indirect means, mediums or media.

29 This is not just an example of cinematic acousmatization, when a sound or voice is heard while its source is kept hidden from view, but also a desynchronization, which subverts the expected temporal progression. The narrative that I construct in the gap between sound-time and image-time is of course paradoxical and non-linear, like the narrative that I might wish to construct based on the montage of the split screen. The desire for a narrative closure is held at bay by an endless suspension created by waiting intervals, or chiasmic structures – spaces for a shared affect of longing. Michael Curran's videos generally work with fragments, loops and repetition: e.g. *Love in a Cold Climate* (2002, 60 mins).

30 I am using a Deleuzian terminology (from his *Cinema* books) to suggest how the notion of 'interval' is helpful to arrest the flux of the moving image and conceptualize, in the passage between frames (or in the gaps between audio and video), a space for thinking new becomings. The interval is for Deleuze the irreducible space in the cinematic time-image between photograms, shots and sequences that arrest the logical passage from image to image. Curran's montage, along with the sensuous flow and elliptic circularity of the desiring machine of cinema, is no less insistent in its own undercutting the possibility of reaching the object. Therefore, we could say that Curran's film is 'arresting', not in any sensational way, but in an intervallic, Deleuzian, way.

31 Curran's use of film violates both the rules of documentary and those of classic cinema, as recalled by Kaja Silverman: 'Classic cinema's success can be measured by the degree to which it manages to substitute fictional fields for the irretrievably ab-

sent one' (Silverman 1988: 12-13). Curran's filmic material is a surrogate inadequate to this task, revelling in the excess of failure.

## REFERENCES

Altman, R., 'The Material Heterogeneity of Recorded Sound'. In: R. Altman (ed.), *Sound Theory/Sound Practice*. London/New York, 1992.

–. (ed.), *Sound Theory/Sound Practice*. London/New York, 1992.

Auslander, P., *Liveness. Performance in a Mediatized Culture*. London/New York, 1999.

Bishop, C., 'Antagonism and Relational Aesthetics'. In: *October*, 110, p. 51-79. Cambridge, 2004.

–. *Installation Art. A Critical History*. London/New York, 2005.

Blesser, B. and L.-R. Salter, *Spaces Speak, Are You Listening? Experiencing Aural Architecture*. Cambridge, 2007.

Bourriaud, N., *Esthétique relationnelle*. Dijon, 2001.

Brewster, M., 'There or Here?'. In: B. LaBelle and S. Roden (eds.), *Site of Sound. Of Architecture and the Ear*. Los Angeles, 1999.

Bull, M. and L. Back (eds.), *The Auditory Culture Reader*. Oxford, 2003.

Chapple, F. and C. Kattenbelt (eds.), *Intermediality in Theatre and Performance*. Amsterdam, 2006.

Connolly, M., *The Place of Artists' Cinema. Space, Site, and Screen*. Bristol, 2009.

Connor, S., 'Edison's Teeth. Touching Hearing'. In: V. Erlmann (ed.), *Hearing Cultures. Essays on Sound, Listening, and Modernity*. Oxford/New York, 2004.

–. 'Sound and the Self'. In: M. M. Smith (ed.), *Hearing History. A Reader*. Athens, GA, 2004. (abridged, originally 'The Modern Auditory I', 1997).

Cox, C. and D. Warner (eds.), *Audio Culture. Readings in Modern Music*. London/New York, 2004.

Crary, J., 'Spectacle, Attention, Counter-Memory'. In: *October*, 50, p. 97-107. Cambridge, 1989.

Curran, M., *Look What They Done To My Song*. London, 2007. (Print + CD)

–. Collection of writings for the Lux Genealogies series. <http://www.scribd.com/document_collections/2383713>

Curran, M., T. Lyons and J. Mooney, *Michael Curran*. (Minigraph Series). London, 2003.

Dixon, S., *Digital Performance. A History of New Media in Theater, Dance, Performance Art, and Installation*. Cambridge, 2007.

Doherty, C., *Contemporary Art. From Studio to Situation*. London, 2004.

Erlmann, V. (ed.), *Hearing Cultures. Essays on Sound, Listening, and Modernity*. Oxford/New York, 2004.

Fensham, R., *To Watch Theatre. Essays on Genre and Corporeality*. Brussels, 2009.

Giannachi, G., *Virtual Theatres. An Introduction*. London/New York, 2004.

Huyssen, A., *Twilight Memories. Marking Time in a Culture of Amnesia*. London/New York, 1995.

Ihde, D., *Listening and Voice. Phenomenologies of Sound*. Albany, 2007.

Kattenbelt, C., 'Intermediality in Theatre and Performance. Definitions, Perceptions and Medial Relationships'. In: *Cultura, Lenguaje y Representación*, 6, p. 19-29. Castellón, 2008.

Kolesch, D. and S. Krämer (eds.), *Stimmen. Annäherung an ein Phänomen*. Frankfurt, 2006.

LaBelle, B., *Background Noise. Perspectives on Sound Art*. London/New York, 2006.

Lastra, J., 'Reading, Writing, and Representing Sound'. In: R. Altman (ed.), *Sound Theory/Sound Practice*. London/New York, 1992.

Lehmann, H.-T., *Postdramatic Theatre*. London/New York, 2006.

Malsky, M., 'Stretched from Manhattan's Back Alley to MOMA. A Social History of Magnetic Tape and Recording'. In: R. T. A. Lysloff and L. C. Gay (eds.), *Music and Technoculture*. Middletown, 2003.

Milner, G., *Perfecting Sound Forever. An Aural History of Recorded Music*. London, 2009.

Petersen, A. R., 'Between Image and Stage. The Theatricality and Performativity of Installation Art'. In: R. Gade and A. Jerslev (eds.), *Performative Realism. Interdisciplinary Studies in Art and Media*. København, 2005.

–. *Installationskunsten mellem billede og scene*. København, 2009.

Pustianaz, M., 'Teatro superstite'. In: Art'O, 12, 27, p. 13-21. Bologna, 2009.

Rancière, J., *The Politics of Aesthetics. The Distribution of the Sensible*. London/New York, 2004.

Schneider, R., 'On Taking the Blind in Hand'. In: *Contemporary Theatre Review*, 10, 3, p. 23-38. London/New York, 2000.

Schwarz, D., *Listening Subjects. Music, Psychoanalysis, Culture*. Durham, 1997.

Sedgwick, E. K., *Touching Feeling. Affect, Pedagogy, Performativity*. Durham, 2003.

Silverman, K., *The Acoustic Mirror. The Female Voice in Psychoanalysis and Cinema*. Indianapolis, 1988.

Sterne, J., *The Audible Past. Cultural Origins of Sound Reproduction*. Durham, 2003.

Tonkiss, F., 'Aural Postcards'. In: M. Bull and L. Back (eds.), *The Auditory Culture Reader*. Oxford, 2003.

Verstraete, P., *The Frequency of Imagination. Auditory Distress and Aurality in Contemporary Music Theatre*. PhD Dissertation. Amsterdam, 2009. < http://www.scribd.com/doc/24130280/Pieter-Verstraete-The-Frequency-of-Imagination>

Voegelin, S., *Listening to Noise and Silence. Towards a Philosophy of Sound Art*. London/New York, 2010.

Weber, S., *Theatricality as Medium*. New York, 2004.

Wigley, M., *The Architecture of Deconstruction. Derrida's Haunt*. Cambridge, 1993.

Wurtzler, S., 'She Sang Live, but the Microphone Was Turned Off. The Live, the Recorded, and the Subject of Representation'. In: R. Altman (ed.), *Sound Theory/Sound Practice*. London/New York, 1992.

# Doubled Bodies and Live Loops

## On Ragnar Kjartansson's Mediatized Performances

Eva Heisler

*Me and My Mother* (2000, 2005, 2010) is a series of videos by the Icelandic artist Ragnar Kjartansson (b. 1976), to which he intends to add an instalment every five years. The first three videos have already been made and show Kjartansson and his mother, the prominent Icelandic actress Gudrún Ásmundsdóttir, standing in front of the family bookshelf as the artist's mother repeatedly spits on him.

The series is an unsettling disruption of the relationship between actor and character: the spitting character is a professional actress following direction *and* a mother who is debasing her son. In the context of the small arts community of Iceland, the videos rely on recognition of the famous actress and the common knowledge that Ásmundsdóttir is an energetic champion of her son. Ásmundsdóttir is recognized as acting out of character because she is generally perceived to be a *good* mother; on the other hand, she is in character because, by acting the role of 'bad' mother, she is supporting her son in his artistic efforts.

The fascination of theatre resides in the doubling of the actor's body, both a fictional character and a physical presence. As Philip Auslander puts it: 'The performing body is

Fig. 1    *Me and My Mother*, 2010. Video, 20 minutes. Courtesy of the artist, i8 Gallery, Reykjavik, and Luhring Augustine, New York.

always doubly encoded – it is defined by the codes of a particular performance, but has always already been inscribed, in its material aspect, by social discourses (e.g. science, medicine, hygiene, law, etc.)' (2006: 90). *Me and My Mother* tests the doubleness of the performing body. Not only is Ásmundsdóttir the 'mother of the actor' as well as the 'mother of the actor's character', her performance also challenges ideologies of the maternal body. Because the performance is repeated at five-year intervals, each enactment resounds with the history of previous enactments and anticipates future instalments. Viewers note the aging of the performers along with the increased technological sophistication of the artist. Even the first performance is now experienced through the lens of subsequent performances, since all three works are exhibited together.

What Jon Erickson has called 'the incorrigible frisson of sign and body' (1995: 62) animates theatrical performance and is particularly striking in Kjartansson's series. They also offer a tongue-in-cheek nod to the traditions of endurance art; in this case, the artist's endurance consists of being able to maintain a straight face and hold still while being spat on by his acting partner (and mother) for four minutes in the 2000 video, ten minutes in the 2005 video, and twenty minutes in the 2010 video. Spit is the residue of voice, its excess. Directed at another person, it signals contempt when words fail. Repeated hundreds of times in the course of *Me and My Mother*, spitting becomes a form of address, a speech the delivery of which is thick with the excesses of a maternal body.

Voice – its excesses and its exigencies – is a central preoccupation of Kjartansson's performance-based works. Vocal performance is one of the primary means through which he explores and tests the body of the performer (and artist). The artist's use of vocal repetition functions as a 'live loop' that generates such an excess of performative gesture that the boundaries between performed character (usually a romantic figure of some sort) and performing subject (the artist) collapse. In this contribution, a brief discussion of the role of 'liveness' in the emergence of performance art is followed by an examination of four performance-based works by Kjartansson that each take as its subject a voice – an operatic voice, a bluesy voice, a crooning voice and a lieder voice. I will point out that Kjartansson's use of exuberant repetition within the context of theatrical conventions mediatizes the liveness that historically has been fetishized in performance art. The paper closes with a consideration of Kjartansson's *The End*, a six-month performance at the 2009 Venice Biennale. While the live performance that is at the heart of *The End* is not a vocal performance, its staging of the romantic image of the painter in his studio extends the artist's preoccupation with mediatized live performance and, as with all of Kjartansson's work, is a conflation of theatre and performance art.

## Performance Art and 'Liveness'

In the 1970s, performance art emerged as one of the most dynamic art forms in the US and Europe. The roots of performance art include futurist and dadaist performances, John Cage and Black Mountain College, Happenings and Fluxus (Goldberg 2001). One of the central premizes of performance art, as summarized by Josette Féral, is 'denial of the notion of representation in favor of a "real" presence of the performance artist, which brings with it the refusal of any role or character' (1992: 146). Because performance art was centred on the body rather than the products of the artist, it was considered more direct and honest, in part because performance was more likely to involve psychological and physical risks. Performance art came to be associated with oppositional and transgressive strategies that confound audience expectations. Adrian Heathfield describes the unsettling experience of live art as follows:

> Whether it emerges from the clash of 'real' time with 'fictional' time, from an actual physical wounding or from the excessive density of enacted events, the charging of attention used by many contemporary Live artists brings the spectator into the present moment of the making and unmaking of meaning. This condition is often decidedly unstable and ambivalent, for whilst the artist's or the spectator's 'presence' in the moment may be a prerequisite, the transient and elusive nature of this presence becomes the subject of the work. You really had to be there, as the saying goes. But often 'being there', in the heart of things, you are reminded of the impossibility of ever being fully present to oneself, to others or to the artwork. Eventhood allows spectators to live for awhile in the paradox of two impossible desires: to be present in the moment, to savour it, and to save the moment, to still and preserve its power long after it has gone. This is a deliberate strategy for many Live artists, bringing the reception of the artwork into the elusive conditions of the real, where the relation between experience and thought can be tested and re-articulated. (2004: 9)

I quote Heathfield at length because he captures many of the claims made for performance art: the cultural capital accrued by viewers who can say that they were there is coupled with the difficulty of knowing just what 'being there' entailed; phenomenological experiences and epistemological questions are entangled and tested; the viewers' unstable experiences become the subject of the work. Heathfield summarizes the aims of live art: 'the embodied event has been employed as a generative force: to shock, to destroy pretence, to break apart traditions of representation, to foreground the experiential, to open different kinds of engagement with meaning, to activate audiences' (ibid. 7). Performance is *ontologically* non-reproductive: this is the claim of Peggy Phelan (1993: 148). In a frequently quoted passage, Phelan asserts: 'Performance's only life is in the present. Performance cannot be saved, recorded, documented, or otherwise participate in the circulation of representations of representations: once it does so, it becomes something other than performance' (ibid. 146).

In contrast to claims for the authenticity and transgressive artlessness of performance art, Auslander challenges the commonplace assumption that the live event and the mediatized event are in opposition to one another. Auslander argues that liveness is a concept that is historically contingent; furthermore, he asserts that what counts as 'liveness' is dependent on experiences of the mediatized. Auslander explains:

historically, the live is actually an effect of mediatization, not the other way around. It was the development of recording technologies that made it possible to perceive existing representations as 'live'. Prior to the advent of those technologies (e.g., sound recording and motion pictures), there was no such thing as 'live' performance, for that category has meaning only in relation to an opposing possibility. (2008: 56)

Auslander points out that 'the very concept of live performance presupposes that of reproduction – that the live can exist only within an economy of reproduction' (ibid. 57). Liveness is not 'an ontological condition' but 'a historically mutable concept' (ibid. 62). In contrast to Phelan, Auslander insists that 'live performance cannot be shown to be economically independent of, immune from contamination by, and ontologically different from mediatized forms' (ibid. 7). In discussing the relationship between early television and theatre, Auslander notes 'the irony that whereas television initially sought to replicate and, implicitly, to replace live theatre, live performance itself has developed since that time toward the replication of the discourse of mediatization' (ibid. 24). This is not simply a case of the use of media technologies at live events but 'live performance's absorption of a media-derived epistemology' (ibid. 37).

This brief summary of competing claims for the status of 'liveness' in 1970s art provides a framework for appreciating Kjartansson's testing of 'liveness' in his performance-based works. Encountering 1970s performance art through black-and-white images that served as evidence of – and fetishized – its liveness, the young artist was particularly fascinated with practices of endurance that tested the body's limits. Whereas 1970s performance art defined itself in opposition to the theatrical and the fictive, Kjartansson recasts the touchstones of 'liveness' and 'endurance' as theatrical 'live loops' that not only test his endurance as artist and performer but also test the spectator's experience of 'liveness'.

## The Vocalic Body: *The Opera* (2001) and *The Great Unrest* (2005)

In *The Opera* (2001), Kjartansson dressed up in eighteenth-century costume and sang improvised 'opera' for five hours a day on a small theatre set representing a rococo interior. Here is the artist's description of the piece:

> I had all the props, a cloth from a lady, a sword, and the champagne I drank. But the whole thing was... improvised. I was eating, drinking, and singing.
> 
> The opera was very abstract, though I followed some stations, like taking a lady's handkerchief, singing, taking the sword, singing and so on. But there was no story but references to women, desire, and war underplayed with sadness... I was in this world constantly for five hours a day. After a while this became a psychological and physical challenge for me. (2009: 67)

Fig. 2  *The Opera*, 2001. Detail of performance installation. Photo: Jóhannes B. Bjarnason. Courtesy of the artist and i8 Gallery, Reykjavik.

The performance, a part of the Iceland Academy of the Arts' graduation show, was held in the echoing expanses of a former meatpacking plant, and Kjartansson's rococo stage was like a set on the lot of a movie studio with many people coming and going. In my memory of the performance, it had the feel of a rehearsal, with its repetitions, brief moments of eating and drinking, and the waxing and waning of performative intensity without clear beginning and end. The extravagance of the artist's costume and make-up corresponded to theatre make-up that must be visible from a distance, but it was unnecessary in Kjartansson's performance because viewers were close: the performance adopted the accoutrements of live theatre but its physical nearness evoked the middle-distance of televised drama.

The artist's claim that his performance of *The Opera* 'became a psychological and physical challenge' – that it was a test of his endurance – is an attempt to frame *The Opera* within the history of 1970s performance art that he had been exposed to in art school. Artists such as Vito Acconci and Chris Burden were examples of testing physical limits that Kjartansson took as inspiration for the testing of his vocal endurance in *The Opera*. At the time, Kjartansson's claim appears odd because endurance art is associated with feats of 'real' bodies (not the bodies of actors); in contrast, Kjartansson sings *faux* operatic refrains in costume. Kjartansson's claim to be an heir to the legacy of 1970s performance art may have been an idiosyncratic reading of this period, shaped by the theatre background of his family – both parents were theatre professionals – and the history of oral performance within Icelandic culture.

Regardless of Kjartansson's curious claim for the connection of his work to 1970s endurance art, *The Opera* becomes particularly interesting in the context of Kjartansson's later works because the artist's 'opera' tests the difference between theatre and performance art. Several levels of presentation are layered in *The Opera*. First, there is the fictional world; the mythic world evoked in opera. Second, there are the gestural conventions used to present the fictional world (crudely summarized by Kjartansson as 'taking a lady's handkerchief, singing, taking the sword, singing and so on'). Third, there are the legacies of 1970s performance art *as assumed (and reassembled) by the artist*: the foregrounding of the artist's physical body; the testing of the artist's physical limits; the duration of 'real' time; the absence of closure; the acknowledgment of, and connection to, the viewers who were wandering in and out of the performance. In *The Opera*, Kjartansson's performance moves between the earnest exuberance of a theatrical performer in character and the earnestness of the performance artist who refuses character.

The Slovenian philosopher Mladen Dolar refers to opera as 'a huge relic, an enormous anachronism, a persistent revival of a lost past' (2002: 3). He argues that the fascination of opera is that of a 'redoubled or mediated fantasy' (ibid.). Opera's mythical setting was a means of creating what Benedict Anderson has termed 'imagined community'. Dolar writes:

> To be sure, today no one believes in this mythological foundation of community, but one does believe in the times when people still believed in it... It is not so much our own fascination that is now at stake as it is the fascination of our ancestors who, supposedly, took opera with the utmost seriousness it deserves, who were interpellated into subjects by it and formed a community relying on it... Opera thus retroactively recreates the mythical past that nobody believes in but yet is dearly needed and piously recreated. (ibid. 4)

I quote this passage at length because the concept of redoubled or mediated fantasy is pertinent to Kjartansson's subsequent works that frequently allude to a romantic past *as staged in the past*. What may have appeared to be the posturing of postmodern irony in *The Opera* marks, in retrospect, the beginning of a series of performances that stage redoubled or mediated fantasies.

*The Great Unrest* (2005) was performed for six hours a day in rural Iceland during the run of the annual Reykjavik Arts Festival. The artist refers to the work as 'an installation with a constant performance' (2009: 70). The setting was a small abandoned building that had once served as a community centre, the site of country dances and amateur theatricals in the mid-twentieth century. Giant painted flames rose from the building's exterior, transforming the entire building into a theatre set.

Fig. 3    *The Great Unrest*, 2005. Installation and performance for the exhibition *Life Time, Material Time,*
*Work Time*, curated by Jessica Morgan at the Reykjavik Arts Festival. Courtesy of the artist, i8
Gallery, Reykjavik, and Luhring Augustine, New York. Photo: Fridrik Örn.

Inside, the artist sprawled on stage in a knight's armour, strumming a guitar and
moaning bluesy improvisations. What appeared to be the remnants of painted backdrops and discarded props were strewn about the building along with old radios and
tape recorders. The thread that held together all these bits and pieces was the artist's

voice, not as bearer of lyrical expression
(because there were no words) but as
spatial presence. Kjartansson's melancholy vocal improvisations activated the
space, generating a vocalic body.

The concept of the vocalic body, influenced by Didier Anzieu's theory of
the sonorous envelope, is theorized by
Steven Connor as the ability of sound to
shape the experience of space; it may be

Fig. 4
*The Great Unrest*, 2005. Installation and
performance for the exhibition *Life Time,*
*Material Time, Work Time*, curated by Jessica
Morgan at the Reykjavik Arts Festival.
Courtesy of the artist, i8 Gallery, Reykjavik,
and Luhring Augustine, New York.
Photo: Fridrik Örn.

associated in an infant's life with the mother's voice but it is also associated with collective experiences of voice. Connor writes, 'The leading characteristic of the vocalic body is to be a body-in-invention, an impossible imaginary body in the course of being found and formed' (2001: 80). Connor discusses the voice's unsettling ability to precipitate itself as an object:

> What characterizes a vocalic body is not merely the range of actions which a particular voice function enjoins on the body of the one producing the voice, but also the characteristic ways in which the voice seems to precipitate itself as an object, upon which it can then itself give the illusion of acting. (ibid.)

Kjartansson is not so much acting the weary forlorn knight as he is acting the weary forlorn knight *as acted in amateur theatricals* in the Icelandic countryside. The knight character is surrounded by (representations of) fragments of theatrical backdrops. (The painted backdrops are constructed to look like remnants of painted backdrops; that is, they are painted backdrops of painted backdrops.) Because Kjartansson's performance is taking place within an installation, the boundaries between the space of performance and the situation of the viewer collapse. The fragments of painted scenery and broken radios are the backdrop to the viewer's experience (rather than a backdrop to a fictive performance that the viewer watches). The viewer experiences a perceptual restlessness: now one is in real time with a real person among real things; now one is privy to a fiction; now I am a part of the fiction; now I stand back and observe a performance.

The backdrops and other bits are deliberate fragments (i.e. faked fragments). The fragment, as Jacques Lacan points out, is experienced as fragment only from a site of illusory wholeness (1977: 4). While Lacan speaks in terms of the emergence of subjectivity and its entanglement in the illusory wholeness provided by the mirror, Kjartansson's fragments (the fragmentary presentation of theatre, and the Icelandic past) allude to a mirage – alternately the mirage of theatre itself and the mirage of theatre's past. Kjartansson's melancholy vocalic body alludes to the collective past of Icelandic countryside entertainment; it might seem to be a nostalgic conjuring of Iceland's rural past but it is, I would argue, more a presentation of nostalgia itself as a mediated fantasy. The mediated fantasy is one of *community*, and art as participating, or generating, that community.

As a live performance, The Great Unrest is motivated in part by the anticipation of its recasting as a story. Kjartansson has remarked that it does not matter that no more than 150 people in a four-week period saw the performance. His claim is that it is the *story* of the performance that matters (Kjartansson 2009: 71). Thus, the 'liveness' of The Great Unrest is a rehearsal for the later 'real' performances that constitute multiple stories recounting experiences of The Great Unrest. The experience, for the viewer, is one of anticipated storytelling. Likewise, the site of the installation/performance is already, by virtue of its location in an abandoned community centre, serving a doubled or remediated fantasy, the live performance of which is mediated again in its projected source of

228

Fig. 5    *God*, 2007. Video installation (video still). Commissioned by TBA 21, Vienna, and Living Art Museum, Reykjavik. Courtesy of the artist, i8 Gallery, Reykjavik, and Luhring Augustine, New York.

stories retold (i.e. the anticipation that the performance itself will be remediated in the future).

## Live Loops: *God* (2007) and *The Schumann Machine* (2008)

*God* (2007) is a video work that features the artist crooning *Sorrow conquers happiness* for thirty minutes against a backdrop of voluminous pink satin and accompanied by an orchestra. Presented as a single-channel projection, the monitor is set up in a space that is draped in pink satin similar to the backdrop in the video. With a tuxedo-clad orchestra and performer singing into an old-fashioned microphone, the performance harks back to the era of big bands and Hollywood musicals. Kjartansson states that he was quite deliberately 'working with cinematic beauty, both acoustically and visually' (2009: 72). As he puts it, 'The sound is velvet smeared with butter, and visually it's pink satin Technicolor heaven' (ibid.). A far cry from the histrionics of opera, this is a voice that softly croons. Kjartansson, who is a trained singer, has a beautiful voice and there is nothing false or mocking in his vocals. However, the seductions of the crooning voice are undercut by the obsessive repetition of the phrase 'Sorrow conquers happiness', as if the performer is consigned to never-ending rehearsal.

The presentation of *God* encompasses several zones of mediatized performance. First, the video is the recording of a live performance, shot in one take, after eight hours of rehearsal (Alemani 2009: 44). The live performance, however, imitates cinematic presentations of singers performing in front of big bands – and these cinematic presentations are themselves representations of 'live' performances meant to generate the experience of intimacy, as if Frank Sinatra or Bing Crosby were singing just to us. However, in *God*, there are no close-ups or reverse shots as there might be in cinema but, as is characteristic of early television, the image is 'frontal and oriented toward the viewer in much the same way as a performance on a proscenium stage would be' (Auslander 2006: 20). Auslander points out that television, until the early 1950s, took its staging from the theatre rather than cinema (ibid. 21). The 'feel' of Kjartansson's video is that of television rather than cinema, and this is further reinforced by the size of the monitor which is about the size of a modest home television set.

Crooning as a style of singing emerged as the result of sound recording 'when it was realized that microphones could not cope with the extreme dynamic ranges possessed by singers used to commanding the large space of the concert hall' (Connor 2001: 82). The sensitivity of the microphone limited range but it enhanced vocal nuances, making 'audible and expressive a whole range of organic vocal sounds which are edited out in ordinary listening; the liquidity of the saliva, the tiny hissings and shudders of the breath, the clicking of the tongue and teeth, and popping of the lips' (ibid.). The use of the microphone increased the power of the voice to project a vocalic body, to invade the listener's space with physical presence. The intimacy of Kjartansson's crooning, however, is destabilized by the thirty-minute repetition of a single line; the refrain is initially perceived as melancholic and obsessive (and thus saturated with feeling and 'voice') but then it is *endured* as the repetition of a loop (and thus robotic and devoid of feeling). Indeed, the loop 'Sorrow conquers happiness' morphs, after the nth time, into a place-holder lyric that might serve as stand-in for any romantic lyric. The artist is a crooning-machine. The use of *God* as a title might strike one as loaded with over-the-top religious signification but *God*, too, functions as a placeholder.

In *God*, the words hardly seem to matter in such excessive repetition: the singing itself is, on the one hand, mechanical and, on the other hand, otherworldly and mantra-like. This is a reminder of the association of music with the sacred (to which the title of the piece seems to allude). Dolar has written about the association of the voice with nature, with the pre-symbolic, and also with the ability to transcend language: 'The voice is endowed with profundity: by not meaning anything, it appears to mean more than mere words, it becomes the bearer of some unfathomable originary meaning which, supposedly, got lost with language' (2006: 31). Thus, it is assumed that the voice precedes the symbolic and has the power to transcend the symbolic; hence, its association with the sacred. Dolar points out that this assumption of the voice's transcendent powers is an illusion:

> The voice as the bearer of a deeper sense, of some profound message, is a structural illusion, the core of a fantasy that the singing voice might cure the wound inflicted by culture, restore the loss that we suffered by the assumption of the symbolic order. *This deceptive promise disavows the fact that the voice owes its fascination to this wound, that its allegedly miraculous force stems from its being situated in this gap.* (ibid. emphasis added)

Fig. 6

*The Schumann Machine*, 2008, Installation and performance for Manifesta 7, curated by Adam Budak in Rovereto, Italy. Courtesy of the artist, i8 Gallery, Reykjavik, and Luhring Augustine, New York. Photo: Wolfgang Träger.

The melancholy and archaic-romantic diction of the lyric – the verb 'conquers' and the romantic noun 'sorrow' – is no more than a cliché wounding. The voice and its repetition reinforces neither the romantic cliché of 'wound', nor the wound inflicted by the symbolic order but the fascination of the wound, the wound as fantasy, a fantasy that the artist's 'live loop' both serves and displaces.

In *God*, Kjartansson presents a video of a live loop, but in *The Schumann Machine* (2008), the artist performed Robert Schumann's *Dichterliebe* six hours a day in a shed located in the courtyard of Manifattura Tabacchi during Manifesta 7 (2008). He was accompanied by the well-known Icelandic pianist David Thór Jónsson, who provided virtuoso performances between two camp beds borrowed from a local boarding school. The tuxedo-clad artist sang earnestly of unrequited love while viewers shuffled through the shed, chattering among themselves, or lounging (and napping) on the camp beds.

The effect of Kjartansson's *Schumann Machine* pivots on a complex layering of contradictory voices. Schumann's 1840 *Dichterliebe* itself is characterized by internal contradictions. To begin with, Schumann's song cycle is based on Heinrich Heine's poems in the *Lyrisches Intermezzo* of 1822-23. The argument has been made that Schumann's compositions do not serve as mere accompaniment to Heine's lyrics; rather Schumann's music 'disrupt[s] and contradict[s]' the poet's voice (Perrey 2002: 6). Heine's lyrics are themselves thick with contradiction, however. Heine's expressions of romantic longing are continually undercut by scepticism toward such longing. Heine employs the conceits and images of Romanticism, but his lyric constructions are perforated with

Fig. 7    *The Schumann Machine*, 2008, Installation and performance for Manifesta 7, curated by Adam Budak in Rovereto, Italy. Courtesy of the artist, i8 Gallery, Reykjavik, and Luhring Augustine, New
York. Photo: Wolfgang Träger.

irony that ridicules the very language out of which the poem is built. As Beate Julia Perrey characterizes Heine's tone, 'Heine's irony cuts through and dismantles,' with the
effect that 'the contents of Heine's poems are themselves rendered worthless' and 'the
reader is left with sudden nothingness' (ibid. 73). In Schumann's *Dichterliebe*, there is a
marked difference in the trajectories of voice and piano accompaniment; Schumann's
music both reflects and resists Heine's voice (ibid. 20). As Slavoj Žižek puts it, Schumann '"dialecticizes" the relationship between the sung melody and its piano accompaniment' (1997: 197). Žižek points out that 'the privileged link between melody and
voice is broken: it is no longer possible to reconstruct the full melody from the solo vocal line, since the melody, as it were, promenades between vocal and piano lines'
(ibid.). The melody cannot be pinned down: 'It is as if the melody's proper place is on
some elusive, intangible third level which merely echoes in both of the levels that the
listener actually hears, vocal and piano' (ibid. 198).

Kjartansson's *Schumann Machine* doubles what is already doubled in Schumann's
*Dichterliebe*. To begin with, there is the pairing of pianist Jónsson and singer Kjartansson; their clowning camaraderie (drinking, smoking cigars, handing out snacks to the
audience) is coupled with professional-calibre performances. In addition, there is the
unsettling coupling of Schumann's *Dichterliebe* and Kjartansson's *Schumann Machine*:
music performance and performance art; song cycle and live loop. It is argued to what
extent Schumann's *Dichterliebe* is a narrative or 'a nonlinear constellation of changing
emotional states' (Hoeckner 2006: 72). The cycle is experienced as two times, the past

love affair that is remembered and the present moment of recounting the past through song. In performance, however, there occurs a 'slippage between story and storytelling in performance' because 'it often appears as if the narrator is reliving and reenacting the events of the past in the present' (ibid.). Kjartansson is not just singing but acting the part of the suffering lover. Schumann recasts Heine's romantic fragments into a cycle; Kjartansson retools the cycle into 'loop'. Through Kjartansson's 'looping', however, the lyric 'I' is hurled from fragmentary self into feedback loop. Thus, *The Schumann Machine* sets up a contrast between the live performance of romantic longing and marathon repetition of that romantic longing, and between the performance of an identity and the gesture of performance itself.

Fig. 8

*Blooming Trees Performance*, 2008. Detail. Oil on canvas, text, black-and-white photographs, performance. Courtesy of the artist, i8 Gallery, Reykjavik, and Luhring Augustine, New York. Photo: Ragnar Kjartansson.

Fig. 9

*Blooming Trees Performance*, 2008. Installation view. Oil on canvas, text, black-and-white photographs, performance. Courtesy of the artist, i8 Gallery, Reykjavik, and Luhring Augustine, New York. Photo: Larry Lamay.

## The Theatre of the Artist

Kjartansson has claimed that his favourite paintings are stage sets. For *The Blooming Trees Performance, Rokeby Farm* (2008), the artist tackles painting itself as performance. The performance took place over a weekend at an Astor estate in upstate New York and included smoking cigars, reading *Lolita*, and painting trees *en plein air*.

Fig. 10
*The End – Venice*, 2009.
Performance installation.
Commissioned by the Center
for Icelandic Art. Courtesy of
the artist, i8 Gallery,
Reykjavik, and Luhring
Augustine, New York.
Photo: Rafael Pinho.

Fig. 11
*The End – Venice*, 2009. Detail.
Performance installation.
Commissioned by the Center
for Icelandic Art. Courtesy of
the artist, i8 Gallery,
Reykjavik, and Luhring
Augustine, New York.
Photo: Rafael Pinho.

Seven landscape paintings were exhibited along with eight black-and-white photographs taken with a 35 mm camera, and a text, all of which serve as documentation of the performance. The photographs were framed with the text written by the artist:

> Took the train to rokeby farm, upstate new york on the 20th of june. Stayed there for two days painting the trees. The sun was fierce on the first day, on the second day there was rain, thunder and quite exquisite light. Did seven canvases and enjoyed myself in the 19th-century mansion. Smoked cigars, drank beer and read Lolita. Returned back to new york city on the 22nd. (Malbran 2009: 52)

The paintings, hanging in a gallery, are evidence of a performance and thus are not vulnerable to aesthetic judgment, being of the same status as documentary photographs. *The Blooming Trees Performance* hence alludes to early performance art when photography served as its only documentation. In this case, Kjartansson uses the photographic conventions of the 1970s performance artist in order to authorize the performer's act of painting.

For the 2009 Venice Biennale, Kjartansson further develops his interest in the per-

Fig. 12 *The End – Rocky Mountains*, 2009. Video still. Video produced in collaboration with the Banff Centre, Canada, and the Stephan and Adriana Benediktson Fellowship for Icelandic Artists. Courtesy of the artist, i8 Gallery, Reykjavik, and Luhring Augustine, New York.

formance of painting. *The End – Venice* (2009) consists of repeatedly painting the same live model throughout the six-month duration of the biennale. Canvases of a solitary figure proliferate, not as paintings but as evidence of Kjartansson's performance of painting. The performance takes place on the ground floor of the fourteenth-century Palazzo Michiel dal Brusa with doors that open onto the Canale Grande; the sound of its water lapping against the artist's 'studio' are amplified by a microphone. A room adjacent to Kjartansson's studio/performance space features a five-channel video installation of the artist and David Thór Jónsson playing a discordant folk-country piece that is entirely instrumental with the exception of one line ('I've got the hell, you've got the heaven') occasionally but barely discerned. Produced at the Banff Centre, *The End – Rocky Mountains* shows the musicians playing outdoors in the frigid and snowy Canadian Rockies. The video plays with stereotypes of the North American frontiersman (like the Walt Disney version of Davy Crockett in his coonskin cap) as well as landscape representations of wilderness and the extravagance and theatricality of pop music videos. In Kjartansson's studio/performance space, viewers can hear the music video, playing on a continuous loop, in the next room; this juxtaposition sets up a relationship between Kjartansson-as-musician and Kjartansson-as-painter, between the sublime mise-en-scène of the Canadian Rockies and the aestheticized mise-en-scène of Venice, between the cacophony of repetitive folk-country improvisation and the redundant romanticism of Kjartansson's acts of painting.

It is important to note that Kjartansson's painting performance is earnest; the artist concentrates effort and skill in his role as painter. While the artist refers to the paintings as 'just props', he also says that 'they are real' and 'hopefully... nice paintings' (2009: 76). As with previous works, this six-month performance is a mediated fantasy. Kjartansson performs the fantasy of the genius-painter-hunched-at-easel. Elaborating on Dolar's point about opera, I would add that Kjartansson's fantasy does not intend to evoke a time when there really were artist-geniuses; rather, it evokes nostalgia for the time when one believed in the cult of genius.

As with *The Great Unrest* and *The Schumann Machine*, *The End – Venice* heightens the exhibition-goer's self-consciousness about his or her role *as spectator* and, hence, as participant in a performance. One strolls about a studio that is also a stage set. One encounters a friendly young man who appears to be earnestly working at his easel, empty beer bottles strewn about, paintings hanging or stacked against the wall. One encounters the performance of an identity (painter) replete with convincing and compelling gestures (acts of painting) and taking place amid the scattered remains of former performances (paintings). Not only is the performer's body doubled, but so are the objects among which one moves; the viewer is not sure if she is encountering paintings or the signs of paintings, and uncertain whether or not this difference is significant.

**Eva Heisler** is Associate Professor at University of Maryland University College's European Division. She has written extensively on contemporary Icelandic art and, since 2006, has served on a research team preparing a five-volume history of Icelandic art (forthcoming). She is a regular contributor to the Atlanta-based international art magazine *Art Papers*.

REFERENCES

Alemani, C., 'God'. In: C. Schoen (ed.), *Ragnar Kjartansson. The End*. Ostfildern, 2009.

Auslander, P., *From Acting to Performance. Essays in Modernism and Postmodernism*. New York and London, 2006 (1997).

–. *Liveness. Performance in a Mediatized Culture*. New York and London, 2008 (1998).

Connor, S., 'Violence, Ventriloquism and the Vocalic Body'. In: P. Campbell and A. Lear (eds.), *Psychoanalysis and Performance*. London and New York, 2001.

Dolar, M., *A Voice and Nothing More*. Cambridge and London, 2006.

–. 'If Music Be the Food of Love'. In: S. Žižek and M. Dolar, *Opera's Second Death*. New York and London, 2002.

Erickson, J., *The Fate of the Object. From Modern Object to Postmodern Sign in Performance, Art and Poetry*. Ann Arbor, 1995.

Féral, J., 'What is Left of Performance Art? Autopsy of a Function, Birth of a Genre'. In: *Discourse*, 14, 2, p. 142-161. London, 1992.

Goldberg, R., *Performance Art: From Futurism to the Present*. London, 2001.

Heathfield, A., 'Alive'. In: A. Heathfield (ed.), *Live. Art and Performance*. New York, 2004.

Hoeckner, B., 'Paths Through *Dichterliebe*'. In: 19th-Century Music, 30, 1, p. 65-80. Berkeley, 2006.

Kjartansson, R., 'The Dead King'. Interview with Christian Schoen. In: C. Schoen (ed.), *Ragnar Kjartansson. The End*. Ostfildern, 2009.

Lacan, J., *Écrits. A Selection*. Trans. Alan Sheridan. New York, 1977.

Malbran, F., 'Blossoming Trees Performance'. In: C. Schoen (ed.), *Ragnar Kjartansson. The End*. Ostfildern, 2009.

Perrey, B. J., *Schumann's Dichterliebe and Early Romantic Poetics. Fragmentation of Desire*. Cambridge/New York, 2002.

Phelan, P., *Unmarked. The Politics of Performance*. New York/London, 1993.

Žižek, S., 'Robert Schumann. The Romantic Anti-Humanist'. In: S. Žižek, *The Plague of Fantasies*. London, 1997.

# Between Solitaire and a Basketball Game

## Dramaturgical Strategies in the Work of Antonia Baehr

Tom Engels

Antonia Baehr is a Berlin-based choreographer, performer and filmmaker. She has created numerous performances with other choreographers and performers like William Wheeler, Valérie Castan and Lindy Annis. Characteristic is her non-disciplinary work and her way of collaborating with different people, using a game structure with switching roles: each person is alternately host and guest.

Antonia Baehr's work does not offer simple narratives. As a choreographer, she focuses on and isolates the seemingly mundane: an everyday movement or action. Like a surgeon, she dissects not only these acts but also the potential that is hidden within them. At a second level her work also deals with the construct of identity, perception and theatrical mechanisms. She researches the fiction of everyday-life performance and the fiction of theatre. Among others, she is also the producer of horse whisperer Werner Hirsch, who occasionally works as a dancer in the French and Belgian contemporary scene.

For her solo RIRE/LAUGH/LACHEN (2008), Baehr asked family and friends to write her laugh scores as birthday presents, which she used as the basic structure for the performance. For seventy minutes, Antonia Baehr explored the realm of laughter. She showed the audience this expression as a sovereign entity, freed from causal baggage – jokes, tickles, narrative, humour, joy – looking at the thing itself: the sound and shape, the music, choreography and drama, the rhythm and the gesture of laughter.

Her latest choreography, For Faces (2010), and her latest film, For Ida (2010), were developed parallel to each other, resulting in two different though related works of art. This time, Baehr focused on the face, a mutable locus where expressions appear and dissolve. Minor changes take place. These movements reveal not only known but also unknown territories of facial expression. The face can be considered a landscape. In this interview, Antonia Baehr explores the issue of two different dramaturgies – those of choreography and film – that from time to time tend to converge in her work.

**Could you start by describing For Ida, your new film?**

In For Ida, you see a multiplication of Henry Wilde, filmed in continuous takes. You see his face four times, next to each other, while he is performing a choreography for the face. The video is a dedication to Ida Wilde by Henry Wilde, her husband. Ida is the one who created Henry and Henry looks like this because Ida dressed him up like that. It's a true story. The film is a little bit like the game of 'solitaire': you play with yourself. I shot the film with a webcam in the south of France in a house where I spend my summers, while nobody was around.

Ida is a reference to a Gertrude Stein character. In *Ida: A Novel*, Stein portrays the life of the most ordinary character imaginable, leading an exceptionally ordinary life – a lot like anybody's life. Stein also worked with multiplication: in her novel, Ida has a twin. There are a lot of different Idas that return in Gertrude Stein's work. The theme of the multiplication of the self is recurrent in art history. Duchamp made a multiple self-portrait with a special photographical device en vogue at that time, called *Marcel Duchamp Around a Table*, quoting *Io-Noi-Boccioni* by Umberto Boccioni. You see him multiplied while smoking his pipe. Parallel to *For Ida*, I made a choreography that resulted in my latest production *For Faces*. The latter is a piece both for the faces of the interpreters and the faces of the audience members. The 'for' in the title is like the 'for' in 'for piano' or 'for orchestra'. It's made to be interpreted. The 'for' in *For Ida*, on the other hand, designates a dedication.

**So you are playing a game with yourself? I can imagine that working on a film solo is very different from making a live performance executed by four live performers.**

I play a game, while asking questions like 'Who is the self?' or 'Who creates the self?'. The starting point for the video was that I wanted to see what sorts of materials and compositions for the face could be interesting and possible to do with the four performers in *For Faces*. It wasn't meant to become a film at all. Secretly I tried out stuff for the piece, creating sequences of facial choreography. Due to the fact that I was creating *For Faces* at that time, I multiplied myself four times in the video. My motivation was very pragmatic at first. I never showed my try-outs to the performers during the rehearsal period, because I didn't want them to copy me. But later on we watched sketches that didn't end up in the final video. And now they are actually doing some of those movements in *For Faces*. And so my two most recent works got interwoven. So there is some classical 'copying' in the sense that the performers do what the choreographer shows

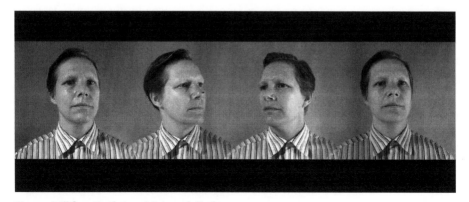

Fig. 1    Still from *For Ida* (2010) © Antonia Baehr.

them, but they copied only small parts from the film, not from me doing it live. In a way, the film and the piece are like the two sides of a record. They are complementary, but they are not conceived for the same audience. Nevertheless, it might be interesting to compare them.

**Your work often deals with the construct of the self by staging characters that do or do not biologically exist. Is video work providing you with a safer playground, or is the stage the ideal place to explore these mechanisms?**

Both function as my playgrounds. It is very different though, working alone or directing four artists. In *For Faces*, for instance, the performers sometimes choreograph their own phrases, by doing a composition in real time. Interaction takes place. When I am alone, I have to find strategies to get along with myself. It's solitaire versus a basketball game. In *For Faces*, I'm the conductor and there is the dynamic of a team. But the strategies are different, both pieces are about the construct of the self. It is the concept of the 'mimetic faculty' that Walter Benjamin talks about. It enables us to imitate, to use others as mirrors. 'Who am I?' – 'I am myself because I've been imitating all these people.' I think this idea is crucial in *For Faces*. The performers are very strong personalities and they are who they are. They do not represent a normative beauty canon, or what 'female' or 'male' are supposed to be. If you look at the four of them, you see quite a complex image. They did not get in the piece through casting. So yes, I think it is very similar to how I questioned myself in RIRE/LAUGH/LACHEN (2008). *For Faces*, on the other hand, is not about me nor about Werner Hirsch or Henry Wilde, but it is also dealing with questions of self-construction through the gaze of others.

**The multiplication of the self also has major repercussions for the technical side of producing *For Ida*.**

*For Ida* was shot with the webcam of my MacBook. The camera does not move itself, and produces a moving image that harks back to the technique of the very beginning of cinema, like Edison's kinetoscope or, even more, the Lumière brothers' *cinématographe*. The image moves within the frame but the frame itself does not move. It is a form of cinema that is close to photography. *For Ida* is closely related to that principle: it is a film that plays with the boundary between still and moving image. *For Ida* refers to portraiture in photography, painting and the passport photograph, but also to the close-up in cinema, the star and the figure of identification. Ironically, I multiplied the singular figure of identification. Furthermore, the webcam operates like a mirror, but one with a slight twist in it. With a webcam, the filmed image can be visible to the filming person while she or he is shooting it, it is just like watching yourself in a mirror. I mainly use it for things like Skype, or at least that is how it became part of my life. When you use Skype, you can see the face of the person you're talking to, but you can also see your own face on the screen while being filmed. I made *For Ida* because I was skyping a lot at that

Fig. 2    Still from *For Ida* (2010) © Antonia Baehr.

time. So the webcam was an everyday-life tool that came to be very useful, but also very inspirational. Although at the same time I did not like this way of communicating: the person on the other end seemed even further away than if we had been talking on the phone.

Also, Skype produces a strange form of narcissism, I felt. The wide-angle camera produces a very ugly portrait and the colours are also of very low quality. But it's quite interesting to see how this very modern tool is a member of several families: that of mirrors, of early film, of surveillance technology, but also of the telephone. Therefore *For Ida* is a silent conversation with oneself, a wordless soliloquy, made in a ritualistic frenzy to exorcise myself of my terrible Skype experiences.

The fact that the film is twenty-one minutes long, filmed in continuous takes and edited without any time-based effects, is also a clear reference to this sort of communication. But it also makes it a contribution to the genre of the 'performance for the camera', a genre that often deals with the artist as author and performer of the artwork at the same time. *For Ida*, being a work that is performed in front of a camera and shot in one continuous take without any effects, relates to the feminist art of the sixties and seventies. For me, it is made in homage to feminist art.

**You have a background in the visual arts. Has that influenced your aesthetics in theatre and video work? Your work always bears that distinct Antonia Baehr signature; it is very atypical and cannot be strictly categorized.**

First I studied media art with Valie Export. I also did a bit of painting and other stuff, and then I went to Chicago, for an exchange. There I was enrolled in the Performance Department, but students were free to take classes in other departments as well. So I studied animation film, participated in theory classes, explored my own performative strategies, etc.: so I gathered a really broad understanding of art and the performing arts. I started with film, but I was never any good at it. My friends were much better, so I stopped. I think this problem arose because of the fact that film uses a really different kind of dramaturgy than live performance. It is amazing how they behave like two completely different languages. Just like German and French: two different languages in which you can say different things as well, and they really require different modes of thinking. This is not only the case for the craft itself, but also for the feeling it produces.

**The ways of communicating with the audience are clearly different. For Faces, for example, always ends with a discussion between you, the audience and the performers. But with For Ida you will never get in touch with the audience. Although both pieces deal with the mechanisms of the gaze, both pieces seem to live totally different lives.**

For Faces is more about deconstructing the mechanisms of the set-up of space and the auditorium. This is something I do in all of my choreographies: asking myself how the architecture of the auditorium is functioning. Cat Calendar (2004), for example, was composed like a diorama, with the audience sitting on children's chairs, looking at a box like you can find them in a museum for natural history. In For Faces, the audience is positioned in an arena, looking at the four performers in the middle. Most of the time I play with these conventions of where to put the audience. The arena in For Faces makes sure that everybody can see each other. The striking difference with a movie theatre is that you are in the dark, alone, but at the same time with the invisible others. You know all the time that what you see on screen is not happening at the same time as what happens in the auditorium. That is a very big difference.

I am really interested in how that dramaturgical language can be used in theatre. For example: one part of For Faces is about the close-up, like in film. In theatre, this functions from human to human, while film, on the other hand, is always communication through a machine. There's a mechanical apparatus that is always involved and most of the time invisible. For me personally, the machinery that we use in performance has to be visible, otherwise I think you don't use the performance language in all its richness and possibilities. You have to make use of everything that is there and make it visible.

**This issue of visibility reminds me of how in For Faces sound indications give the audience clues as to the structure of the performance. You can hear the performers making sounds that trigger expressions or a series of movements. In For Ida this works completely differently due to the fact that you did not have the issue of liveness imposing on the creation.**

In For Faces, the sounds the performers make in the third movement are there to orient themselves in time, since they cannot hear or see each other – which is a particularity of this quartet. The sounds were merely developed as a tool in the learning process of the dance. We meant to take them away later on, once the performers knew the dance well, and work with a click track instead. But then we realized that the performers had created a beautiful piece of music with these sounds. This was a particularly fun experience for musicians/composers Andrea Neumann and Sabine Ercklentz; to realize they had

Fig. 3    *For Faces* (2010). Photograph: Anja Weber.

created a musical composition without intending it. The fourth and last section works the other way around. It is about finding sounds that produce movement. Here, the acoustic composition is the basis for the motions, while in part three, the sounds serve the composition and execution of the moves.

In *For Ida*, the unison is more precise than in *For Faces*, and there is more of it. Since the face is of the same person, it seemed interesting to observe difference through similarity. The four faces make the same movements, and doing so, we can see their differences. That's the whole 'magic' of unison, isn't it? Technically speaking, *For Ida* is made with a click track of instructions that I listened to while filming myself. I translated the score into verbal instructions and recorded them. I don't know if it this technical aspect of the 'making of' is relevant at all, but it seems funny that in order to make this silent self-portrait, I was hearing the computer talk to me in my own voice throughout, telling me what to do.

**Cameras can zoom in, but eyes cannot. Did you find a strategy to transpose film techniques to the theatre?**

In film, the montage and the close-up are used to define the dramaturgy of the film. In live performances, and in *For Faces* in particular, the eyes of each audience member choose another place to look at. In this sense, the eye of the spectator functions like the lens of a camera zooming in. The activity of the spectator's gaze in *For Faces* is similar to that of the director of photography in the process of making a film. In *For Faces*, someone is looking at the eyes, others at the feet, others still at the nose. People choose their close-ups very differently. And in film you normally get clear directions where to look.

That is why I would like to show For Ida in a big cinema, which would mean that the audience cannot really see the four faces at the same time, and consequently really become obliged to wander through the image, never being able to get the whole picture. In For Ida, you get four frontal faces throughout the whole work. You never see the back of a head, like you do in For Faces. Those two different notions make for the differences between the two pieces. In For Ida, the multiplication happens through the duplication of the self. In For Faces, this happens though the multiple perspectives of the audience through the arena that determines the visual structure. No two people see the same performance.

**Bill Viola says that we people live in time like fish live in water. For me, this idea is clearly expressed in both For Faces and For Ida. You dedicate time to an expression on a face, or just to the face itself. That is something you would not do on the street if someone passes by. How different is it to work with time in theatre and in film? Do you want to look for the same kind of time experience?**

I would speak about time and space, or a combination of both. In For Faces, you are sitting in an arena and there are four people in front of you that you can look at, but they do not look at you. What the performers and the audience do is very similar. They are almost in the same position. You don't have to react like you have to do in real life. If someone smiles at you and you don't smile back, that is a strong gesture. In the performance, we are safe. We can contemplate or we can observe ourselves, how we become reactive. When I watch them, my face also starts to move, like theirs. Then I think: 'Oh, what am I doing?' I contemplate them, the others, but also myself and my own position in theatre. I contemplate what it is to be a human being. You're not allowed to do that in real life, because that's voyeurism. This freedom of contemplation gives you what the cultural historian Aby Warburg calls 'Denkraum', a space to think. It opens up perception, because you're calm. You have time and space to think. Warburg was very interested in the reproduction of the Medea image in art history. She symbolizes the moment of thinking, the moment before she kills her children. That moment of reflection, of taking time to think, is something we are not used to in the movie theatre. Not that I mean to say that film denies reflection, but it clearly is another relationship towards a constant flux of images that we are talking about. That is why I also want to bring that Denkraum into the movie theatre.

Since the movie does not happen in real time, there is a difference in responsibility for the audience. For example: if I fall asleep during a film screening, I do not disturb the film. In a performance, however, the audience has an immense responsibility towards the performers and the creation itself. It is in their hands. If someone becomes very loud, then he is going to disturb. That is the dilemma in the performance LAUGH, because laughing is so contagious. Your neighbour starts to laugh, but actually you just want to listen to the laughter of the performer. I love to go to experimental films and sleep or take notes. And there is the possibility of watching movies over and over again, of course. The contract that the spectator signs with regard to the artwork is a different one in the cinema and in the theatre.

**The contract between the audience and the performers is very specific in _For Faces_. There is even an unconscious biological contract being made by the 'mirror neurons' in our brains. These neurons are activated when we perceive movements or gestures, and they cause a similar reaction, for instance in our faces. I read this as an attempt to bring life and art closer together.**

The situation in _For Faces_ is similar to an everyday-life constellation. People are sitting in front of other people. We experience this all the time: in the subway, at a dinner table, in face-to-face encounters in cafés or anywhere else, when we are not speaking to each other, when we cease to use words to back up our experience. But in _For Faces_, the theatrical contract makes the situation different from a quotidian one. In making the difference between life and art as small as possible, I make it as big as possible. What I mean by that is that the power of the theatrical contract becomes visible and the audience can physically experience it. The spectators might observe themselves mirroring the facial movements of the performers' faces in their own faces. Then the spectator becomes the object of self-observation. Or, on the other hand, the viewer might contemplate the performers' faces and those of the other spectators sitting across from him or her as if they were objects, sculptures, or paintings. Or one might just fall asleep too. Each spectator experiences the theatre's fourth wall differently in this piece. But the fourth wall is clearly there. The piece does not ask the audience to participate, unlike

Fig. 4    _For Faces_ (2010). Photograph: Anja Weber.

this kind of theatre in which the actors ask the audience to sing along or clap their hands or come onstage. The particularity of *For Faces*' setting might enable us to scrutinize the theatre, but also life in itself, through comparison, and because here in the theatre, we have time to think and observe. We are not asked to react immediately.

**There is also a practical difference between performance and video work: the reproducibility of the work. With the proper distribution channels for your film, everybody can see your work. With performances, that is different. Does this matter to you? You position yourself in the art scene in an entirely different way if you leave artistic relics.**

It totally matters. I started to do live art because it was too confusing not to know for whom I was going to do the work. While doing performances, I really knew that I was doing it for very concrete persons, for all those people present in the room. It was very comforting to know: 'It's going to be for them.' That simplified not only the situation but also my capacity to produce work. Actually, any work of art is for anybody, also when it is live art. But there is another sense, like writing someone a letter, or thinking about somebody that you are doing it for. The piece is for Ida. Just like in the Sixties when it was a habit to give scores as birthday presents. *For John Cage* (1982), for instance, is a beautiful score that Morton Feldman gave to John Cage as a birthday present.

There is the problem of how to document live art on video. It's a whole problem in itself. What I am doing here is approaching the problem from the opposite side, in the sense that I am not doing it at all. The registration of the piece is finished before the actual piece. They are related, the two, but it is not the idea of documenting. That is where everything goes wrong. That is where people do not get that it is really a different language. You cannot just aim a camera on a performance in order to catch it.

**There are numerous performance DVDs nowadays, from Merce Cunningham, Marina Abramovic, or very recently Wim Wenders' 3D movie *Pina*. It seems that those registrations are transforming or even replacing our memory. Do we have to learn to live with the ephemeral aspect of performance again in this era of audiovisual expansion?**

I changed my opinion about this. At first I was really against this idea of documenting performances and, by that, denying the ephemerality of live art, but now I do not know. We are now so thoroughly surrounded by moving images. We use Google and YouTube constantly. Now artists, but also the audience, have easy access to a really broad range of material. So our way of thinking, making and composing has changed because of that and there is actually no escape, or you have to isolate yourself in the mountains. But we can observe the differences that it makes. *Holding Hands* (2000) for instance, a piece performed by William Wheeler and myself, consists of pieces made with a video camera as a working tool. First we filmed the rehearsal and then watched the videotape. Again and again. A camera functioned as the outside eye. That way of working produces pieces that are very flat. It has one vanishing point, like e.g., *Self-Unfinished* (1998) by

Xavier Le Roy and many other pieces of that time. For *For Faces*, it was very remarkable that I lost all the videotapes of the rehearsals and that we almost never used a television or camera to give feedback on the work. The set-up is round, so it completely escapes the camera logic. You cannot put it in one image. When I see people and how YouTube and those other flat images inspire their work, I think how different *For Faces* is. There is so little that we took from video during the creation of *For Faces*. It changed our vocabulary completely. There is a little part that we transposed from Trisha Brown from video, but mainly paper and colour pens became our working tools. The piece is so complex that we just would not be able to make a simple movie version out of it.

**Tom Engels** completed his master's degree at the Department of Theatre, Performance and Media Studies of Ghent University. He is an editor of *Oral Site* and has worked with artists like Needcompany, Antonia Baehr and Eszter Salamon. In 2011, he will be a dramaturge for Adam Linder and Rodrigo Sobarzo's *Such Gathering*. In 2012, he will be Eleanor Bauer's assistant for *A Dance for The Newest Testament*.

# Index of Subjects

# Index of Names